Who Rules
the Joint?

Who Rules the Joint?

The Changing Political Culture of
Maximum-Security Prisons in America

Charles Stastny
Gabrielle Tyrnauer
Harvard University

LexingtonBooks
D.C. Heath and Company
Lexington, Massachusetts
Toronto

Library of Congress Cataloging in Publication Data

Stastny, Charles.
   Who rules the joint?

   Bibliography: p.
   Includes index.
   1. Prisons—United States—History. 2. Prison administration—United
States—History. 3. Prison reformers—United States—History. 4. Power
(Social Sciences) I. Tyrnauer, Gabrielle. II. Title.

| HV9466.S7 | 365'.973 | 78-14157 |
| ISBN 0–669–02661–1 | | AACR2 |

Published simultaneously in Canada

Printed in the United States of America

International Standard Book Number: 0–669–02661–1

Library of Congress Catalog Card Number: 78-14157

To Our Parents

Contents

Figures
and Tables

Foreword

In the two hundred years following the remodeling of the Walnut Street Jail in Philadelphia in 1790, there have been five eras in the evolution of penology in the United States, each lasting the length of a generation of approximately forty years. Each era presented a different design for the rehabilitation of offenders; each failed to achieve the ideals for which it strove. But each produced the seeds of the future for the next era. These are the five eras, with their outstanding features:

1. 1790–1830: Early American prisons. *Features:* Meditation and moral instruction.
2. 1830–1870: Pennsylvania and Auburn systems. *Features:* Discipline, religion, judicial reprieve (probation). Solitary and silent models.
3. 1870–1900: Reformatory era. *Features:* Vocational training, education, parole. Separation of youthful and older offenders.
4. 1900–1940: Industrial prison. *Feature:* Habits of industry.
5. 1940–1980: Case-work prison. *Features:* Programs of rehabilitation. Classification of prisoners.

The present era (1980s and beyond) is attempting to integrate all that has preceded it. Hopefully it may place a new emphasis on resolving significant problems underlying criminality in each individual offender and on determining an agency of control in corrections. *Who Rules the Joint?* provides rich insight and valuable information for correctional administrators and practitioners, teachers, students, and researchers in criminology, as well as for all those concerned with the improvement of conditions in U.S. prisons. In this stimulating study, Charles Stastny and Gabrielle Tyrnauer have introduced a new and critical perspective on the events of these successive eras by showing the struggle for power that has developed among those involved, particularly through an intensive case study of one penitentiary. The authors present this power struggle, as a background to the present era, through the work of three men—Thomas Mott Osborne, Howard B. Gill, and William R. Conte—and their labors at Auburn and Sing Sing (New York), Portsmouth (New Hampshire), Norfolk (Massachusetts), and Walla Walla (Washington). Many other leaders in the past fifty years might have been chosen to demonstrate the contributions that this century has produced. Among them, the following are outstanding: Sanford Bates, Austin MacCormick, Frank Loveland, Mary Harris, Miriam Van Waters, Albert Fraser, Walter Thayer, A. Warren Stearns, Herbert Parsons, Kenyon

Scudder, Edgar Doll, J.W. Ellis, Lewis Lawes, and Vernon Housewright. To these wardens and administrators can be added those leading criminologists whose research and observations have brought new insights and established new standards for corrections in the United States. Included in such a list are Negley Teeters, Harry Elmer Barnes, Edwin Sutherland, Donald Cressey, Ruth Cavan, Nevitt Sanford, Thorsten Sellin, Marvin Wolfgang, Ralph Brancale, and Sheldon and Eleanor Glueck.

Cutting across the vast welter of ideas, ideals, and personalities, Stastny and Tyrnauer present an original and significant analysis that effectively shows the struggle for power among nine groups in this very complicated field:

1. *Wardens or administrators*—especially those with dominant personalities.
2. *Prisoners*—who have emerged as a powerful counterforce, particularly when they acquire decision-making functions.
3. *Custodial guards*—in charge of security (escapes), exclusion of contraband, and controlling disturbances.
4. *Guards in personal contact with prisoners*—acting as lay counselors in the cell-houses, shops, and so on. (The unionization of guards and their increasing contention for power has proved another disruptive force in correctional administration.)
5. *Professionals*—bringing their specialties to bear on the treatment of prisoners, but as advisors, ideally.
6. *State commissioners of corrections*—newly established in many states, their philosophy of corrections often aims to reshape the approach of prison officials.
7. *Governors and legislators*—who have a direct political stake in the condition of prisons, especially with the growing threat of unrest and pressure from the public and the courts.
8. *Outside community influences and the mass media*—now more and more penetrating the formerly closed world of prisons.
9. *Judges*—no longer restrained by the hands-off doctrine, they have issued since 1965 some 2,000–3,000 court decisions affecting correctional administration.

The interplay of these nine forces is still the most significant characteristic of today's corrections, and the authors of this book effectively highlight the past and present development of American prisons through the struggle for power among these often conflicting groups. It is too early to say which of these agents will become the dominant factor—a question Stastny and Tyrnauer do not attempt to resolve in any final way. Their study, however, provides significant evidence of the renewed importance of the judiciary, especially concerning doctrines developing around the Eighth Amendment ban on "cruel and unusual punishment." The *center of control* in any human process, according to Charles Sherrington, eminent British physiologist and philosopher, lies with that agency which provides the common path for all persons involved and which can interfere with any and all agencies engaged in the process. It appears to me that the judiciary can and should become the leading force in corrections in the United States, completing a circle that began two centuries ago.

From the dominance of the harsh and arbitrary court of Bloody Lord Jeffries to the inept leadership of the executive branch of the government, the history of corrections for the past two hundred years has been a sorry story of political mismanagement. With the courts again asserting their authority to change corrections through judicial decrees and with law and professional schools increasingly offering courses for training correctional specialists, a new leadership is emerging. By the year 2000, it seems clear that the judiciary could again come to dominate the correctional field, this time, it is hoped, under the most intelligent and highly trained leaders in the legal profession and on a solid grounding of humane standards and legal rights.

Although Stastny and Tyrnauer reach conclusions more gloomy than my own expectations, I have become convinced through my own life-long work in this field that we can succeed if we implement four practical bases:

1. Differentiation in architecture for different classes of prisoners.
2. Continuous programs of "acculturation" that bring offenders to absorb the accepted norms of society.
3. Greater emphasis on the discovery and resolution of the significant problems underlying criminality in each individual prisoner.
4. A center of control over corrections, which will provide an effective professional leadership.

With a philosophy of corrections built on these four pillars—and with the participation of all significant forces, including the prisoners—penology in the United States could become a positive rather than a negative element in our society. If we are to take heed of Dostoevsky's observation that prisons are the test of the civilization of a nation, the achievement of such a correctional regime may well represent a new level in American culture.

Howard B. Gill
Institute of Correctional Administration
Boston, Massachusetts

Preface and
Acknowledgments

This book began with Attica. Before that, neither of us had been professionally involved with prisons or prison problems. When Attica exploded in September 1971, we were living in upstate New York, not far from the prison. For us the four-day siege and its bloody aftermath were local as well as national and international news. We followed the events intently and pondered whether there might have been a different outcome.

Our work ended in Nürnberg, a city in which an international tribunal a generation ago judged those who had carried the abuse of incarceration to its ultimate extreme. This gives us other things to ponder: whether the basic structural changes we had perceived underlying the shorter or longer cycles of reform and reaction were as irreversible as they seemed to us in the course of this study. Pre-Hitler Germany, after all, was known to have one of the most enlightened penal systems of its time.

Mauthausen is a picturesque Austrian town on the Danube, best known for the prison that bears its name. The structure, with its high walls and towers and its isolated rural setting, physically resembles the average American maximum-security prison. And some of the problems that confronted its administrators—security, overpopulation, classification, allocation of resources—were similar. But there the resemblance ends. For Mauthausen—as one of Hitler's concentration camps—solved many of its technical problems, as well as those of the state that created it, through mass extermination. What was the missing link between this penal system of the Third Reich and its predecessor of the Weimar Republic? Could it happen in other times and places as well?

When we began our research in 1972, prison reform was a mobilizing cause for a reforming society. Conditions within the grim fortresses, it was widely believed, must be changed so that there would be no more Atticas. A particularly interesting reform experiment had been implemented in the Washington State prisons not long before Attica. After the tragedy in New York, it received widespread media attention as a hopeful alternative to the existing system. The authoritarian regime of the prison was to be transformed into a democratic community. Prisoners would become citizens in the full sense of the term.

In tune with this spirit, we undertook our research. Our training and teaching careers in political science and anthropology provided the lenses through which we focused on the phenomena of power and culture within the walls of America's most total institution. In the course of our research, the circumstances changed, the times changed, and so did our perspective. A study of past prison-reform experiments revealed that they were often short-lived; and indeed the reforms that we were studying were abolished halfway through our decade of research and were replaced by as authoritarian a regime, it seemed, as that which had preceded them. The brief social contract among the factions of the prison gave way to unrestrained violence, a war of all against all.

Our research was built around a developing prisoner political consciousness—derived in part from the generally heightened politicization of the 1960s—and a gradually democratizing inmate polity within prison walls. We did not seriously entertain the possibility of a return to a closed prison at Walla Walla. We saw men who had known neither trust nor responsibility in their lives transformed by the opportunities for political participation and self-expression permitted them at Walla Walla during the reform period. We assumed that the movement of renovation was basically unidirectional, despite occasional setbacks.

As history short-circuited our original approach, we groped about for new meanings in the masses of data we were accumulating. We knew that our methodological approaches as well as our theoretical perspectives were changing, but we were not sure where they would lead us. Robert Merton has pointed out that hypotheses and analytical categories often must be transformed in order for one's data to "fall into place." We began to see recurring cycles where we had been attuned to straight lines of progress. Later, however, the cycles gave way to a conception of spirals. Twentieth-century technology had broken down the isolation of the fortress prison. Regardless of how thick the walls and how autocratic the administration, the penitentiary could never again revert to the kind of total institution it once had been. But we came to see that there can be downward as well as upward spirals. The same technology might also create the prison of total surveillance, the nightmare of 1984.

Our new perspectives on "detotalization" and "retotalization" made it possible for much of our data to fall into place. We developed the concept of the *interactive prison* as the successor to the *total institution,* reflecting our increasing dissatisfaction with the early microstudies of prison society that had provided the original model and point of departure for our own study. We began to move toward a conflict perspective. The Washington State Penitentiary experiment in self-government was not only an attempt by enlightened administrators to displace an anomalous authoritarian regime with a democratic one but became more clearly the product of changes affecting all of American society.

Just as the prison reforms of the early 1970s were the product of an American society in ferment, so the retrenchment policies rode in on the conservative wave that swept America in the latter part of the decade and climaxed in the election of Ronald Reagan to the presidency. The concept of rehabilitation became discredited and the "nothing works" school of thought took its place, leading to a renewed emphasis on the custodial functions of prisons. The federal courts, which in recent years played an increasingly important role in maintaining order and minimum standards within American prisons, began to edge back under pressure toward the previously repudiated "hands-off" doctrine—that is, the judicial policy granting unrestricted autonomy to prison administrators. It strikes us that a weakening of the judicial function, perhaps especially in this area of American life, presents a threat to the fundamental constitutional conception of the separation of powers.

Thus, the outlook for prison reform, as we have suggested, was more hopeful at the beginning of this study than at its conclusion. But in personal and intellectual terms, the experience has been rewarding. Without the stimulation and assistance we received from a range of individuals and organizations, the research and preparation of this book would not have been possible.

The project was launched through a grant from the College Center of the Finger Lakes. It was clearly designed as a collaborative project from the outset, even when grants were awarded to us as faculty members of different teaching institutions. In the early phases of our work, we were guided, encouraged, and befriended by associates of McGill University's Forensic Psychiatry Clinic: Lydia Keitner, Guy Mersereau, Judith Princz, and its director, Bruno Cormier. Especially important for our acquisition of a broader understanding of criminal justice was our association with the University of Montreal's School of Criminology and Centre International de Criminologie Comparée, under the direction of Denis Szabo and Alice Parizeau.

The fieldwork brought us into contact with many prisoners and staff members at prisons all over North America. The residents at the Washington State Penitentiary were our principal sources and voluntarily shared with us their hopes and fears, as well as their sometimes extraordinary insights into the walled world in which they lived. We thank especially Harold Billington, John Mullinex, Jim Moi, Dave Riggins, Willie Peele, Mike Pryor, and Chester Woods. Special mention must be made of Don Anthony White, who became, in the course of our long association, a virtual research assistant on both sides of the walls. He was a conscientious and capable collaborator. Superintendent B.J. Rhay and Associate Superintendent Robert Freeman were both generous in sharing their long-term knowledge and perspectives with us. Minority Affairs Director Vincent Lombard and Father James Cummins, first chaplain and later associate superintendent of treatment, were also helpful.

Numerous state administrators in Washington's Department of Social and Health Services guided and assisted us in our research. William Conte, who headed the state's correction system for five years (1966–1971) and was widely regarded as the Father of the Reforms, generously provided us with materials and critiques. We also are indebted to Donald J. Horowitz, the late Milton Burdman, Roger Maxwell, and Don Johns.

We greatly benefited from our association with the members of Institutional Legal Services, especially Steve Scott, John Ziegler, and Barbara Miller. Other members of the legal profession who assisted us were Tim Ford, Michael Lewis, Bertha Houser, and David Danelski.

It was really our association with Harvard University that made the preparation of this book possible. It began at the Center for Criminal Justice and was completed at the Center for European Studies. We thank the directors of the CCJ, Lloyd Ohlin and James Vorenberg, now dean of Harvard Law School, for providing us with assistance, guidance, and a stimulating ccmmunity of colleagues engaged in similar research. We also thank Stanley Hoffmann, director of the CES. While at CCJ, we received a contract from the American Justice Institute, which made the transcription of our many recorded interviews possible. The director of this project, the late Robert Montilla, provided continuous encouragement, as well as financial assistance. Kathy Waldbauer and Robert Allison lent their labors and talents, which went far beyond the original typing assignment, to this project.

Many other professional colleagues provided helpful comments on this work in its various stages. These include Benedict Alper, Kathleen Adams, Joseph Hickey, Renée Kasinsky, and Clarence Schrag. A very special role has been played by Howard B. Gill, the dean of American prison reformers.

Archibald Tweedle has been an invaluable helper on this project over the last few years, providing us with typing, editorial assistance, and, above all, witty commentary on the passing scene. Susan Alamgir also gave friendship in combination with technical assistance; we owe her much. Michael Nussbaum contributed long-distance research assistance at short notice. For their skills and devotion during the final stages of the manuscript preparation, we thank Louise Lippard and Linda Speare. We are grateful, for graphic assistance, to Giovanni Knöpfli of Bern.

The Sozialwissenschaftliches Institut at Nürnberg University and the Institut für Kriminologie at Heidelberg University provided the authors with congenial professional bases in the final stages of this work. We thank colleagues at both institutions—especially Gerhard Wurzbacher, Friedrich Heckmann, Ullrich Fischer, and Dietlinde Lessner-Abdin at Nürnberg; Hans-Jürgen Kerner, Thomas Feltes, and Helmut Jenssen at Heidelberg.

There is no way we can adequately express our gratitude to friends on two continents who have provided hospitality, comment, and encouragement during the various phases of the writing. These include Constance Phillips and Ramiro and Carlos Valdes of Somerville, Massachusetts;

Henryka Kurzepa of Cincinnati; Samir Adbin of Nürnberg; Marie Luise and Hans Hartung of Erlangen; Noa V. Zanolli of Bern; Satu Stierlin and Klaus Schadewaldt of Heidelberg; and Ulla Schild of Mainz.

Finally we thank Minnie Brown Stastny, who became a true partner in our research enterprise. Without her faithful newspaper clipping service, especially over the periods when we had no other access to Washington State news, this book could not have assumed its present form. It was a labor of love, which proved indispensable. Our fathers, who gave strong encouragement to our collaborative work from the beginning of our professional and personal association, did not live to see the completion of this book. We think of them very much at this time.

Since it is customary for authors to thank their spouses for support, both material and moral, we must pause to thank each other. This book has been written under difficult circumstances. The right of spouses to professional collaboration, which is basic to this book, became a legal issue in the course of our research. We trust that before long the law will clearly establish this right on an equal basis and that this book provides justification for our own professional collaboration.

1

From Attica to Santa Fe: The Explosive Decade

A perfected model it is, this prison life, with its apparent uniformity and dull passivity. . . . Hidden by the veil of discipline rages the struggle of fiercely contending wills, and intricate meshes are woven in the quagmire of darkness and suppression. —Alexander Berkman (1912)[1]

For four days in September 1971, the attention of the world was riveted on a prison uprising in a rural New York State community named Attica. When it was over, forty-three men were dead and over eighty wounded. After its investigation, the New York State Special Commission of inquiry (the McKay Commission) called it "the bloodiest one-day encounter between Americans since the Civil War."

A decade later the details have faded. But to many people, Attica remains a vivid symbol of rebellion and repression in American prisons and it continues to be evoked in the debates over the future of corrections in the United States. The McKay Commission set the tone: "Attica is every prison and every prison is Attica."

No previous prison riot had been so widely reported in the media or had made such a deep impression on public consciousness. It was generally expected that the tragedy would create a climate favorable to implementation of the reforms recommended by the commission, changes that were "inescapably necessary" in order to reduce "the frustration and desperation that drive men to rebellion." Prisoners, the commission insisted, must be granted all the rights of other citizens except those the courts have specifically taken away; they must be given social responsibility "directed at elevating and enhancing their dignity, worth and self-confidence."[2]

But the promise of the immediate post-Attica period was not fulfilled. Superficial changes were made in the New York State system: uniforms and titles were changed, impotent inmate advisory councils were set up. There were some initial attempts to improve officer training, recruit more minority staff, and improve some of the conditions of imprisonment. Far more public energy, however, was devoted to bringing to trial those Attica inmates accused of criminal acts in the course of the uprising. At the same time, the prosecution of law enforcement officers charged with illegal actions was sidestepped.

1

Even while recommending specific reforms, the McKay commission expressed considerable skepticism about the possibility of enhancing human dignity within the walls of America's huge nineteenth-century-style fortress prisons. In fact, here it approached the position of "abolitionists," such as Gary Wills, who hold prisons unreformable. Critic Wills refers to American prisons as the "failed experiment" of the Enlightenment.[3]

The cause of prison reform declined in popularity in the following decade. The ideal of rehabilitation, on which so much of it had been based, was undergoing ideological attacks from both the Left and the Right, while the fiscal conservatives in state and federal government were slashing correctional budgets. Prisons once more moved from near the center of public concern to its periphery.

Then in February 1980 another bloody prison riot erupted. For thirty-six hours the inmates of the New Mexico Penitentiary at Santa Fe held hostages and rampaged through the prison, smashing and burning as they went, torturing, mutilating, and murdering fellow prisoners. The toll was thirty-three dead, all inmates killed by inmates. As many as two hundred others were beaten and raped, while the majority ran, terrified, to safety outside the walls, taking refuge among the state patrol surrounding the institution.[4]

The New Mexico attorney general, assigned to conduct an investigation of the causes and course of the riot, produced a two-part report describing the upheaval in detail and focusing on the underlying conditions over the preceding decade.[5] This study did not have the scope of the Attica Commission's report, but it was similar in its calls for reform. The report's perspective on the preceding ten years was distinctly critical of the popular "hard line," contrasting the first with the second half of the decade:

> Order in the early 70s was partly the result of a series of formal and informal incentives which were used by the administrators to motivate inmates to accept and cooperate in the orderly operation of the institution. . . . During the late 70s, many of the formal and informal incentives were removed by the administration. The result was a forced reliance on coercion as the primary method of inmate control.[6]

The principal cause of the riot, according to the attorney general's report, was "the disruption of incentive controls over inmates," which "disrupted the nonviolent power sources of convict leaders." The consequence was the emergence of "a new group of violent inmates," whose effect was to fragment the inmate population "into small self-protective cliques with no strong central leadership."[7]

It was this absence of any clear prisoner leadership which provided the most striking contrast with the Attica uprising. Although the inmate body at Attica was split into many groups, they managed to collaborate to keep order in the yard. With the exception of the secret killing of three inmates and the death of one guard from injuries sustained in the initial outbreak, the hostages and the inmates were not harmed during the four days that preceded the armed assault. At Santa Fe, inmate leadership was weak and began to muster some initiative only after the slaughter had run its course.

But paradoxically, at Attica, where inmate leaders were in a reasonably favorable position to commit their following to an agreed settlement—and where the outside observer team could influence the mediation—the negotiations reached an apparent impasse and Governor Nelson Rockefeller ordered a military invasion. At Santa Fe, on the other hand, although assaults of the prison were planned and set to go several times, they were always canceled, Governor Bruce King at one juncture rejecting the advice of California experts that the prison be stormed.[8] All the hostages were released, and the prison was reoccupied without a single shot. The weakness of the inmate leadership at Santa Fe did not deter the authorities from continuing to negotiate with it right up to the end. A lesson of official caution, if nothing else, had been learned from Attica.

Whatever the important differences between Santa Fe and Attica, both massacres were dramatic expressions of changes going on in the larger society, nationally and even internationally. In his keynote address to the American Correctional Association a few months before the Santa Fe outburst Charles Silberman spoke of an intensifying crisis of legitimacy and its impact on the prison system:

> What has happened is that contemporary prisoners—especially black prisoners—are unwilling to accept the kind of mutual accommodations and understandings between inmates and staff that, in the past, had kept the pressures toward anarchy and violence under some sort of control. In effect, inmates have withdrawn the consent on which prison government has always rested. Instead, they are protesting the conditions under which they live and are demanding a wide variety of changes; at times, they seem to be rejecting the legitimacy of prison government itself. The result has been a widespread breakdown in order and control.[9]

The relationship between the breakdown in order and control and the crisis of legitimacy in the prison, as well as in other American institutions, continues to be debated, but the mounting chaos and violence are evident to all. Neither politicians nor criminologists nor administrators have succeeded in providing a formula for coping with the destructive eruptions that punctuate the existence of penal institutions with increasing frequency and intensity.

The first part of this book is an exploration of how the American prison came to its present impasse and an account of past reformers' attempts to divert its course into more constructive channels. The second part deals in depth with the most recent of such reform experiments at Washington State Penitentiary at Walla Walla.

Between Attica and Santa Fe, a remarkable prison reform experiment ran its course. For a while, it became a beacon of hope. By the time Attica exploded, the first Resident Government Council at the Washington State Penitentiary (WSP) was preparing to leave office. Over the next four years, there were to be seven others. The grim yard at Walla Walla was transformed. Drab uniforms gave way to colorful civilian clothes, shaven heads and faces to shoulder-length hair and beards, idleness to bustling activity. Inmate leaders could be seen dashing about with attaché cases, or escorting visitors freely about the institution. A formerly forbidden patch of grass inside the walls became the "People's Park." Uncensored newspapers were published; political campaigns were freely conducted; lectures were made around the state by prisoners who had not seen the outside of the massive walls for ten or twenty years. A month after Attica a *New York Times* feature story pointed to this experiment in Washington State as the hopeful alternative, which might eventually lead to the removal of guards and walls.[10]

But four years later self-government at Walla Walla was moribund. The walls did not tumble down, the guards remained, and life in the old fortress penitentiary grew increasingly violent. The stream of outside visitors dried to a trickle, and the media reported only the more dramatic incidents of disruption. Although WSP managed to avoid volcanic explosion, such as those at Attica or Santa Fe, its cumulative hostilities led to repeated prisoner outbreaks followed by administrative retaliation.

In May 1980 a federal judge supported the inmates' contention that incarceration in WSP at Walla Walla constituted "cruel and unusual punishment," and hence was unconstitutional. A special court master was appointed to oversee the implementation of the judge's orders, which were designed to bring the prison up to minimal constitutional standards.[11] In the space of a decade, WSP's national image had plummeted from that of the best of maximum-security prisons to one of the worst, from an exemplar of prison reform to an institution struggling to become a lawful prison.[12]

What lessons can be drawn from this dramatic change? How are they related to the lessons of Attica and Santa Fe and to those deriving from reform efforts of the past? The second part of this study focuses on the reforms at WSP in an attempt to find some answers to these questions. We will see how both the brief success and the ultimate failure of the bold experiment in Washington State was related to the outside events and forces that increasingly have shaped the era of what we call the interactive prison.

The reform experiment at Walla Walla will be viewed in several perspectives: as the heir to past attempts to bring democracy to the autocratic prison setting; as an expression of the new and radical forces in American society; and as a marker on the road from Attica to Santa Fe.

The liberal reform experiment at Walla Walla attempted to set up a model of civic responsibility for which there are few real correlates in contemporary American society, let alone in its penal institutions. Nevertheless, the experiment generated new visions, new opportunities, new plans. It transformed a few lives and created a temporary truce among the conflicting forces in the prison's social structure. These, we feel, are reasons enough for closely examining the reform experiment, attempting to understand its inner workings and its eventual breakdown, while keeping sight of its multiple connections with other social forces within the prison and beyond its walls.

Liberal reform is no longer in favor. The critics of Walla Walla's experiment from the Left argued that the reforms were co-optative or merely palliative and did not go nearly far enough.[13] The attack from the Right held that by loosening the reins of authority, the reforms led to violence.[14] The cry arose, in Washington State as elsewhere, for more punishment and longer sentences; rehabilitation was pronounced dead. Violence rose sharply despite the swing toward tighter controls. It might be said, to paraphrase the McKay Commission, that today every prison is Santa Fe and Santa Fe is every prison. It is not a hopeful prospect.

In our research we have attempted to bring to bear the perspective of political science and anthropology in addition to the sociological insights that have been so central to penology. Early prison fieldwork, although conducted by sociologists, was very much in the ethnographic tradition. The temptation to view the prison, one of the most isolated of institutions in modern society, as a self-contained cultural system analogous to that of primitive tribes proved irresistible to the social ethnographers of the Chicago school.[15] While this perspective provided some valuable insights, it was bound to change as social theory together with social reality was transformed in the wake of World War II. As communications improved, social theory became more interactionist, and the "prison community" became the "prison in mass society."[16]

As the concept of culture is central to the anthropologist's perspective, so is power to that of the political scientist. All cultures have their political components, their distinctive ways of responding to power and of allocating values authoritatively. In order to comprehend the changes in the power system of the penitentiary, we must study the political culture in which that power is embedded. In few social institutions does power traditionally show itself as nakedly as in the prison. The line between the rulers and the ruled begins as absolute, and distance is enforced by sanctions on both sides. Even the most cordial relations between individuals in such a system cannot escape the constraints of what is essentially a caste system.

The periodic reforms punctuating American penal history have represented attempts to reduce the social distance between the controllers and the controlled—to introduce some sort of shared decision making, which would partially realign the political process with the system prevailing in the rest of society. But the essential line did not disappear; the veto power of the keepers was not surrendered. Thus for the most part, liberal reformers sought to provide a useful intercaste communication device rather than to effect substantial redistribution of power or fundamental social change.

Nevertheless a redistribution of power within prisons has been taking place, an unintended product of the social forces at work. This process of a developing political consciousness and the differentiation of groups coincided in various places with particular reform movements and was nourished by them while they lasted. Thus the inmate governance experiment in Washington State acted as a wedge in the heavy steel door of the traditional prison society and became the principal catalyst for the more deeply penetrating structural change that has outlived these reforms.

Notes

1. *Prison Memoirs of an Anarchist* (New York: Schocken, 1970—originally published by Mother Earth, 1912), pp. 272-273.
2. *Attica* (New York: Bantam, 1972), pp. xi-xii, xvi-xvii.
3. Gary Wills, "The Human Sewer," *New York Review of Books,* April 3, 1975, p. 3.
4. For a description and analysis of the New Mexico upheaval, see Michael S. Serrill and Peter Katel, "Anatomy of a Riot: The Facts behind New Mexico's Bloody Ordeal," *Corrections Magazine* (April 1980):pp. 7-16, 20-24.
5. "Report of the Attorney General on the February 2 and 3, 1980 Riot at the Penitentiary of New Mexico," pt. 1 (June 1980), pt. 2 (September 1980).
6. Ibid., pt. 2, p. 5.
7. Ibid., p.6.
8. Ibid., pt. 1, pp. 51-52.
9. Charles Silberman, "Race, Crime, and Corrections," *Proceedings of the American Correctional Association, 1979* (College Park, Md.: American Correctional Association, 1980), pp. 5-14.
10. *New York Times,* October 18, 1971, p. 24.
11. Decision of a Federal District Court (*Hoptowit* v. *Ray,* May 1980), Judge Jack Tanner. Subsequently, an appeal was made by Washington to the Ninth Circuit Court of Appeals. In early 1982 a three-judge panel of this court handed down a ruling severely limiting the scope of Tanner's decision and returning it to the lower court. For more detailed discussion see chapter 8.
12. The phrase *lawful prison* is taken from a position paper prepared

by John P. Conrad and Simon Dinitz for the Seminar on the Isolated Prisoner, Academy for Contemporary Problems, Columbus, Ohio (1977), pp. 51–53. It refers to a prison that both conforms to the law as prescribed by the courts and maintains an orderly regime.

13. See Frank Browning, "Organizing Behind Bars," *Ramparts* (February 1972):40–45.

14. See the nine-part series, "Fury in the Soul," in the *Spokane Spokesman Review,* November 18–26, 1979, especially the views reported in the initial article.

15. For discussion of the influence of the Chicago school of sociology on American criminology, see John Irwin, *Prisons in Turmoil* (Boston: Little, Brown, 1980), pp. 30–33.

16. Donald Clemmer, *The Prison Community* (New York: Rinehart, 1958—first published 1940); James B. Jacobs, *Stateville: The Penitentiary in Mass Society* (Chicago: University of Chicago Press, 1977).

Part I
Perspectives on
the American Prison

2

The Penitentiary—
An Idea, A Reform?

John Howard's *State of Prisons,* published in England in 1777, was viewed as a landmark in the movement for prison reform. Howard is credited with having coined the term *penitentiary* and became known as the Father of the Penitentiary.[1]

How is it that the penitentiary, which became the prototypal form for confining persons convicted of serious criminal offenses, was hailed then and thereafter as a progressive step in social development? Eventually prisons would be subjected not only to the harshest of judgments on their failings, but also the very *raison d'être* of the prison as an institution would come into question. Yet in the late eighteenth century, the displacement of corporal punishment, together with its ultimate form, capital punishment, by imprisonment seemed to constitute a notable humanizing advance.[2]

In the mid-1780s Pennsylvania led the way in the area of criminal law by reducing the list of capital crimes, and within a few years execution would be applied only to first-degree murder. At the same time, most forms of corporal punishment—mutilation, whipping, branding, the pillory—were abolished, with imprisonment substituted as the punishment of societal choice.

Prior to this turning point, prisons, as places of incarceration, had not generally been considered as a form of punishment. Historically they had been used mainly for detaining persons prior to trial or pending exile or preparatory to execution. Thus confinement served essentially as the control mechanism antecedent to trials and until the sentence was carried out. As a holding operation a prison stay was in theory, if not always in fact, of short duration. Now prison itself would constitute the criminal penalty, and incarceration would often be a long-term experience for those convicted.

The penal philosophy underlying the adoption of an imprisonment regime in place of degradation and bodily mutilation rested on several bases. First, there was the *social-contract* conception, which inspired much of the Enlightenment approach. Applied to this area, it meant that criminal deviancy should be treated as a rupturing of the bonds that held civil society together. This breach of contract required swift retribution if the social fabric was not to unravel, and incarceration was generally deemed a sufficient penalty in a humane society. Second, in an approach deriving from

11

the premises of the Age of Reason, there must be rational application of rationally conceived laws. In this context, there should be due proportion between the crime and its punishment. Man, as a reasoning, self-willing creature, must be held responsible for his acts, and punishment must fit the offense rather than the offender. Finally, the custody and correction functions of imprisonment were seen as being essentially complementary; the right form of punishment would lead naturally to reformation of the individual.

For the secularist, what was good and true could be apprehended through the rational faculty. The lesson wrapped up in the punishment could regenerate the lawbreaker (rehabilitation), as well as give pause to those who witnessed the consequences of lawbreaking (deterrence). From a religious perspective, embraced by the idealistic Quakers and others, imprisonment appeared as sufficient punishment and as an opportunity for doing redemptive penance on earth, while the example of individual suffering served as warning to others. In short, whether the outlook was theological or secular, simultaneously with the birth of the American nation, imprisonment came into its own. The spirit of the age supported the belief that the prison offered the best mode for controlling and correcting the behavior of the violators of society's norms, granting free will to each individual.[3]

The penitentiary was the institutional embodiment of the new approaches toward law and order growing out of the Enlightenment era. The theories underlying the prison-as-reform idea in America during the late eighteenth and early nineteenth centuries had both religious and secular sources. On the religious side, the Quakers were perhaps the most prominent.[4] Not only did they have a long history of opposition to the brutality of the English criminal code, but a hundred years earlier, under William Penn, they had already experimented with substituting incarceration at hard labor for the capital and corporal punishment contained in the Anglican law.

In 1718 these Pennsylvania innovations were cut short by a swing back to British standards in the colony, but the American Revolution brought the rationalistic and humanitarian views embedded in the Enlightenment—and accelerated the movement to abandon the punishments of public execution, physical torture, and the subjection to public humiliation. The intellectual giants of the Enlightenment era helped to create not only what Carl Becker has called "the heavenly city of the 18th century philosophers" but also what another writer has termed "the heavenly prison of the philanthropists."[5]

As a social-control system, the objective of the penitentiary was to separate the individual who violated society's values from all contact with potential sources of corruption. The walled penitentiary seems well adapted to achieve the dual purpose of severing the prisoner's connection with the outside world and with his fellow inmates through the isolation of a solitary cell and a wall of silence. The structural requirements of this institution were that the convicts be totally sealed off from the world at large. The walls themselves were to be an unbreachable physical barrier, and this principle of impermeability was to encompass non-physical penetration as well. In this vein, James G. Blaine, prison commissioner for the state of Maine in the 1850s and later a perennial presidential candidate, maintained that "information upon events of current interest, and glimpses of the outer world, have a tendency to unsettle the convict's mind and render him restless and uneasy."[6] Thus the interdiction of social contact with the world at large was a *sine qua non* of this *total institution.*[7]

In the original conception of its creators, the "society of captives" within this walled enclosure was composed of essentially atomized individuals.[8] This society approximates an undifferentiated collection of persons unconnected with each other except for their presence within the same institutional construct. They are effectively barred from interacting or communicating or aggregating into groups.

This process resembles that which has been observed by students of comparative politics in totalitarianizing societies.[9] The atomization or pulverization of all subgroups tends toward the isolation of members of the society from each other and from any influences except the political center, the party-state. The sociological model of a total institution, as in Goffman's construct, shares at least two important characteristics with the classic closed system of totalitarianism: impermeability to external influence and the elimination of all autonomous subgroups. Thus the closed institution as a sociopolitical category is antipluralistic just as is the closed totalitarian society.

There is, however, a crucial difference. In the latter, the atomized individuals are reintegrated into a new superauthoritarian organic whole, complete with a dynamic totalitarian ideology, party, and leader. It is, in brief, this dynamic quality of a mass society in revolutionary motion toward ideologically prescribed goals that is characteristic of the totalitarian species of authoritarianism. But a penitentiary clearly lack such dynamism. While the ideal conception of a modern prison includes commitment to the reformation of prisoners, individually and collectively, this is scarcely equivalent to propulsion of the masses toward ideologically prescribed goals. Typically maximum-security prisons are static institutions whose rulers tend to resist change in the status quo. Consequently it would be misleading to pursue this analogy too far, much less equate the penitentiary regime with totalitarianism.[10]

Thus the ideal penitentiary contains a population in near-total isolation from the outside world, with each member in strict separation from the others and committed to the objective of reformation. These features, though never completely realized, gave the character of "total"-ness to the original penitentiary concept.

In historical terms, how were these original philosophical conceptions to be institutionalized? Existing prisons were ill adapted to use for long-term incarceration. They were essentially jails in the form of small local places of detention, fit only for short-term warehousing and not for the additional functions prescribed by the new ideology of imprisonment.

A possible alternative to the typical jail was the so-called bridewell (or house of correction) originating with London's St. Bride's Well in 1552 and designed to control vagrancy and other lesser evils through confinement at "forced labor."[11] These workhouses, orginally quite distinct from gaols, had had a spotty history, reverting frequently to corporal punishment. This was true also of houses of correction in the American colonies, including Quaker Pennsylvania, to which the English model had been carried. Eventually the distinction between jails and workhouses became quite indistinct. Consequently when the reformers proceeded to implement their idea of a penitentiary in that setting, they soon ran into serious difficulties.

Philadelphia's Walnut Street Jail was a prime example of the difficulties encountered in applying the penitentiary ideal to a setting designed for different purposes. By the second decade of the nineteenth century, the whole movement was threatened with failure. The system, with its principle of solitary confinement to an individual cell, seemingly could not work at the Walnut Street Jail. Overcrowding had made the single-cell standard impossible to maintain, and this was compounded by inadequate funding and personnel, resulting in the disruption of industry and discipline. Without adequate work for the growing number of prisoners, this model prison and "cradle of the penitentiary" had rapidly been corrupted. There was an outcry calling for the reintroduction of corporal punishment, which, had it succeeded, would have defeated the expectations for the new system of punishment before it was securely launched.

Clearly the idea of the prison could be rescued only by a fresh reform, which took the form of a wave of new construction of penitentiaries. It was, contemporary observers agreed, an achitectural triumph. The first of the gigantic stone fortresses to be built was the one at Auburn, New York; it opened in 1817 and is still standing. The pioneering Philadelphia Society for the Alleviation of the Miseries of Prisons (founded 1787) moved in a similar direction. In the 1820s, two large bastilles were established in Pennsylvania: Western Penitentiary (Pittsburgh, 1826) and Eastern Penitentiary, familiarly known as Cherry Hill (Philadelphia, 1829). The Cherry Hill institution became the physical embodiment of the Pennsylvania (or solitary confinement) system, which competed during the next half century with the rival Auburn (or silent, congregate) system for hegemony in American corrections.[12]

There is considerable irony in depicting the erection of such grim monstrosities as somehow marking the culmination of a reform thrust. Yet the significance of these developments is hard to overestimate. The philosophical roots, beginning with the abandonment in principle of corporal punishment and the virtual abolition of the death penalty, only later came to institutional fruition in the form of a new bastille, the penitentiary. But this achievement did not come easily. In the immediate period after the American Revolution, the legal and conceptual basis had been laid for this change, but there had been little to go by in the way of structural blueprints. What alterations then occurred in internal prison arrangements, as Rothman has pointed out, "were only minor or confused departures from colonial arrangements."[13]

There were a few examples at an early stage of departures from the typical large house model for incarceration. The Charlestown Prison (1805) in Boston was one of the earliest to represent the changing direction, which was to culminate in the penitentiary. But this was an exception, one of the first tentative departures from the kind of enlarged household design that was then the prison standard. Well into the nineteenth century, the ideals of the penal reformers still remained untranslated into reality either in the outer form of the prison or the inner arrangements for single cells prescribed by their theories. The general verdict on the system as it stood in 1820 was that it had almost completely failed: "Institutionalization had not only failed to pay its own way, but had also encouraged and educated the criminal to a life in crime."[14]

Yet, by the following decade, the penitentiary system in the United States was to win not only national approbation but become a subject for international investigation and study. Such celebrated observers as Alexis de Tocqueville and Gustave de Beaumont, while once referring to the American penitentiary as a "spectacle of the most complete despotism," saw it as a leading social artifact of the world's newest democracy and an important model to be emulated.[15]

Notes

1. See Blake McKelvey, *American Prisons: A History of Good Intentions* (Montclair, N.J.: Patterson Smith, 1977), p. 16. For a collection of interesting studies dedicated to the John Howard bicentennial, see John C. Freeman, ed., *Prisons Past and Future* (London: Heinemann, 1978).

2. This view of the humanistic character of the penal reforms that followed the American Revolution is not universally shared. Today's advocates of the "new penology" see the origins of the modern prison as reflecting the basic interests of an emergent ruling class, intent on centralizing

power in the state through structuring an instrument of repression adapted to the purposes of that class. See Paul Takagi, "The Walnut Street Jail: A Penal Reform to Centralize the Powers of the State," *Federal Probation* 39 (December 1975):18–26.

3. For a different view of the rationale for the uses of imprisonment, see David J. Rothman, *The Discovery of the Asylum* (Boston: Little, Brown, 1971).

4. Takagi, "Walnut Street Jail," pp. 18, 21. Takagi, however, asserts that the claim to priority of the Quakers is largely mythical, part of the "belief system on the origins of the American prison." Although the Quakers and their ideas had "some influence," according to Takagi, the Philadelphia Society for Alleviating the Miseries of Public Prisons was, in fact, dominated by Episcopalians.

5. Carl Becker, *The Heavenly City of The 18th Century Philosophers* (New Haven: Yale University Press, 1932); Carl Wilson Pierson, *Tocqueville and Beaumont in America* (New York: Oxford University Press, 1938), p. 457. For discussion of Enlightenment era thought in its relation to crime and punishment, see Harry Elmer Barnes, *The Repression of Crime* (New York: George H. Doran Co., 1926), pp. 90–93, 335–336.

6. Quoted in Rothman, *Discovery,* p. 96.

7. The term *total* has been so widely used in relation to prisons that its source must be noted: Erving Goffman, *Asylums* (Garden City, N.Y.: Doubleday, Anchor Books, 1961), pp. xiii–xiv, pp. 1–124.

8. The term derives from Gresham M. Sykes, *The Society of Captives: A Study of a Maximum Security Prison* (Princeton, N.J.: Princeton University Press, 1958).

9. The so-called totalitarian model as a tool of political analysis has been discredited to some extent; at the least, it requires modification to surmount its theoretic inadequacies. See Carl J. Friedrich, Michael Curtis, and Benjamin R. Barber, *Totalitarianism in Perspective: Three Views* (New York: Praeger, 1969).

10. A distinction should also be drawn between the generally static character of a prison regime and the kind of dynamic "ideological totalism" described by Robert J. Lifton in his study of thought reform during the "cultural revolution" in Maoist China. See R.J. Lifton, *Thought Reform and the Psychology of Totalism* (New York: Norton, 1969), pp. 419–437. The kind of private penitence ideally required of a penitentiary prisoner is quite different from the public and communal confession of the thought reform subject. Similarly, the process of "re-education" in an American penitentiary is typically individualistic, whereas in China it was linked to the collective community. Nevertheless, the psychological momentum toward this "individual totalism" within the subjects Lifton studied cannot be wholly different from the kind of behavior modification twentieth century Western prisons have attempted with their inmates.

11. McKelvey, *American Prisons,* p. 2.

12. There is a large scholarly literature on the Walnut Street Jail and the origins of the Pennsylvania prison system. See Negley K. Teeters, *The Cradle of the Penitentiary: The Walnut Street Jail at Philadelphia, 1773–1835* (Philadelphia: Pennsylvania Prison Society, 1955). For a revisionist view, forcefully argued, see Takagi, "Walnut Street Jail." On Eastern Penitentiary, see Negley K. Teeters and John C. Shearer, *The Prison at Philadelphia: Cherry Hill—The Separate System of Penal Discipline: 1829–1913* (New York: Columbia University Press, for Temple University Publications, 1957).

13. Rothman, *Discovery,* p. 89.

14. Ibid., p. 93.

15. G. de Beaumont and A. de Tocqueville, *On the Penitentiary System in the United States and Its Application in France,* trans. Francis Lieber (Philadelphia: Carey, Lea & Blanchard, 1833). The "despotism" reference is on p. 47.

3 A Prison Typology

American prisons can be seen through the prism of four types of institutional regimes. In terms of their power configuration, these types range along a continuum from a concentration of power (unicentric pattern), through two intermediate forms of power distribution (bicentric and tricentric), to a wide dispersion of power (polycentric pattern). In taking as its point of departure the nature of relationships internal to the prison polity, this typology focuses on the basic issues of power, authority, and purpose. Conceptually, as we move through two centuries of development, the original *enlightenment prison* embodies a unicentric model; the durable *warehouse prison* fits the bicentric; the recurrent *remedial prison* represents the tricentric; and the polycentric principle is reflected in the *interactive prison*. Examining these four models in sequence, we find the political culture within the prisons which they represent characterized by increasingly diffuse power distribution and a growing differentiation of functional roles within the prison polity.

The descriptive terms employed in this typology have historical referents, though they are not intended to point to a strictly chronological sequence. The first type is the product of the Enlightenment era. It corresponds most closely to the original idea of the penitentiary. Whereas in Chapter 2 we examined the penitentiary in terms of its social history, here we will study it in terms of its power configurations. These relations of power were not, of course, the primary objective of the penitentiary's inventors, but developed as a by-product. While the moral philosophy and religious ideology that were so closely connected with the creation of the enlightenment prison disappeared into history, the name, the architectural style, and frequently the disciplinary regime of the penitentiary survived their original function and philosophy to become the prototype of American prisons.

The unicentric enlightenment prison concentrates power in a single place within a monolithic structure—at the top—where there is a monopoly of power and authority in the prison warden, a kind of Platonic "philosopher-king." While charged with guiding the prisoner-penitent toward the light of redemption, in reality, however, the warden of the penitentiary more often resembled Machiavelli's prince than Plato's philosopher-king.

Opportunities for the formation of inmate groupings that could challenge the concentration of power in the warden are foreclosed by the silent and solitary nature of confinement within this type of prison. At the same time, there is little interference from above. As long as a warden remains in power, the prison is recognized as his sovereign domain.

Over time the ideal of reformation that justified the autocracy of the enlightenment prison gave way to the simple purpose of isolating offenders from the society that they had offended. In what we here term the warehouse prison, they were stored away behind massive walls, originally designed as much to protect their souls from worldly contamination as to ensure their detention. If there was an idea behind this form of imprisonment, it was essentially incapacitation. The prisoners were human merchandise to be kept in storage for as long as society deemed just or feasible.

In this warehouse prison we find a dual (or bicentric) power relationship: between the prison authorities on the one hand and the convicts on the other. The warden of what has been called the "big house" has the role of a dictator, but seldom can he rule in an absolutist manner. Given the numerical ratio between keepers and kept, plus the development of communication among prisoners, the warden's limited task of maintaining security and stability becomes possible only through tacit recognition of and accommodation with *de facto* inmate power. This prison has retained the form of the enlightenment prison but regards its reformative goals as utopian. And with inmate groupings beginning to emerge from a previously atomized convict body, the stakes become the division of the prison's scarce values, to be accomplished without challenging the prison status quo in any fundamental way. And that status quo resembles the traditional authoritarianism of political theory: heavily coercive with a consensual basis provided by an elite having a stake in the system.

The third form, the remedial prison, is closely associated with the so-called medical model. The prisoner once more becomes a human subject; reformation once again becomes a goal. "Treatment," based on modern scientific knowledge of the human psyche, becomes the means of achieving this goal. In place of "imprisonment" we have "corrections." The remedies for criminal behavior are seen as consisting of a combination of work, educational programs, and counseling, all designed to correct the underlying psychological problems and environmental influences that launched the prisoner on his criminal career.

This type of prison is characterized by a tricentric power configuration: a custodial network, a treatment network, and an inmate ("client" or even "patient") network. Theoretically in this model, science should reign supreme, and the treatment staff, on the basis of its monopoly of the tools of correction, should have decisive authority. In practice, the preexisting power of the other two parties in the triangle, in particular that of the custodians, diminishes the power of the rehabilitators, despite the lip-service paid to their roles.

In declaring its objective of correction, this type of prison has reasserted a reformative purpose. At the same time, the inmates' collective interests and individual rights are largely disregarded. The inmate now had a "right" to treatment and to humane conditions of imprisonment. The rights of prison inmates as citizens of a state and members of a community were not yet acknowledged.

Finally, what we call the interactive prison represents the highest degree of power diffusion, polycentrism. The prison here comes to reflect the interests and divisions of class, race, ideology, and other factors found in the outside society. Moreover, these outside forces and institutions, including public opinion, cultural trends, and the judiciary, have a steadily increasing impact upon the prison community. This marks an important difference from the other three prison types, in which the inmate body had been, to a high degree, isolated from the outer world. The walls are now much more permeable, allowing for more and more interaction between the realm within and that without, as well as intensive interaction within the prison polity itself.

Some of the changes that took place in this most recent phase of the prison's development were deliberate: the products of administrative reform efforts aimed at opening up the closed prison society or the results of lawsuits designed to restore civil rights to those behind the walls. At the same time, other forces were at work, which reflected broader social trends. For example, the formation of guards' unions, in the context of public-service employees' organization for collective bargaining, further divorcing the interests of prison employees from those of their managers; the reorganization and bureaucratization of state departments of correction; and the rapid growth of all forms of mass communications were some of the developments that led to the pluralization of the prison polity.

The major characteristics of this fourfold prison typology are summarized in table 3-1.

The Enlightenment Prison

General Characteristics

The prison projected by eighteenth-century philosophers was intended to establish a humane regime for the prisoner. In the negative sense, it meant the absence of capital and corporal punishment. The penitentiary, in its original pure form, emerged as the intentional framework of penological ideas during the Age of Enlightenment. When perfected achitecturally in

Table 3–1
A Prison Typology

Prison	Power Configuration	Main Function	Principal Features
Enlightenment	*Unicentric:* Keepers over prisoners	Reformation: Penitence leading to redemption, development of work habits	Isolation Atomized prisoner body Silence system Warden autocracy Labor
Warehouse	*Bicentric:* Keepers versus convicts	Incapacitation	Custody, surveillance "Balance of power" Static polity Convict code Prison labor
Remedial	*Tricentric:* Keepers and Remediators and Inmates	Rehabilitation: "hospital" and "school" models	Treatment/training Indeterminate sentence Special role of treatment staff Programs Education
Interactive	*Polycentric:* Mass society: Prisoners, keepers, guards' unions, courts, legislatures, mass media, etc.	Simulated community: the "open" prison	Detotalization Permeability Diffusion of power Pluralism Judicial intervention/prisoners' rights

the 1820s, the *Pennsylvania model* could justly lay claim to being the closest approximation of the ideal model.

Although such a regime would appear contradictory to the very nature of a democratic society, there existed, as we have seen, a developed rationale for consigning those who offended against the social order to a type of quarantine.[1] While the humane approach to this problem abjured corporal and capital punishment, at the same time it could not run the risk of further corruption of the criminal within society or of criminals corrupting each other; hence the justification for total isolation behind impenetrable walls, and within individual secure cells. And even when this extreme of human isolation was modified through adoption of what came to be known as the congregate or Auburn system, the isolation principle was preserved by the rule of strict silence.

The penitentiary, then, was designed as a setting for enforced penitence, where the redemptive process of meditation and Bible reading would lead the sinner to the light of truth. The theoretical purpose of imprisonment was solely the moral reformation of the prisoner. In the absence of this purpose, Beaumont and Tocqueville wrote, "this would not any longer be a penitentiary system but only a bad system of imprisonment."[2]

The design and implementation of the Pennsylvania system in the first half of the nineteenth century called for total isolation of the inmate, incarceration in single cells (solitary confinement), and, after initial hesitation on this point, solitary work done in the prisoner's cell. The convict's separation from his fellow inmates was made complete through the use of a hood over his head while en route from his cell.

The Auburn system was principally a variant of the Pennsylvania system. In historical retrospect the similarities appear more significant than any of the reputed differences, which led to a half-century of debate over the respective merits. The difference in the New York model came mainly in its introduction of the so-called congregate system of labor during the day. The inmates worked in large rooms with other prisoners but returned to their cells at night. The congregate system used a rigid rule of silence to block association of the inmates, so that, though they occupied the same living space during the day, they remained isolated from each other. The Auburn model claimed advantages of a practical nature: supporters argued that it was cheaper and had less severe effects on the inmates than the unrelieved solitary confinement of the Pennsylvania system, which was charged with driving prisoners insane.[3]

The dominant assumption behind the penitentiary, either in the Pennsylvania or the Auburn form, was that the convicts must be isolated from each other. According to Beaumont and Tocqueville's observations on both these penal systems, "it is incontestable that this perfect isolation secures the prisoner from all fatal contamination."[4] Through maintaining isolation, if not always physical separation, the two systems tend to merge as a single conception of institutionalized banishment from the external world and apartness of each prisoner from his fellows. With prisoners wholly cut off from the main society, the "encompassing or total character," according to Goffman, "is symbolized by the barrier to social intercourse with the outside and to departure that is often built right into the physical plant."[5] To the extent that the early American penitentiary could achieve its own prescribed objectives, it would fulfill these features of the model Goffman has described.

In historical experience, this barrier to social intercourse with the outside was marked by the high walls of the penitentiary. In the Jacksonian era, the aim was to make this isolation as complete as possible. Visitors and mail for prisoners were under a virtually total ban.[6] Some relaxation came in the 1840s; one censored letter could be sent out every six months by a Sing-Sing convict and one every four months from the new Clinton Prison at Dannemora, New York. An inmate could also have one relative visit during his entire prison tenure. All books (except the Bible) and all newspapers remained strictly contraband.

It proved easier to maintain the impermeability of the walls than to keep the prisoners wholly isolated from each other. The congregate Auburn system was undermined as the absolute rule of silence was relaxed in the latter part of the nineteenth century when isolation could no longer be maintained through blocking intercommunication and interaction among prisoners working together in the same room. The separation model tended to give way to something less extreme. The inmates of the penitentiary remained shut away from the outside world, but no longer was there a total absence of a *society* among the captives.

Power Distribution in the Enlightenment Prison

The principle of power distribution in the enlightenment prison is *unicentric.* Theoretically if every prisoner is really in solitary, there can scarcely be any participation in the penitentiary polity by the body of prisoners. The inmates are subjects, even slaves, atomized and rendered powerless. If instead of being perpetually confined to a single cell, the prisoners are isolated behind a wall of silence, such solitude equally renders them inert and impotent. In terms of rulers vis-à-vis the ruled, such a prison, in which the prisoners are powerless and devoid of rights, would seem a perfect model of the concentration of the instruments of force and all other resources of power at the top.

While rudiments of community may seep into the silent system, in the solitary version the inmates can scarcely constitute a society of any sort since they are permitted no form of interaction. Thus a real question arises as to whether we are here dealing with anything that can properly be termed a polity—that is, a society in its political aspect. There remain certain attributes of an authoritarian-type governing system; these include a pattern of regimentation (for example, the military style in the Auburn system), enforced discipline, compulsory practices relating to penitential functions, and forced labor. But certainly there is a stark contradiction in finding such a coercive universe within an institution that professes humanistic goals. To the extent this model can be implemented in practice, the inmates are entirely foreclosed from aggregating into groups. This is perhaps the ultimate in a totalist model for the prison.

As a prison type, this enlightenment model could be realized in practice only for short periods and then never fully. Yet fragments of this model have remained in prison regimes down to the present. Solitary confinement is still widely used in one form or another and typically constitutes a kind of prison within a prison. Similarly the separate prison ("maxi-maxi") for the especially dangerous prisoner creates the kind of isolate situation postulated by the original penitentiary—with the difference that the idea of offender regeneration has been abandoned altogether.

Even assuming a relatively open prison, the availability to the keepers of various lock-up and lock-down options affects the power equation and holds out the threat of plunging the kept back into some kind of closed society approximating the traditional absolutist prison. There are other measures available to superior power, which may press the system in the direction of totalization. These include suppression of inmate groupings, interdiction of communication, and stringent censorship. Wherever such policies prevail, the inmate body tends to be to that degree more atomized, and we find at least a partial resurrection of the enlightenment prison.

The Warehouse Prison

General Characteristics

Once the ideal of prisoner reformation is abandoned, the penitentiary becomes essentially a kind of storage warehouse for society's rejects. The warehouse metaphor points to the emphasis on the incapacitative and retributive purposes of this custodial kind of prison. Of course, custody has always been a prominent and usually dominant feature of the prison system. The typical pattern for exercising the strictest supervision over inmates' daily lives has included such elements as marching in lockstep and wearing prison stripes, while enforcing stringent prison discipline. The extent to which particular prisons have conformed to such a model varied. But as a type, the traditional custody-oriented model remains in all probability the most persistent of any species of prison system. It was the elevation of the custody-as-punishment function that led to the development of the warehouse prison, which reflected obvious disillusionment with the optimistic expectation that regeneration was possible through the employment of reason and the exercise of free will. Despairing of these hopes, what is left are collections of down-and-out humans confined in huge bastilles, essentially left to their own devices.

The past half-century has seen the appearance of an extensive social-science literature examining the inmate society and culture found in this kind of prison. Beginning with Hans Reimer and Donald Clemmer in the 1930s, pioneering studies of the prison community have dissected the social system within that type of "pen" which John Irwin has recently epitomized as the Big House.[7] After around 1950, according to Irwin, the Big House largely faded into history (memorialized by the stereotypes of old movies). Yet it continued to be the model for many state prisons, reflecting the persistence of this species of prison regime both before and after the few decades (1930s to 1950s) when it was the dominant type.[8]

A sharp contrast between the enlightenment prison and the warehouse prison is evident in the fact that the early penitentiaries had been consciously constructed to carry out an idealized plan. The protagonists of the Pennsylvania model had such pride of creation that they viewed any tampering with its purity as a repudiation of the fundamental idea of what a penitentiary must be. To the separate-system advocates, compromising this core principle of the penal regime was the beginning of a total deterioration. As the deviationist Auburn system spread widely in the United States, the congregate feature, together with often-insufficient efforts to enforce the silent system, led increasingly to the mutual "contamination" of prisoners.[9] And it was through this process that the warehouse prison emerged in the mid-nineteenth century. Although isolation from the outside remained essentially intact, inside the walls the road was now opening up for the development of a complex prisoner polity.

For the remainder of the century and into the first quarter of the next, the hallmark of adult imprisonment was hard labor, which prevailed until the pressures of complaints from free labor and legislative enactments largely eliminated this component from the open market and reduced the convicts to idleness. Corporal punishment as the means of maintaining discipline again became the open practice, although the prisons of the enlightenment period (especially those on the Auburn pattern) had already revived corporal punishment. Solitary confinement now largely took on the special character of disciplinary punishment, featuring both mental and corporeal torture.

Meanwhile a subtle shift had taken place in the justification for the isolation of the penitentiary prisoner from society. Originally, since it was a corrupt society that had led to his downfall, the inmate's quarantine was primarily to protect him from any further contamination from the outside. This was also the rationale for building prisons in rural areas, far from corrupt cities. Many nineteenth-century moralists believed that laboring in the fields in the fresh country air would have a salutary effect on the soul of the convict. With its transformation to a warehouse prison, the same penitentiary with its impenetrable walls was now to keep the society free of corruption by the prisoners. Thus the paramount goal was not the convict's salvation but the protection of society—and these two goals became more and more opposed.

Power Distribution in the Warehouse Prison

The distribution of power in a warehouse prison reflects a *bicentric* pattern. A custody regime in a warehouse prison characteristically relaxes the effort to isolate the inmates from one another. Although the prison administration has an interest in keeping the inmate body as atomized as possible for reasons of security, the attempt to block the formation of groups or to break up those that have formed is pressed mainly when they threaten disruption. The warehouse prison accords with Goffman's total institution in that there is a functioning society inside even while the inmate inhabitants are cut off from the outside. The inmates of the warehouse prison are sealed in a large container and thereby barred from intercourse with, as well as departure to, the outer "free world." To the extent that inmate society has been atomized and natural groupings pulverized, the inmate is then resocialized into the inmate culture (Clemmer's "prisonization") by indigenous forces within the inmate world.[10] An underground society (and polity) coexists side by side with the rulership of the formal prison hierarchy. This peculiar system could not readily be characterized as totalitarian in that it is much less a monolith than a "duolith." What is apparent is that this warehouse prison stood in stark contrast to the idealized enlightenment penitentiary; there was "no solitude, no silence, no penitence, no reform."[11] Thus the warehouse prison resembles an original penitentiary that has lost its soul—retaining the form but emptied of its substance.

Where the enlightenment prison rests in principle on a pattern of power distribution in which total power and authority are concentrated in one place, the warehouse prison is based on a "dual-power" relationship between the inmate polity and the prison administration. The peculiarity of this arrangement is that it combines illegitimate covert authority on the one hand with legitimate overt authority on the other, under a rubric of a strange sort of partnership.

Despite the official monopoly of authorized force in the hands of the prison authorities, the actual power relations in the prison world are of a different order. The guard force is greatly outnumbered by the prisoners and, even granting the option of calling upon reinforcements from the outside, it is constantly vulnerable to being overwhelmed. Consequently the formal relation of forces merely establishes the general context within which the operative social and political system takes shape. On an informal and unofficial basis, the inmate body is ceded a sort of self-rule, often dominated by "con-bosses," who control the distribution of scarce values within the system. The old saw about prisons—that "the cons run the joint"—was meant to apply to this situation.

Certainly such a partnership is an uneasy one in many respects, yet the collaboration in maintaining a stable order has often been remarkably successful. This is not to say that the equilibrium is immune to upsets. But as long as the kind of balance of power required by the system is sustained— and there are strong interests on both sides in its maintenance, corrupt though it be—stability ordinarily can be maintained and disruptions of the power relations can be obviated. In the warehouse prison, the administrations controls the periphery and the inmates dominate the internal polity. Thus sheltered by the harsh isolation of the internal realm as against the outside free world, this unusual dual power relationship tended to persist.

The early literature on the prison social system and inmate culture was based largely on observation of the warehouse-type prison. Surprising as it may seem, the inmate forces typically espouse a conservative ideology, stressing maintenance of the status quo. Richard Cloward suggests that "the official system accommodates to the inmate system in ways that have the consequence of creating *illegitimate opportunity structures,*" that is, varying political roles, apportioning power and status to the individual inmates within a covert society based upon deprivation and degradation.[12]

It may be questioned whether such an inmate polity has taken on the genuine character of a civil society, even in terms of the authoritarian conception of Thomas Hobbes rather than the liberal construct of John Locke. The inmate realm is perhaps not quite "the war of all against all" depicted in Hobbes's state of nature; still, the claims of power and status emerge in a milieu marked by coercion and intimidation rather than by free consent. The stakes in the system are reflected in the accommodations for personal benefit reached by individuals and groups in the inmate elite and acquiesced in by the prison administrative establishment. The de facto legitimacy of this dual power arrangement is based on tacit and informal acceptance of a static and undisrupted status quo sustained by common interest.

Retributive at its core, the warehouse prison finds its rationale in the requirements of social defense. The very weakness of the warehouse prison's claim to legitimacy invites its displacement.

The Remedial Prison

General Characteristics

Approximately a century after the American Revolution, the reform motif made a strong comeback. Noteworthy landmarks of this resurgence included the founding in 1870 of the National Prison Association, today called the American Correctional Association, and the establishment of the model reformatory at Elmira, New York, in 1876, with Zebulon Brockway as warden.[13] The ensuing century was to see the professed emphasis in America's approach to punishment on the need to treat, to correct, to rehabilitate the confined criminal, who was now to be regarded more as a secluded patient than an incarcerated prisoner. A speaker at the 1870 founding Congress of the National Prison Association set the tone:

> A criminal is a man who has suffered under a disease evinced by the perpetration of a crime and who may reasonably be held to be under the

dominion of such disease until his conduct has afforded very strong presumption not only that he is free from its immediate influence, but that the chances of its recurrence have become exceedingly remote.[14]

For the ensuing hundred years, the medical model has held sway; the imprisoned are considered in some sense "mentally ill" and the goal of their confinement must be to treat them as patients and remake (or rehabilitate) them into healthy and whole individuals.

The metaphor, however, raises more questions than it answers. How and by whom is the treatment to be carried out? In a field where diagnostic and prognostic knowledge and techniques are notoriously undeveloped, on what premises would the proper "cure" be based?

The concept of a remedial prison is a more-inclusive category than suggested by the medical analogy. The original enlightenment prison was also remedial in aiming at the ultimate reformation of the prisoner. In these terms, the enlightenment prison certainly operated on a principle of correction that sought to remedy lawless behavior, utilizing the instrument of incarceration. The crucial distinction lay in contrasting notions on the source of change in the lawbreaker's behavior.

The enlightenment conception prescribes that the offender is to be given the opportunity in prison for his personal regeneration. Under the right form of penitentiary custody, the inmate eventually will grasp society's norms through meditation and repentance. These norms, reflected in the criminal law, are derived from the principles of natural law. This notion of rehabilitation rests on the proposition that silent and solitary contemplation can lead to repentance. Even with the fading of the ideal penitentiary, a crude rationale of rehabilitation through labor was ready to take its place in the Auburn model.

What was distinctive about the later approach was the belief that remedial action must be applied to the prison inmate from the outside (or from above); and the treatment must be based on the most advanced scientific methods. The remedial prison was a child of philosophic positivism.

The key features in which positivism contrasts with classicism, which underlay the enlightenment conception, are a deterministic view of human behavior (as against free will), inductive methodology buttressed by empirical research (as against formalistic legal codes derived through rationalistic deductive method), and the belief that punishment should fit the criminal (rather than the crime).[15] The corollary of this final characteristic is the advocacy of the indeterminate sentence as indispensable to the individualized treatment model.[16]

Given its commitment to scientific knowledge, the remedial prison brings the expert into a central position, because only through expertise can the laws of human behavior be understood, the reformation of individuals directed along the correct path, and discretion exercised scientifi-

cally. All of these elements infuse the "perfected reformatory" depicted in
the early twentieth century by Zebulon Brockway:

> The common notion of a moral responsibility based on freedom should no
> longer be made a foundation principle for . . . prison treatment. . . . To-
> gether with abrogation of this responsibility goes, too, any awesome regard
> for individual liberty of choice and action by imprisoned criminals. Their
> habitual conduct and indeed their related character must needs be directed
> and really determined by their legalized custodians. . . . The perfected re-
> formatory will be the receptacle and refinery of antisocial humans who are
> held in custody under discretional indeterminateness for the purpose of the
> public protection.[17]

Expertise thus plays a key role in running the prison. This approach required "a passionless scientific procedure" and even "penalties for official
malfeasance" if there is too frequent recidivism among discharged prisoners.[18] But what sorts of training would reshape the inmates' behavior in
the right direction? For Brockway, one of the leading prison reformers of
the second half of the last century, the remedy was to be found in an industrial training school, other forms of education, and intensive physical training.[19]

The treatment idea has taken many forms over the past century. Virtually anything can be provided with a rationale that will make it into a
treatment, including punishment. By the 1950s, when the idea of implementing therapeutic programs in prisons became popular, the repertoire of
possible remedial devices included numerous types of psychological thera-
pies (such as psychotherapy, reality therapy, and various kinds of behavior
modification), as well as environmental therapy (group therapy and milieu
management).[20] All of this treatment aimed to achieve what was now universally termed rehabilitation. In 1954, in the wake of a wave of prison
riots, the American Prison Association changed its name to the American
Correctional Association, signaling a commitment to rehabilitative goals.[21]
Correctional institutions became the predominant designation for prisons
by the middle of the twentieth century.[22] While the name remained unchanged, the correctional idea suffered a sharp decline. The wave of violence that erupted at Attica and elsewhere in the early 1970s led to some
immediate improvements in the conditions of imprisonment. However, it
did not stimulate a renewal of the remedial prison. Rather it led critics of
the correctional system in quite different directions.

Power Distribution in the Remedial Prison

Many of the difficulties of the remedial prison lie in the peculiarities of its
tricentric power distribution. This rests on a triad made up of prisoners,

treatment staff, and custodial personnel. The remedial prison is distinguished from the warehouse prison by the addition of a third bloc, the treatment staff, to the duality of the keepers and the kept of the custodial model. The treatment staff, with its monopoly of expertise, in principle should have ultimate power and authority of decision making in the remedial prison. The theoretical predominance of the treatment staff in the correctional facility is legitimized by its monopoly of the knowledge and skills to bring about the "cure."

In reality, however, the treatment side of the triad was rarely conceded a dominant position, much less a monopoly of power. The custodial function retained its primacy in maximum-security institutions. And despite the ascendancy of positivism in academic criminology of the late nineteenth and early twentieth centuries, the scientific reformation of human behavior in a prison setting remained a dubious enterprise. The guards, untrained in the methods and ideology of treatment, often thought it worthless and resented downgrading of their own custodial roles. This discrepancy between the ideal dominance of the correction side and its actual subordination to the requirements of custody constitutes a source of tension between the treatment staff and the guard staff. The two groups ordinarily had separate organizations, lines of authority, and relationships to inmates while pursuing divergent, often contradictory values and purposes.[23]

The simple triadic relationship posited here is little more than a starting point from which to explore the definitions and interrelations of the different segments of prison society. The first question is one of definition. Who belongs in the treatment category? Psychologists and psychiatrists, case workers and counselors, group leaders and social worker therapists and other psychological helpers (sometimes including a sector of the guards) are typically assigned to the treatment component. But how widely one casts one's net depends on the particular treatment ideology one adopts.[24]

By the 1950s, rehabilitation, by whatever definition, was the prevalent approach; there were few in what was by now known as corrections who did not give at least lip-service to it. However, treatment in adult prisons was a negligible factor before this time despite the stated intention of the National Prison Association, since its founding in 1870, to make rehabilitation the primary aim of imprisonment. The ideal of reformation was translated into programs primarily in juvenile institutions, following the model of the Elmira Reformatory under Zebulon Brockway. There were a few experimental treatment programs in adult prisons between the 1870s and the 1940s, but they did little to restructure fundamentally the warehouse prison.

Although treatment staff and their programs played only a minor role in the power structure of even the more progressive prisons, a number of treatment methods did develop during these early years. Parallel with this was an ever-widening scope of discretionary authority of correctional personnel, inherent in the indeterminate sentence and classification schemes.

After World War II, more funds and more professional personnel became available for developing programs.[25] Also with the implementation during the Great Depression of legislation restricting commerce in products of prison labor, treatment programs could serve the function of filling the time vacuum that this had created, thereby avoiding the curse of the "idle shop." Thus, by the 1950s the groundwork for the preeminence of the rehabilitation model had been laid, and the prestige, if not always the power, of the treatment personnel was greatly enhanced.

This breakthrough for the rehabilitative model after World War II was far from complete, however, and achieved very mixed results. Although there is little doubt that the treatment side succeeded in enhancing its authority vis-à-vis custody, its real power position was often something very different from what it appeared to be.

In some cases, the mere presence of therapists would be paraded as proof of the prison's commitment; the creation of this impression seemed, in many cases, to be the main function of the treatment personnel.[26] Even when professional staff began with the goal of achieving the stated purposes of the remedial prison, the actual circumstances of prison life—the frustrations, hostility, and rejection on all sides—typically led through defeatism and cynicism back to conformity with custodially oriented norms.

Although the initial expectation might have been that the more prominent role for the helping and remedial side would promote a constructive relationship between the treaters and their clients (or patients), in actuality the life of a remedial prison more often than not features conflict between the treaters and the treated. The manipulative aspects of the therapeutic model, with its authoritarian implications (such as in behavior modification), are often resented by the inmates, who confound the game by "conning" the counselors.

The conflict between inmates and professional staff, however, does not undermine the remedial prison to the same extent as does the more open and structural conflict between treatment and custodial staffs for institutional supremacy. This conflict has been accelerated in recent years through the formation and growing militancy of officers' unions.

Thus power relations in the remedial prison—relations that include both custody and treatment personnel as well as their involuntary clients— are far more complex than in the warehouse prison. Moreover the prison polity is increasingly enmeshed within a wider political web, encompassing state correctional agencies, organized labor, legislatures, mass media, and public and interest-group opinion.[27] No longer can the penitentiary exist as the isolated fiefdom of a largely autonomous warden. Nor do we find a stable balance of power within the remedial prison. There is little indication that the emphasis on rehabilitation makes for greater harmony and stability than in the traditional warehouse prison context; on the contrary, the remedial prison is often a more conflicted environment.²⁸ Substantial progress has been made in identifying the sources of conflict as they exist in particular institutions and as they form persistent patterns.²⁹

Although the warehouse prison found its formula for relative peace between prison authorities and the inmate body, it is unclear that this result was either desirable or sustainable over the long run. A key precondition was, evidently, the high degree of isolation from the outside world, symbolized and in fact maintained by the massive walls. Then with the lessened security of a more "open" prison, frequently created within the very same fortress structure, came multiple destabilizing factors, many of these growing out of the increased contact with the outside world. But it is doubtful that there is any way back to the simpler ways of the traditional warehouse prison once the medical model of individual attention and treatment has begun to transform the basic milieu. Whatever the covert forms of oppression cited by its critics, however contradictory the coexistence of custody and treatment, it was in the remedial prison, with its educational and rehabilitation programs, that the first chinks in the massive walls of the penitentiary appeared. This evolution pointed the way toward a new configuration of forces reflective of the outside society and its political values.

The Interactive Prison

General Characteristics

The interactive prison reveals features that mark it off from the other models of the prison. It is distinctly modern, as evidenced by such contemporary creations as guards' and prisoners' unions. And while many of its contours were at least partly foreshadowed in earlier prison types, today's prison is being decisively reshaped by the communications technologies that have revolutionized American society during the past half century.

A variety of labels have been proposed for broadly similar constructs: *pluralistic, balkanized, violent, contemporary, new.*³⁰ The designation *open prison,* despite ambiguous usage, comes closer. But "open" to what and for what? Our label, *interactive,* is surely not problem-free; however, the basic notion of interaction—defined as mutual or reciprocal action or influence—has the merit of focusing not only on the one crucial characteristic distinguishing this type of prison from the typically isolated prisons of the past, but also on the dynamic qualities of today's social institutions.

The formerly impermeable walls have become penetrable to the products of the mass media, to the organizational technologies of modern mass society. Under the impact of such forces prison inmates look increasingly to outsiders—often of very different social origins from their own—with whose help they can pursue cultural, educational, vocational, social, and self-realization projects linked both to their fellow captives and to the outside.[31] Finally, no longer are the imprisoned as if civilly dead; the courts, abandoning their long standing hands-off policy, have ruptured this wall of silence, and reconnected the inmate to the world of civic status and citizens' rights.[32]

Thus the interactive prison provides an institutional setting different from all earlier ones, which, regardless of their objectives, approximated the model of what Goffman called a total institution.[33] This latest model is far less clear in its goals than either the remedial or the enlightenment prison, less secure in its custody, and less isolated than the warehouse prison. In its present form it departs from the positivistic individualized medical model of the remedial prison, reverting instead to the premises of antideterminism—together with a standard of "just deserts" for the offender—once found in the enlightenment prison.

But above all, it was the emergent role of groups, rather than individuals, which marked the social and political life of the interactive prison. Groups meant identity, power, and security for the inmate in the interactive prison. Since many of these groups were based on ethnic affiliation, they provided the prisoner with a link to both past and future outside the walls, thus intensifying the interaction between inside and outside. Groups rather than individuals became the principal unit in the society of captives within the interactive prison.

Nevertheless, it was the remedial prison—with its concepts of individual rehabilitation through education, participation, and psychological treatment—that began the process of opening the prison and creating the milieu in which a pluralistic political culture could develop. It was inside the remedial prison that the networks began to form which then played a vital role in the communications and power distribution of the interactive prison. The interactive prison evolved in a period of intensive politicization within what was still the remedial prison. Consequently its polity also oriented itself to the diverse arenas of power, outside the walls, such as the courts, the administrative bureaucracies, the state executives, and legislatures.

But where will all the overt and covert activity and communications of the interactive prison lead? With its undefined goals and shifting power bases, a sense of purpose is difficult to discern. It becomes problematic even to specify the functional basis of the institution, other than the traditional one of custody. There is no clear notion of how to prevent violence or how to cope with it when it comes, except by violent countermeasures. The prison as a social institution remains in part retributive, in part incapacitive, and only ambivalently rehabilitative.

Power Distribution in the Interactive Prison

The hallmark of the interactive prison is a *polycentric* distribution of power. In the three other types of prison discussed previously, power is either highly concentrated or divided in such a way as to serve the purposes of the model. The physical and social context of all these prior models is congenial to institutional totalism. A diffused power model, on the other hand, by definition cannot generate a total institution. In practice, of course, these prisons of the past were never as total as their conceptual bases would presuppose. But in the interactive prison, as a power diffusion model, this result is contradicted. The deconcentration of relatively consolidated power (if not monolithic, certainly authoritarian in one way or another) requires a process of redistribution of power. The name we suggest for this evolutionary process is *detotalization.*

This detotalization, broadly speaking, takes a course that has striking similarities to a "thaw" in a totalitarian system. From a rigidly coercive system, the political culture opens up into some sort of pluralistic system and to political consciousness. The competing interests may have been present covertly all along, but now they acquire an overt form and a quasi-legitimacy. The effects on the political culture are likely to be pervasive, long-lasting, and extremely difficult to reverse. The transformation of a warehouse prison, for example, into a more "open" arena could only be reversed at the price of atomizing the prisoners' groups and forcefully recompressing the inmates into an authoritarian framework (in short, "retotalization"). It is unlikely that this could be accomplished without a great deal of violence.

Closely related to detotalization, but to be distinguished, are the changes brought about by democratization and liberalization. The terms as we use them here are not interchangeable, though they overlap in many respects. *Democratization* is a political process whereby the prisoner is transformed from subject to citizen. This is a complex process, which entails expanded participation in the prison polity and a widening of its political base. While it would be absurd to claim that democracy has come to the prison, there is a sense in which the leadership of the prison must increasingly take account of its constituencies—inmates, guards, and other staff components.

The courts have been giving a push to this development. The movement is not all in one direction; but prison inmates do seem to have advanced toward a sort of quasi-citizenship, together with a deepened "engagement of the governed in their own governance."[34] But the degree to which this can or will go forward, as well as the forms it is to take, is far from clear.

Is the prison polity to construct a representative government? In essence, this is what is meant by political liberalization. While the responsiveness of the system is linked to the degree of political democracy—that is, the breadth of the political base—the responsibility of the government to the governed depends on the working of parliamentary (or constitutional) institutions. Only infrequently have prison polities erected more than rudimentary instruments of formal governance; but those experiments that have been attempted can provide some insight into the possibilities and the problems of particular formulas for political liberalization.

In the dynamic process leading to an open polity, there are three levels. The surface level is the institutional or superstructural dimension, where liberalization of the polity takes place, if at all, through the construction of constitutional frameworks. This is the plane on which liberal reforms occur; if the political structures work, responsible government has been installed. Conversely if the system degenerates or collapses, then the challenge on this level is to recreate a better and more durable superstructure.

The next level, democratization, involves a process broader than institutionalization. Of course, the participatory role can expand or recede, thus increasing or decreasing the responsiveness of the system. In principle, a reversal on this plane would amount to degrading "citizens" to "subjects." Finally, the level of detotalization is the deepest and most basic dimension. A structural process is involved here. This is the plane on which the end of isolation has its most profound impact on the prison community, independently of any particular regime. This process involves an end to atomization through a process of group formation, eventually leading to a pluralistic prison polity.

Beginning in the 1960s, dramatic changes took place in the familiar prison culture. Its monolithic character, governed by the formidable convict code, became fragmented; the starkly oppositional quality of the culture gave way to a multiplicity of competing norms and loyalties. The conflicts and consciousness of the civil rights movement made race an increasingly important factor in the relationships among inmates and between inmates and staff. Perhaps most significant was the emergence, in either legitimate or illegitimate form, of inmate groups or organizations. In only a few cases have there been analyses of these phenomena highlighting the political side. Particularly within the prisons of states with large urban centers, such pluralization of the inmate polity tended to reflect the power distribution in ghetto streets. Jacobs has described the volatile process by which gangs (and what he terms "super-gangs") came to dominate an Illinois penitentiary.[35]

What we have been describing has mainly to do with the challenge from below to the formerly absolute power and authority of the prison regime, headed typically by the warden. We must also consider the challenge to that authority from above, from outside the prison polity. Although this concerns many elements—central state bureaucracy, legislatures and governors, interest groups, the media, the public—here we will focus on one institution that has made a striking impact on the prison: the judiciary. Since about 1960 the courts, especially the federal courts, have assumed an active role in building a body of inmates' rights, placing limits on the authority of prison administrations, and thus bringing the life of the prison within the ambit of the U.S. Constitution. This judicial activism is particularly true of the lower federal courts. The United States Supreme court, as well as the state courts, have played a much less important role. Inevitably, there is a substantial gap between decision and implementation, between promise and fulfillment for the inmates.

An overview of two decades of judicial involvement reveals two broad phases. During the 1960s, having largely abandoned a hands-off stance, the courts moved toward enhancing the status of prisoners as persons. Constitutionally this meant that inmates were to be accorded First Amendment rights (religion, speech) and "due process" under the Fourteenth Amendment. In a rare and belated pronouncement in this area, the Supreme Court in 1974 stated, "There is no iron curtain drawn between the Constitution and the prisons of this country."[36]

The earlier bid for religious rights by Black Muslim prisoners had established the initial bridgehead for First Amendment guarantees. A suit was initiated in 1962 by a Muslim leader at Stateville, Thomas Cooper, charging that he was being held in segregation as punishment for his religion and, for the same reason, was being denied access to the Koran and Muslim literature. The partial victory which Cooper won in the courts after five years of litigation had effects not only on major trends in the law, but boosted the Muslims' prestige in prisons and had an impact on the status of inmates generally.[37]

Another pioneer in the area of prisoner litigation was Martin Sostre. Originally a Moslem and then a political radical, he persevered in his law suits over two decades, becoming the first United States inmate to be designated by Amnesty International as a political prisoner, and being granted a pardon in 1976. Sostre's law suit concerning the right of Muslims to practice their religion was upheld in 1964; and in 1970 a court granted him relief from harsh treatment that appeared clearly to stem from dislike of his radical politics.[38]

In 1974 the Supreme Court pronounced for the first time on the issue of due process in disciplinary hearings. In a suit brought by Nebraska prison inmates, the high court, while firmly rejecting any right to counsel in such proceedings, outlined a minimal list of procedural requirements, including at least twenty-four-hours' written notice to the inmate of the charges against him.[39] That same year the Supreme Court placed certain restraints on what was formerly the unlimited authority of prison officials to censor prisoners' mail.[40] Two years earlier, a federal district judge in a Wisconsin case involving the right to correspondence by mail had ruled in the inmate's favor, arguing that "those convicted of crime should continue to share with the general population the full, latent protection of the 14th Amendment."[41] The applicable legal standard for placing any restriction at all on the exercise of these rights would be a "compelling governmental interest" in treating prison inmates differently. On appeal, however, a circuit court substituted a "rational relationship" standard, which was considerably more permissive (to state authorities)—meaning that prison administrators were given ample scope to do virtually as they wished.[42]

As to prisoners' rights of association, in 1972 a federal district judge issued a restraining order in Rhode Island against any attempt to interfere with the meetings at the prison of the National Prisoners Reform Association (NPRA), an organization with both inmate and noninmate members.[43] The authorities presented no evidence that the NPRA differed (except for its interracial character) from many other organizations allowed to meet with outside members. But if prison reformers and activists saw this as a prelude to the extension of such organizational rights by the higher courts, they were to be disappointed.

In 1977 the case of a prisoners' union in North Carolina came before the Supreme Court. The district court had found the state department of corrections' regulations unconstitutional, designed to crush the union. The Supreme Court, in overruling the lower court, conceded maximum discretion to prison administrators to restrict organizational rights. The Court took the position that the state need show only a rational basis—not a compelling state interest (the usual first Amendment test)—for interfering in these rights. Justice William Rehnquist, speaking for the majority, chided the district court for not having given "appropriate deference to the decisions of prison administrators and appropriate recognition to the peculiar and restrictive circumstances of penal confinement." Justice Thurgood Marshall, in dissent, viewed this decision as having essentially foreclosed further reform in prisons through court intervention.[44] It is clear that the Supreme Court majority was drawing a tight line on political rights, this decision representing a long step back toward the discredited hands-off doctrine.

Thus the constitutional status of prisoners in the United States has become something less than "citizen" but rather more than "subject." This "intrusion of the legal system" aimed at putting limits on the absolutist authority of prison administrators to the gain of the prisoners.[45] At the same time this judicial activism entails an increase in judicial power and raises the issue of separation of powers.[46] The controversy over this development can be seen most sharply in the courts' treatment of the Eighth Amendment, the ban on "cruel and unusual punishment." In the 1970s, this hitherto neglected provision of the Bill of Rights was pressed into service as the principal ground for declaring entire prisons and prison systems unconstitutional. By the end of the decade, federal court decisions of this kind had affected half the states.[47] Particularly controversial were Judge Frank Johnson's tough decisions, threatening to close Alabama's prisons unless they were brought up to minimal standards of human treatment. The strong opposition of the governor, George Wallace, who accused the judge of aiming to create a "hotel atmosphere" in the prisons, quickly politicized the issue: "Why should a judge worry about whether they [the prisoners] have enough room to sleep in? They can sleep on their heads, as far as I'm concerned."[48]

Wallace's opposition, however, did not deter Judge Johnson; and his example has spread to other areas of the country. But these issues are not likely to fade, given the basic questions of power and authority involved. Historically the judicial function has usually been exercised by negative commands. Today the courts have mandated actions of an affirmative nature and must then oversee their implementation. But the more fundamental issue of whether courts should be acting in spheres that had traditionally belonged to administrators remains in the center of the controversy. An academic critic has said in relation to Judge Johnson and others:

> The courts are still engaged in expanding rights and reducing powers. With what effect? . . . The overall effect of judicial intervention in social-policy administration is to reduce the responsibility and range of discretion of administrators and service workers; . . . one may well wonder whether social policy has been improved by judicial intervention.[49]

In June 1981, the U.S. Supreme Court ruled eight to one that "double-celling" in an Ohio prison does not violate "contemporary standards of decency" under the Eighth Amendment. In overturning the lower court, the Court majority argued that *cruel and unusual* does not necessarily forbid more than one man in a cell, but turns on the "totality of circumstances" in a particular prison.[50] Justice Thurgood Marshall, in his dissent, wondered if this was a "step toward abandoning" the courts' overseer role in the Eighth Amendment area.[51] The tone of this decision, even more than its exact terms, was discouraging to those who have looked to the courts in this area. Nevertheless, this retreat is not likely to take the judiciary out of the interactive prison.

Notes

1. The eighteenth-century Enlightenment gave birth to what has become known as classical criminology, most closely associated with the name of Cesare Beccaria, an Italian. Beccaria's principles were rooted in

social contract theory, which posited civil society as having brought an end to the presocial "war of all against all" (Hobbes). Thus punishment was to function as a social-control device to prevent the disruption of the social fabric and mend it if necessary. For a succinct summary of classical criminology, see Ian Taylor, Paul Walton, and Jock Young, *The New Criminology: For a Social Theory of Deviance* (New York: Harper Torchbooks, 1973), pp. 1-3.

2. G. de Beaumont and A. de Tocqueville, *On the Penitentiary System in the United States* (Philadelphia: Corey, Lea, and Blanchard, 1833), p. 2. For a succinct but detailed description of the Pennsylvania and the Auburn systems, see Harry Elmer Barnes and Negley K. Teeters, *New Horizons in Criminology,* 2d ed. (Englewood Cliffs, N.J.: Prentice-Hall, 1951), pp. 399-412.

3. Charles Dickens, *American Notes* (London: Macmillan, 1903). While convinced that "in its intention . . . it is kind, humane and meant for reformation," Dickens described the effects of the solitary system in chilling terms and held "this slow and daily tampering with the mysteries of the brain to be worse than any torture of the body." Ibid., p. 86. Dickens' observations on the effects of solitary confinement, together with more recent psychological studies, were cited to support the testimony of an expert witness in the suit brought by inmates of the Washington State Penitentiary (*Hoptowit* v. *Ray,* 79-359—ED Wash., 1980). See Richard R. Korn, "Report on Conditions at WSP at Walla Walla," Appendix, pp. 34-41.

4. Beaumont and Tocqueville, *Penitentiary System,* p. 23.

5. Erving Goffman, *Asylums* (Garden City, N.Y.: Doubleday, Anchor Books, 1961), pp. 4, 13.

6. David J. Rothman, *The Discovery of the Asylum* (Boston: Little, Brown, 1971), pp. 94-95.

7. Hans Reimer, "Socialization in the Prison Community," in *Proceedings of the American Prison Association, 1937* (New York: APA, 1937), pp. 151-155; Donald Clemmer, *The Prison Community* (New York: Rinehart, 1958—originally published 1940); John Irwin, *Prisons in Turmoil* (Boston: Little, Brown, 1980), chap. 1. For an extensive listing of sources on the prison social system during its heyday in the 1940s and 1950s as a research focus, see Richard A. Cloward et al., *Theoretical Studies in Social Organization of the Prison* (New York: Social Science Research Council, 1960), pp. 5-7.

8. Irwin, *Prisons,* pp. 1-3.

9. Barnes and Teeters, *New Horizons,* pp. 412-416. See also Rothman, *Discovery,* p. 102.

10. Goffman (*Asylums,* p. 13), observing the total institutions of the mid-twentieth century, rejects the term *desocialization* as being "too strong, implying a loss of fundamental capacities to communicate and

cooperate." Instead he uses the less extreme *disculturation,* which seems close to Clemmer's *prisonization,* discussed in Clemmer, *Prison Community,* pp. 298–315.

11. George Wilson Pierson, *Tocqueville and Beaumont in America* (New York: Oxford University Press, 1938), p. 702. This is Pierson's summation of how Tocqueville and Beaumont would perceive the American penitentiary a century after their famous visit.

12. Richard A. Cloward, "Social Control in the Prison," in Cloward et al., *Social Organization,* pp. 33–41. Cf. Gresham M. Sykes and Sheldon L. Messinger, "The Inmate Social System," in Cloward et al., *Social Organization,* pp. 10–11, and Irwin, *Prison,* pp. 12–14, where the author provides a similar but somewhat more elaborate listing of prisoner types.

13. For a brief account of the early development of Elmira under Brockway, see Blake McKelvey, *American Prisons: A History of Good Intentions* (Montclair, N.J.: Patterson Smith, 1977), pp. 131–138. See also Zebulon R. Brockway, *Fifty Years of Prison Service: An Autobiography* (New York: Charities Publication Committee, 1912).

14. Quoted in Jessica Mitford, *The American Prison Business* (Harmondsworth, England: Penguin Books, 1977), p. 100.

15. For a brief discussion of these contrasts, see Sue Titus Reid, *Crime and Criminology* (Hinsdale, Ill.: Dryden Press, 1976), pp. 104–128.

16. In recent years, disillusionment with the indeterminate sentence has become widespread; and criticism of it has been a major focus accompanying the decline of the treatment-oriented prison model and the emergence of a neoclassicist school of realists. Concerning the neoclassical revival, see the collection of writings in Leon Radzinowicz and M.E. Wolfgang, eds., *Crime and Justice,* vol. 3: *The Criminal Under Restraint,* 2d rev. ed. (New York: Basic Books, 1977).

17. Quoted in *Struggle for Justice: A Report on Crime and Punishment in America* (Prepared for the American Friends Service Committee) (New York: Hill and Wang, 1971), pp. 37–38.

18. Ibid.

19. See McKelvey, *American Prisons,* pp. 131–138.

20. For a brief summation of these treatment modalities, see Reid, *Crime,* pp. 550–559.

21. See McKelvey, *American Prisons,* p. 327.

22. See Irwin, *Prisons,* pp. 37–65.

23. Cressey distinguishes three distinct staff groups: one for "keeping" the inmates (custodial), another for "serving" them (treatment) and a third for "using" them (industrial). See Donald R. Cressey, "Adult Felons in Prison" in Lloyd E. Ohlin, ed., *Prisoners in America* (Englewood Cliffs, N.J.: Prentice Hall, 1973), pp. 117–150. While this three-fold break-down of the "keepers" suggests some further complexities in power relationships,

for our present purpose we retain the focus on the basic custody-treatment axis as it relates to the "kept."

24. In Elliot Studt et al., *C-Unit: Search for Community in Prison* (New York: Russell Sage Foundation, 1968), the authors outline (pp. 10–19) five models derived from distinct ideologies: custodial, educational, individual psychotherapy, group treatment, and resocialization, the last being their own experiment in using all available resources to change the prison society into a different sort of community.

25. See Irwin, *Prisons,* p. 40.

26. See Thomas O. Murton, *The Dilemma of Prison Reform* (New York: Holt, Rinehart and Winston, 1976), pp. 115–117. The narrow research role assigned to state criminologists working in Illinois' prisons—which have included such well-known names as Lloyd Ohlin, Saul Alinsky, and Donald Clemmer—is underlined in James B. Jacobs, *Stateville: The Prison in Mass Society* (Chicago: University of Chicago Press, 1977), p. 19.

27. See Peter H. Rossi and Richard A. Berk, "The Politics of State Corrections" in David F. Greenberg, ed., *Corrections and Punishment* (Beverly Hills: Sage, 1977), pp. 69–88. See also Richard McCleery, "Correctional Administration and Political Change" in L. Hazelrigg, ed., *Prison within Society* (Garden City, N.Y.: Doubleday, Anchor Books, 1969), pp. 113–149.

28. J.E. Thomas, comparing the traditional (warehouse) prison and the rehabilitative (remedial) one, notes that in addition to "the sheer intrinsic stress" of prison work, rehabilitative policies introduce "increasing uncertainty and uneasiness" on the part of staff. J.E. Thomas, "A 'Good Man for Gaoler'? Crisis, Discontent, and the Prison Staff," in John C. Freeman, ed., *Prisons Past and Future* (London: Heineman, 1978), p. 58.

29. Among recent literature, see Edith E. Flynn, "From Conflict Theory to Conflict Resolution: Controlling Collective Violence in Prisons," *American Behavioral Scientist* 23 (May-June 1980):745–776; G. David Garson, "The Disruption of Prison Administration: An Investigation of Alternative Theories of the Relationship Among Administrators, Reformers, and Involuntary Social Service Clients," *Law and Society Review* 6 (May 1972):531–561; Hans Toch, *Police, Prisons, and the Problem of Violence* (Rockville, Md.: National Institute of Mental Health, 1977), pp. 73–89.

30. On the application of "balkanized" see Jacobs, *Stateville,* p. 159. Irwin, (*Prisons,* p. xiii) uses the term "contemporary"—apparently for lack of a more substantive term—as the final entry in his general historical sequence; however, he goes on to label the "last stage" of the current social processes as "the violent prison" (p. xiv). John Conrad and Simon Dinitz (*Position Paper on the Isolated Prisoner,* Columbus, Ohio, 1977) speak of the "new prison" (p. 16.).

31. A striking example of an educational interchange was the formation of the "Soledad-Santa Cruz Collective." University of California at Santa Cruz students met as a college class inside the California prison in the

early 1970s. See Karlene Faith, ed., *Soledad Prison: University of the Poor* (Palo Alto: Science and Behavior Books, 1975).

32. See Ronald L. Goldfarb and Linda R. Singer, *After Conviction* (New York: Simon and Schuster, 1973), pp. 364-369.

33. On total institution, see Goffman, *Asylums.*

34. David Fogel, *We are the Living Proof,* 2d ed. (Cincinnati: W.H. Anderson, 1979), p. 209. Fogel, in presenting his so-called "justice model," here argues that: "The prison is not an ideal setting for democracy, but . . . [it can] be more democratized."

35. See Jacobs, *Stateville;* Erik Olin Wright, *The Politics of Punishment* (New York: Harper & Row), 1973; Theodore Davidson, *Chicago Prisoners: The Key to San Quentin* (New York: Holt, Rinehart and Winston 1974); Ronald Berkman, *Opening the Gates: The Rise of the Prisoners' Movement* (Lexington, Mass.: Lexington Books, D.C. Heath and Company, 1979); Irwin, *Prisons.* A recent study of prison organization in five maximum-security institutions, focusing on the guard and administration components as well as the inmates, was conducted by Robert Montilla and James G. Fox. See James G. Fox, *The Organizational Context of the Prison* (Sacramento, Calif.: American Justice Institute, 1980).

36. *Wolff* v. *McDonnell,* 418 U.S. 539 (1974). For at least a decade after lower federal courts had begun to abandon the hands-off approach, the high court had given only its tacit approval.

37. See the description of this legal saga in Jacobs, *Stateville,* pp. 64-67.

38. *Sostre* v. *McGinnis* 334 F. 2d 906 (1964); *Sostre* v. *Rockefeller* 312 F.Supp. 863 (1970).

39. *Wolff* v. *McDonnell.* See also Alvin J. Bronstein, "Reform Without Change: The Future of Prisoners' Rights," *Civil Liberties Review* 4 (September-October 1977):32-33. Bronstein observes that these guarantees were "substantially less than had been ordered by many lower state and federal courts."

40. See Bronstein, "Reform," p. 36; *Procunier* v. *Martinez* 416 U.S. 396 (1974).

41. *Morales* v. *Schmidt,* 340 F.Supp. 544 (WD Wis., 1972) quoted in Sheldon Krantz, *The Law of Corrections and Prisoners Rights* (St. Paul: West, 1973), pp. 328, 329, 336-338.

42. Ibid., p. 329, 336-338. The philosophy reflected in this federal judge's opinion goes perhaps as far as any judicial statement in extending the constitutional rights of prisoners. His view contemplates the modification (or abolition) of the prison system, if necessary. See also Goldfarb and Singer, *After Conviction,* pp. 678-679; Berkman, *Opening the Gates,* pp. 42-44.

43. *NPRA* v. *Sharkey* 347 F.Supp. 1234 (1972). See Krantz, *Law of Corrections,* pp. 391-398.

44. *Jones* v. *North Carolina Prisoners Labor Union,* 409 F.Supp. 937

(1977). The dissenters argued that: "If the mode of analysis in today's decision were to be generally followed, prisoners eventually would be stripped of all constitutional rights, and would retain only those privileges that prison officials, in their 'informed discretion,' deigned to recognize. The sole constitutional constraint on prison officials would be a requirement that they act rationally. Quoted in Scott Christenson, "Prison Labor and Unionization," *Criminal Law Bulletin,* 14 (May-June 1978):244.

45. The phrase *intrusion of the legal system* is taken from Jacobs, *Stateville,* chapter 5.

46. Goldfarb and Singer (*After Conviction,* p. 365) list three rationales that had underpinned the hands-off doctrine: the separation of powers principle, the courts' lack of expertise in penology, and "the fear that intervention by the courts [would] subvert prison discipline."

47. Among the more prominent cases in this area have been: for Arkansas, *Holt* v. *Sarver,* 309 F.Supp. 362 (1970); for Alabama, *Pugh* v. *Locke,* 406 F.Supp. 318 (1976); for Rhode Island, *Palmigiano* v. *Garrahy,* 443 F.Supp. 956 (1977); and for Washington, *Hoptowit* v. *Ray,* 79-359/ED Wash. (1980).

48. See Martin Tolchin, "Intervention by Courts Arouses Deepening Disputes," *New York Times,* April 24, 1977.

49. Nathan Glazer, "Should Judges Administer Social Services?" *Public Interest,* no. 50 (Winter 1978):76, 80.

50. *Rhodes* v. *Chapman,* 29 *Crim. L. Rev.* 3061 (1981). See *New York Times,* June 16, 1981. Justice Powell, speaking for the Court majority, said that "the Constitution does not mandate comfortable prisons." The cells in question are sixty-three square feet, in relation to the sixty square feet per person standard of the American Correctional Association, as well as other national and international bodies.

51. Signs of retreat at the Supreme Court level had appeared as early as 1976 in the case of *Meachum* v. *Fano,* (427 U.S. 215) which rejected a Massachusetts' prisoner's claim that due process protections apply to transfer from a medium to a maximum facility. See David Gilman, "U.S. Supreme Court Ruling May Foreshadow Reduction of Judicial Involvement in Corrections," *Corrections Magazine,* December 1976, pp. 49-51.

4 Ventures in Prison Democracy

Reform does not consist in a gentle indoctrination of benevolent feelings. Reform means the taking of a bone from a dog; reform means belling the cat. —John Jay Chapman, *Eulogy to Thomas Mott Osborne,* 1927.

Beginning with Tocqueville and Beaumont, observers have commented on the disparity between the "perfect despotism" of the American prison and the democratic (ideally, at least) society to which the prisoner was expected to return. The traditional American prison, Norman S. Hayner noted in 1940, is the "antithesis of the normal community" and in no way prepares one who spends time in it for return to the community.[1]

Hayner wrote at a time when the enthusiasm for reform and rehabilitation seemed to be ebbing; the trend was toward heavier sentences and a stricter prison regimen. In this atmosphere, not very different from today's, Hayner reminded his readers that "the prisoner comes from a community" and after an average stay of two to three years "will return to a community." While he deplored the lack of innovation in prison administration, he cited one recent exception: the experiment with the community prison at Norfolk, Massachusetts, conducted by Superintendent Howard B. Gill in the late 1920s and early 1930s. Gill's "supervised community within a wall" was the second of two major attempts during the first part of the twentieth century to transform entire prisons into a closer approximation of the free community to which the prisoners would return.[2]

The first and best known of these experimenters was Thomas Mott Osborne, the former mayor of Auburn, New York, who in 1913 had put his ideas into action within the penitentiary that a century earlier had made his town famous in penal circles around the world. Subsequently as warden at Sing Sing and commandant at the Portsmouth, New Hampshire, Naval Prison, he repeated the experiment.

Although there were important differences in the approach of these two pioneers, the common theme was the creation of a community-like prison society designed to prepare prisoners for life on the outside. The inmates were to be citizens, not mere subjects of a despotic regime. They were to share responsibilities for the community and participate in its processes. Both Osborne and Gill made serious attempts to introduce basic democratic practices into the prison.[3]

45

When one examines the details of these experiments, it is hard to avoid the conclusion that the personalities of these two reformers were a key factor in the situation. As outsiders to the prison system, they both brought with them enthusiasm, fresh views, and unorthodox approaches to prison management. In addition, both had the support of liberal governors and state administrators, at least at the start of their prison experiments. Gill maintains that an important element in Osborne's early success was the powerful position he and his family occupied in Auburn and that, conversely, his downfall at Sing Sing was in part due to the lack of a strong political base there.[4]

The political climate changed while both men were in office. As the pendulum began to swing away from public acceptance of innovation and reform, both were forced out of their positions of leadership. While the changes in governance they introduced survived them for a time in a weakened form, it was not long before they disappeared almost completely.

These experiments in community prisons took place in the context of the remedial prison and were built on the foundation of the individualized treatment approach. They also formed a bridge to the succeeding era of the interactive prison. The models for these community prisons derived from both "hospital" and "school," without attempting to draw a distinction between the two.[5] Treatment and education were complementary tools to be used in the service of rehabilitation.

Osborne's method consisted of an educational process based on participatory democracy that would train prisoners to be responsible citizens. Gill used a psychological-social problem-solving process, foreshadowing the therapeutic community, that sought to bring the inmates to confront the sources of their criminality through both individualized and group treatment methods.

The differences of both from the typical remedial prison model lay in the deliberate attempt to elevate the inmates to a nearly coordinate role in the process. Whereas the classic *medical model* places the "doctor," with his or her superior knowledge and skill, in the dominant role, the greatly expanded role for the "citizens" of the community prison alters that relationship. The analogy of the medical model is not abandoned, but the relationship between treater and treated becomes more nearly equal. Thus the prison power relationship in both experiments aimed at the ideal of democracy in internal decision making.

Osborne's Mutual Welfare Leagues

Osborne's approach to democratization of the prison was based on a philosophy of civic education.[6] He claimed to have reached the conviction as early as 1904 that "self government was the practical remedy for the evils of the prison system" but had not yet worked out how this conception could be put into practice.[7]

Osborne started with a generalized model of the community within an institution, a conception based on the George Junior Republic, a coeducational institution for juvenile delinquents who were to learn responsibility through participation in a self-governing community. Osborne was associated with the Republic almost from its establishment in 1895 and served as board chairman for many years. He considered William R. George, the founder, to have opened him to the possibility of using self-government principles and institutions (courts, legislatures) as a basis for reforming the prison system.[8]

In 1912 Osborne read Donald Lowrie's *My Life in Prison,* a book that affected him deeply and turned him into a crusader for prison reform. With a view to implementing his developing ideas, he contrived to have his friend, Charles Rattigan, appointed warden of Auburn Penitentiary. Shortly afterward Osborne became chairman of the New York Commission on Prison Reform. At this point, Osborne "came to the conclusion that if [he] wished to learn . . . [his] subject, [he] must get down to its foundation and find out what the life of a prisoner was really like."[9]

Thus Osborne came to spend a week in Auburn prison as an ordinary inmate named Tom Brown. It was an exercise in self-education.[10] Upon emerging from behind the walls, Osborne was determined to reorganize life inside this fortress penitentiary, the birthplace a century earlier of the Auburn system. As a first fruit of this experience, he vowed to avoid the "fatal blunder" of instituting a prepared plan of self-government handed down from above. Instead he had come to realize that

> if a plan of self-government was to work at all, it must be worked by the prisoners; and they would certainly work their own plan better than they could some outside plan—no matter how perfect. I understood that the only self-government that would be successful in prison was the self-government which the prisoners themselves would bring about.[11]

Even after retiring from active prison work, Osborne continued to maintain, "It is not in human nature to submit to reform from without."[12] Yet at the same time he stressed that "prisons must be educational institutions":

> We must provide a training which will make them, not good *prisoners,* but good *citizens;* a training which will fit them for the free life to which, sooner or later, they are to return. . . . Not until we think of our prisons as in reality educational institutions shall we come within sight of a successful system.[13]

By the end of 1913, Osborne, with Warden Rattigan's support, had gone back inside Auburn to initiate the first Mutual Welfare League. Osborne met alone in a constituent assembly with forty-nine elected inmate-delegates, the first time that prisoners had convened "without guards and been encouraged to discuss . . . the problems of the institution in which they were confined.[14] Two weeks later, the proposed by-laws, drafted by an inmate committee, were read to a plenary assemblage in the chapel, while "the guards . . . watched curiously and perhaps apprehensively nearly 1,400 convicts planning to take from them their old authority and assume it themselves."[15]

On Lincoln's birthday in 1914, the forty-nine prisoners elected by secret ballot to Auburn's new Mutual Welfare League recited the following oath: "I solemnly promise that I will do all in my power to promote in every way the true welfare of the men confined in Auburn Prison . . . and that I will endeavor to promote friendly feeling, good conduct and fair dealing among both officers and men."[16]

Osborne believed that this kind of inmate experience in self-government, which he was to attempt to replicate at Sing Sing and Portsmouth, "gives them a civic ideal" and leads to reformation.[17] The old warehouse prison, which he had set out to displace, gave no scope for such training and therefore could not serve a reformative purpose. The prisons that were the scene of Osborne's experiments—in particular the two New York penitentiaries—were among the toughest laboratories that could have been selected. Yet in the opinion of many observers, the inmate self-government systems worked amazingly well for a period.[18]

At Auburn, institutional rules were in the hands of an elected representative body of the prisoners. An inmate quasi-judicial panel, chosen by the elected body, meted out discipline. The prisoners, through numerous committees, shaped sizable areas of internal policy, including programming of entertainment and recreation, operating a job-placement bureau, and even instituting a monetary system using tokens as exchange medium.[19]

Probably the most difficult issue in the establishment of the inmate self-government system at Auburn concerned violation of prison rules. Osborne abandoned his original idea of a prisoners' court modeled after that of the George Junior Republic. Instead a simpler type of grievance committee, with inmates as members, was adopted featuring an investigation rather than a trial format because, said Osborne, "Many of the League members had already suffered from a surplus of legal procedures . . . and we [decided to] start by throwing aside the whole simulacrum of a court."[20] The committee dealt essentially with minor offenses; but the deputy warden continued to sentence inmates for the same acts, constituting a kind of double jeopardy. Osborne's solution was to obviate the overlap by granting to the League, through its grievance committees, exclusive jurisdiction over all but major offenses.[21] The crucial factor was that a significant portion of the judicial function was delegated to the inmates, with final appeal to the warden. Osborne's revolutionary experiment at Auburn created a national sensation, with the wide publicity spurring a popular debate on penal ideology.

In the fall of 1914, Osborne was offered the position of warden at Sing Sing, an institution in political and administrative chaos. Osborne had initiated the democratizing changes at Auburn in a private capacity; he had not been responsible to administrative superiors. At Sing Sing, as the warden, he would be squarely within the political hierarchy reaching to the state governor. His friends urged him to refuse the job, an extremely difficult one, but Osborne consulted a group of League friends at Auburn, who voted that he accept. Finally the matter was decided for Osborne when he learned that the Sing Sing inmates had signed a petition endorsing him.[22]

In December 1914, Osborne took over as Sing Sing's warden. The difficulties of handling this particularly tough prison seemed overwhelming, but after installing much the same self-government system that had been initiated at Auburn, Osborne realized similar success.[23] There was one new feature in the Sing Sing League that Osborne considered an improvement over Auburn:

> A judiciary board was established in place of the eight grievance committees, and court was held every afternoon during the hour of recreation, whenever there was any business to transact; and to the judiciary board were trusted *all cases of discipline*—with an appeal to the warden's court, consisting of the warden, the principal keeper and the doctor.[24]

Clearly Osborne had set out to give a measure of power to the inmates by granting them a decision-making role in several important governance sectors. A contemporary of Osborne's described inmate politics under the Mutual Welfare League at Sing Sing:

> The warden's day was filled with appointments with Committee Chairmen who wanted assistance or advice. The Chairmen quickly came to realize that a great deal of power lay in their hands if they knew how to wield it. Not only were they the trustees of the wishes of their fellow inmates, but the prison officials came to regard them as responsible makers of institution policy. Some of them became adept in the art of getting what they wanted without appearing to ask for much.[25]

Appointment of all committees and of their chairmen was the prerogative of the executive board, a nine-member body chosen by the fifty-five member elected board of delegates. This board received the reports of committees; removed and replaced members on them; ordered and supervised special elections necessitated by their release, transfer, resignation, recall, or suspension of a delegate; handled relations with staff and even undertook investigations of trouble spots within the prison. Tannenbaum believes the vitality of this political life pointed up the fact that Sing Sing prison had become a community—"a community behind prison walls, guarded by armed guards, but yet a community with the problems, the needs, the conflict of motive and ambitions that is the essence of community life."[26]

Siege and Departure from Sing Sing

Osborne had been developing his unique brand of prison democracy at Sing Sing for little more than a year when he was indicted, in December 1915, on a number of charges by a Westchester County grand jury. The charges included perjury and neglect of duty, the latter involving "failure to exercise general supervision over the government, discipline, and police of the prison." A final charge alleged that Osborne "did not deport himself in a manner as to command the respect, esteem, and confidence of the inmates of the prison and that he did commit various unlawful and unnatural acts with inmates of Sing Sing Prison."[27] Osborne's response was to fight the charges. He refused to resign prior to legal disposition and the state authorities were reluctant to remove him. The agreed interim arrangement was that Osborne would take an extended leave of absence during the legal battle and that he would be replaced by Dean George Kirchwey of Columbia Law School. Kirchwey was a disciple of Osborne's on prison reform and was committed to carrying on Osborne's experiment in inmate governance during what turned out to be a six-month absence for Osborne.

In the broadest sense, Osborne was made vulnerable to the concerted assault on his Sing Sing administration because of the dramatic and vigorous way in which he pursued his reform goals. He clearly was well in advance of his contemporaries and had the temerity to launch democratization experiments in the toughest of maximum-security penitentiaries. Exposed as he then was to criticism, he was not well protected politically once he left the Auburn scene. Commitments he had received from a newly elected governor at the time he agreed to take the Sing Sing position proved worthless; and the superintendent of the state prison system emerged as a close collaborator of those conspiring to oust Osborne. Thus Osborne's experiment was exposed to the heaviest of political cross-currents. Further, while the drastic nature of the internal changes had certainly generated resistance and opposition within the prison polity among the guards and previously favored inmates, the fury of the personal assault on Osborne was largely a product of outside forces.[28]

These external enemies had linked up with a small core of disgruntled inmates, who were opposed to the policies of radical democratization Osborne had initiated. Tannenbaum describes a "class struggle" that occurred after Osborne abolished the special privileges of the former prisoner elite.[29]

The inmate populace had divided into the "highbrows" and the "roughnecks." The former, called "silk stockings" by the lower-class "roughnecks," consisted of the bankers and other professionals or upper-class persons who had landed in prison but still retained important outside connections. In contemporary terms, it was the white collar criminals vs. the street criminals.

An inmate "Honor League," dominated by the upper-class elite, had been set up prior to Osborne's arrival. Regarding this earlier system as a fraudulent imitation of inmate self-government, Osborne moved to deprive this group of its power position and thereby created enemies who proceeded to put together the dossier to be used against him. An ex-banker inmate, Tannenbaum reports, said of Osborne, "He wanted . . . jail birds . . . he wanted criminals to run the Mutual Welfare League."[30]

The grand jury indictment brought a storm of protest and pro-Osborne activity in the public forum and through the press. Two public meetings were held at Carnegie Hall, featuring ex-convicts and many pro-Osborne dignitaries. The president of Harvard wrote a glowing testimonial to the *New York Times.*[31]

In the end, the case never came to a trial. When the perjury count was dismissed by the presiding judge, the legal case began to unravel. The Osborne side was soon maneuvering to force the district attorney to bring the case to trial so that Osborne would be vindicated. But the district attorney withdrew all charges and Osborne resumed his position as warden of Sing Sing. Three months later, still being harassed from the state capital in Albany, Osborne resigned.[32]

Successors and Critics

Osborne's successors saw prisoner participation in a different light. When newly appointed Warden Lewis E. Lawes arrived at Sing Sing on January 1, 1920, he moved quickly to bring the self-government system under the tight control of the prison administration and to revamp a political arena that he saw as becoming "mortally dangerous." Lawes wrote:

> Self-government in prisons must not be allowed to descend to the level of ward politics. . . .If it is to become a basis for character building, it cannot be permitted to encourage campaigns . . . that will arouse passionate partisanship with all the evils and intrigues of practical politics. I found the League membership divided into two party camps. The energies of both parties were concentrated toward corralling sufficient votes for election purposes. . . . The judges [of the League court], sad to relate, were not

always of the highest calibre. They were . . . hand-picked, [by inmate poli-
ticians] and did not examine facts with impersonal impartiality.[33]

Thus to ensure that the League would not be working at cross-purposes with
his administration, Warden Lawes "abolished party politics" and decreed
that "breaches of discipline would be handled only by . . . [the] Warden's
Court." The primary sphere of the League would be "to regulate the leisure
hours of the prisoners."[34]

This major line of criticism recurs in present-day analyses of Osborne's
experiments. Joseph Hickey and Peter Scharf point out that what Warden
Lawes here describes constitutes the "iron law of oligarchy," the classic
thesis propounded by Roberto Michels in 1915 holding that political elites
eventually dominate all political systems.[35] Michels asserted that "a system
of leadership is incompatible with the most essential postulates of democracy." Oligarchy, he claims, "derives from the tactical and technical neces-
sities which result from the consolidation of every disciplined political
aggregate. . . . It is the outcome of organization."[36] This is even more the
case within prison polities, Hickey and Scharf argue, given the accentuation
of "internal constraints against democracy" in that artificial environment.[37]

Michels's law, though retaining a widespread influence, has not proved
verifiable in any scientific sense and remains controversial down to the
present. The late Alvin W. Gouldner viewed Michel's "assumption that
organizational constraints have stacked the deck against democracy" as the
product of a subjective "pathos of pessimism," not as the result of rigorous
analysis:

> The very same evidence to which he called attention could enable us to
> formulate the very opposite theorem—the "iron law of democracy." Even
> as Michels himself saw, if oligarchical waves repeatedly wash away the
> bridges of democracy, this eternal recurrence can happen only because men
> doggedly rebuild them after each inundation.[38]

Yet the persistence of *tendencies* toward oligarchical domination of
democratic institutions can scarcely be denied. The criticism of Osborne,
however, reaches further. Hickey and Scharf also characterize Osborne's
"rather romantic" view of the typical inmate as "a hybrid of a Rousseauian
noble savage and a well-meaning village Rotarian." And they charge him
with stigmatizing the guards by excluding them from his participatory
scheme.[39] This was, according to Gill, the basic fault of the Osborne plan.

Most doubts expressed by Osborne's critics then and now center on the
intrinsic difficulty of introducing such far-reaching innovation into a maximum-security penitentiary. Possibly, it has been argued, this scheme might
have succeeded in a medium-security institution or within a carefully con-

trolled experimental environment, involving less than an entire penitentiary.[40] Barnes and Teeters believe that the "nonreformable" (incorrigible)
inmates must be excluded from any self-government system; but they concede it is hard to fault him since methods to make such classifications were
as yet poorly developed.[41]

Yet for all the criticisms of his penal philosophy and administration,
Osborne remained a character of great fascination for later historians as
well as his contemporaries. During the trial his personal eccentricities were
blown to scandalous proportions and contributed to his downfall. Chamberlain commented: "Only a genius could have marshaled against himself
so many powerful forces. He had an utter disregard for appearances and
this gave his enemies a peg on which to hang their slanders." The world of
prison administration never looked kindly on radical innovators. Much less
on an eccentric possessing what Chapman described as "a messianic element in his nature."[42] Osborne was a fighter, a muckraker, and ultimately a
political threat to powerful interests on both sides of the walls.

Gill's Norfolk Plan

Birth of a Prison Community

In 1927 a state prison colony was established at Norfolk, Massachusetts,
twenty miles south of Boston. The old Charlestown Prison in Boston,
dating from the beginning of the nineteenth century, had long since been
condemned. The building of Norfolk Prison offered the first opportunity to
begin transferring a few inmates from Charlestown to a new environment.

The first twelve prisoners, carefully selected from the Charlestown
population, arrived on the site in June 1927. In September the construction
of the enclosing wall, which the prisoners themselves would build, com-
menced. In November, Howard B. Gill became its first superintendent.[43]
Gill had graduated from the Harvard Business School in 1914, and, as a
private business consultant in the 1920s, he had made a nationwide study of
prison industries for Herbert Hoover, then secretary of commerce. When
Sanford Bates, the Massachusetts commissioner of corrections (who was
soon to become the first head of the Federal Bureau of Prisons), presented
Gill with the plans for a standard fortress prison, Gill balked, protesting
that he wanted above all to avoid the grimness of cell-blocks. Given a deadline for producing an alternative design, Gill returned with a cottage-dormi-
tory blueprint for inside the wall—a radical plan for its day—which became
the Norfolk architectural model.

As early as 1928 Gill took the innovative steps, which led to the creation
of what he called a "community prison." His actions were not designed

consciously as an experiment, nor did he come to his task as an advocate of inmate self-government. Gill's conception of inmate participation grew out of a practical situation. The building of the prison wall had fallen badly behind schedule and a combined committee of inmates and engineers was appointed to plan and expedite construction. Out of the success of this collaboration grew Gill's conviction that joint participation was both administratively sound and therapeutic.

Although Gill freely acknowledges the influence of Osborne, whom he met in 1925, he was to make significant departures from Osborne's model. Norfolk's pattern of prison governance—including the involvement of the guards and the use of inmates in custodial functions took several years to be worked out. Gill's basic penological approach was clear from the start: he wanted to create, through trial and error, a prison community that would be as close to a normal community as possible, except for the necessary supervisory functions.

Gill, very much in the reform-therapeutic tradition, stressed the importance of classification of prisoners, of individualized treatment, and of a group cottage living arrangement—all as part of the community organization structure.[44] The concession to the custodial function of the prison was confined to two basic rules: no escape and no contraband. Thus, conceptually, custody was to be constricted to the smallest possible sector, with treatment to occupy the rest of the field.

Gill believed it was crucial that he have control over the makeup of the inmate body and thus over the quality of the incipient prison community. For most of the years at Norfolk he was allowed to reject unpromising prisoners, returning them to the Charlestown Prison. The beginning point of inmate classification for Gill was the distinction between tractable and intractable. For Gill, the test lay in the distinction between cooperative and antagonistic behavior, and he maintains that his capability to weed out the troublemakers was "the very heart of my success":

> I could get rid of my problems, those that wouldn't cooperate with me. . . . You cannot run the prison with normalcy . . . if you have these other people who are always fighting you running according to the convict code, adopting an adversary relationship, antagonistic, trying to con you all the time. . . . Those that were left were fairly normal people. . . . Cooperative, loyal, they did their work. . . . [It was a] closed community, of course, under wraps, but a fairly normal atmosphere.[45]

The degree of control Gill had over the composition of his inmate population was obviously far greater than Osborne had at Sing Sing. Once the prison community had been restricted to "reformable" prisoners, the building of Gill's community prison rested on the implementation of supporting policies. "Normal living and development of personality must transcend custodial needs"; and, most important for basic policy making, "community life at Norfolk is a joint undertaking, and . . . is based on joint responsibility of staff and inmates."[46]

An inmate council was put into operation shortly after Norfolk's establishment. Initially its main function was ensuring against escape or dealing in contraband.[47] Council members were elected from the prisoners who were building the houses and erecting the wall. Joint committees (prisoners and staff) were at first set up as expedients for dealing with particular problems. Norfolk's venture into the concrete practice of inmate participation began in the "oval," the open prison outside the wall; only in June 1931 was the council expanded to embrace representatives from behind the now-completed wall.

At first the council met without staff representation, once by itself each week and once with Superintendent Gill. Within a year, Gill concluded that this organizational pattern, modeled on Osborne's was unsatisfactory. Gill described this original council structure, in which the inmates collaborated with the warden in policy making to the exclusion of the guards, who were only afterward told what to do, as "a pyramid set upon its apex":

> We soon found [at Norfolk] . . . that the Osborne approach doesn't work. I shifted at once from a council that met with me and then told the guards what to do to a council where the guards were on an equal footing with the inmates and told *me* what to do.[48]

In the fall of 1929, the elected council was recalled; and Gill introduced what he considers his most important innovation relating to governance, the principle of staff representation.[49] Through this process, the principle of joint participation, joint interest, and joint responsibility was combined with a serious effort to forestall the alienation of the guards, which had often been considered an inevitable failing of self-government schemes. Gill felt that the pyramid had now been placed on a solid base—the guards and the inmates—while the warden was at the apex. He then added several related elements to support the overall design. From 1930 on, officers were divided into watch officers (essentially custodial) and house officers (primarily treatment, including collaboration in the governance system); staff screened nominees to the council; and the warden retained ultimate control over decision making, inhering in his authority to modify or to veto the policy recommendations of the council.[50]

Although the powers of the council were basically advisory, they were defined broadly. Gill, however, insisted on a careful distinction between matters of general concern to the community, which were to be within the council's purview, and issues involving individuals. For the council to deal with the latter would destroy the system, in Gill's view. Nevertheless he believed the individual and the collective aspects were complementary: socialization, brought about through instrumentalities of joint participation, operating through the guidance of the Community Service Division; and individualization of treatment, which involved problem solving, to get at the sources of each inmate's "criminality," carried out under the aegis of the Case Work Division. In addressing his staff on this theme, Gill stated:

> There are two functions of our organization—case work and community service work. . . . They are the machinery by which . . . the therapeutic functions of the institution are carried over to the inmates—through case work to the individual, through community service to the inmates in groups or as a whole.[51]

In March 1934 at a hearing before the governor and commissioner, Gill quoted from his own 1929 annual report to the commissioner summarizing the governmental features of the Norfolk system:

> As a direct outgrowth of the group system, an inmate organization, called the Council, has developed and together with the Staff constitutes the community government of the institution. . . . This community organization operates on the principle of joint-responsibility in which both officers and inmates take part. . . . The Council has advisory powers only and final action always rests with the Staff. . . . However, in the sixteen months during which the plan has been in operation, the two have never failed to agree finally on any decision. . . . [This] is due to the . . . sincere part played in it by the officers, who [contrary to the usual circumstances] are wholeheartedly a part of it and who act as a proper balance wheel. . . . [But] it is not an "administration affair," and the very concrete advantages derived for the men by the cooperation of the Council and Staff continually demonstrate its vitality.[52]

Within this framework, the Norfolk plan proposed to give the inmates "as much responsibility as they could stand."[53] Carrying out this project, however, did not prove easy. At an early stage (the fall of 1929 council), the power of recommending transfers between the living units was being exploited by inmate politicians, who were on the council, in an effort to stack votes for a pending election. Gill soon forced a confrontation, which led to the recall of this council and the adoption of his crucial joint participation pattern on all committees and on the council itself. Nevertheless, according to contemporary observers, "this staff participation in no way lessened the vigor or latitude of the discussion" among the inmates.[54]

To Gill, there appeared to be a cyclical swing between effective and ineffectual councils. Norfolk's official historian, Thomas Yahkub, sees the period up to 1930 as a formative stage with a continued upward movement to the end of 1931, "the heyday of the council system." From then on, there were regressive tendencies, fed by ever heavier influxes from Charlestown and dispirited councils, which "could not see much else to be done."[55] Gill himself saw variations in the quality of his working relationships with the councils:

> I had the final say, to be sure, but I was very careful not to negate after they really showed careful consideration. Now it's true that once or twice we had a group of bad actors get ahold of the council. . . . I simply sat back on my haunches and said I refuse to cooperate with you. And we had a stand-off for a period of two to three months.[56]

Overall, however, Yahkub believes that this council system promoted a sense of responsibility and cooperativeness during the six-year period of its existence under Gill's leadership. This was especially so among those inmates housed in minimum-security conditions outside the wall in the so-called oval, later known as the farm colony. Thus through teaching "the rudiments of community living," the system was frequently effective as a form of group therapy, in the opinion of Norfolk's official and unofficial chroniclers.[57]

Superintendent Gill's Dismissal

Yet, finally, the Norfolk experiment could not be isolated from the shifting political currents of state and local politics. Here was an institution that, as an early model of a community prison, exemplified an advanced form of remedial prison and a precursor of the interactive prison. As such, it outraged the traditionalists on the corrections scene.

Commenting on the final period of Gill's tenure (1933–1934), two prominent penologists, sympathetic to Gill, call it "a most painful ordeal of outside criticism."[58] According to Carl Doering, editor of the 1940 *Report* on the Norfolk experiment:

> The end of the experiment was reached amid a storm of intense and bitter feeling on each side. The staff was divided against itself and the inmates. . . . Had Mr. Gill been reinstated, he probably would have restored order, but the editor doubts that he would have been willing to sacrifice . . . any part of his plan—which certainly would have been necessary as the population increased to its planned maximum of 1200. . . . Gill would not have been willing to fill the shoes of a conservative prison warden; he was interested in spreading and realizing his ideas.[59]

Yahkub, a staunch backer of Gill, was nevertheless resigned to "the hopelessness of the experiment." While supportive of Gill's purpose and program, he feared the worst from the effects of the sociopolitical setting within which Gill was working. He felt that "a complete reorientation of society's attitudes is necessary before such men [prisoners] can be patiently, considerately, and effectively treated."[60]

In the fall of 1933 the commissioner of corrections, Francis B. Sayre, resigned to become an assistant secretary of state under President Roosevelt. This opened the way for the statehouse politicians, in particular, Francis X. Hurley, a politically ambitious state auditor, to launch an attack on Gill. They lodged a series of scatter-shot charges against Gill that were aired in the press. The accusation was that the Norfolk inmates were being mollycoddled in a hotbed of petty corruption.

At the end of January 1934, Gill was pressured into withdrawing (not resigning) as superintendent, pending a public hearing on Hurley's allegations. In early March, a public hearing before the Massachusetts governor and the commissioner of corrections was held in the presence of a large and partisan crowd. He had the support of numerous public-spirited groups and individuals. Eyewitnesses describe the hearing-room confrontation as a highly dramatic one. Gill responded, patiently and fully, to the charges. One was that he had "allowed a speech to be made by an employee" at Norfolk's Armistice Day banquet that derided the motives for U.S. entry into World War I. That such charges had been brought, many of no greater seriousness, was obviously embarrassing to the governor and the commissioner.

In conclusion, Hurley had written in his report: "During the whole investigation I kept in mind that, when all the verbiage is stripped away and when all the nice words used in the science of penology are reduced to ordinary terms, the inmates at Norfolk are criminals."[61] Gill responded at the conclusion of the hearings: "According to Hurley, the men at Norfolk are criminals. We hold that the criminals at Norfolk are men."[62] Although there was no question that Gill had been completely vindicated, he was summarily dismissed a month after the conclusion of the hearings.

Prison Democratization: Old and New Criticism

The Osborne and Gill experiments were similar in their attempt to broaden the base of the prison polity by introducing a degree of democratization into the prison, thereby transforming a diffuse and alienated population into a community. Osborne went much further in the direction of a judicial role for the inmates, turning over to convict judges a large part of the disciplinary function.[63] This feature, promptly ended by Warden Lawes at Sing Sing, was perhaps the most criticized feature of Osborne's self-government model.[64]

The most troublesome issue in all prison self-government experiments was the role of staff, particularly guards. Osborne was concerned with redeeming criminals through an experience in being citizens of a community, which left no place for the guards in the self-government scheme. But if the concern was to make the community become a more harmoniously functioning entity, then the staff could hardly be left out of account. Gill moved rapidly in the direction of inmate-staff collaboration, dividing the guards into a custodial and a treatment component. Many observers are still highly skeptical about placing guards in a role where they must behave simultaneously as custodians and therapists.[65] Whatever the difficulties, however, the community prison clearly presupposes the cooperation of the staff at all levels.

Underlying most of the objections to the Mutual Welfare Leagues and the Norfolk plan was their "excess of democracy." The powerless were given some power and were admitted to the circle of decision making, even if in only a limited way.

The "new" criticism comes from the opposite direction and faults experimenters in prison participation schemes, such as Osborne and Gill, for not going far enough. The criticism views the representative features in the older council systems as weak instruments, absent a union of prisoners.[66]

The most far-reaching criticism rejects the treatment model for its admitted failures in rehabilitating inmates, its intrinsically authoritarian features, and the inherent contradiction in any institutional system that strives for both treatment and custody, in particular the hospital model. Inevitably, the critics charge, such reforms are co-opted by the authoritarian system within which they are implemented.

Historian David J. Rothman, one of the spokesmen of the new criticism, devotes the last chapter of his study, *Conscience and Convenience,* to Gill's Norfolk, which he describes as the final "grand effort to implement the Progressive reform program for the deviant." Rothman sees the Norfolk experiment as "a powerful parable" of an entire era of reform in America's institutions and as a "final indictment of the Progressive system." He places on Gill essentially the entire symbolic responsibility for the fall, the "degeneration to the hole." It is this "hole," the hallmark of super-custody and atomized isolation, which marks the final collapse of the original promise of "the model institution that realized the most advanced and scientific system of incarceration."[67]

How correct is Rothman's critique? The Progressive era in America, which Rothman dates from the 1890s to World War II, was a period of intense reform activity affecting all of society's institutions. As Rothman sees it, a wide gap emerged between intent (rooted in "conscience") and results (colored by expedient "convenience"). The reformers' intention, according to Rothman's analysis, was caught up in the belief that the prison could be transformed into a community or, alternatively, a hospital. And while Rothman appears more attracted to the former—of which Osborne's Mutual Welfare League seems to him the best example—than he is toward the latter, in practice the distinctions become blurred.[68]

Rothman views the reforms of the Progressive era largely as exercises in futility. Their failure to make a permanent liberalizing impact, resulted, above all, from custodial needs overtaking the rehabilitative design. The community prison was still a prison, a "supervised community."[69] Gill, Osborne, and others of this era never pretended that they could abolish the custody side. But they believed that they could find a pragmatic balance, through trial and error, if permitted by their political superiors to carry through their general design on its own terms.

Rothman was not the first to criticize the pragmatic solutions that had been made. The 1933 Osborne Association report on Norfolk found it "hard to understand just why this otherwise modern institution should have been enclosed within a wall which denies much of its progressive spirit." Although the inspection team was on the whole favorable to the Norfolk plan, saying it marked "an important step forward in the history of American penal methods," they found it difficult to reconcile Norfolk's break with traditional architecture and management methods alongside "the high wire-topped wall and fortified gatehouse [which] marked it indelibly as a prison.[70]

Rothman's basic criticism of the Progressive formulas centers on the "ultimately most problematic assumption" that custody and treatment could coexist.[71] He insists that the conflict between the goals of rehabilitation and custody has invariably undermined the reform program as applied.[72] At Norfolk, Rothman concludes, "treatment did not temper custody but fell victim to it."[73] He finds the principal—almost sole—evidence for this conclusion in the so-called "Diary" of Norfolk for the years 1932 and 1933. This "Diary" was established as a kind of open forum for both the professional staff and Gill himself. It was intended as a place to air every viewpoint, criticism, and complaint, outside of regular administrative channels.[74]

The differences between the Gill and Rothman assessments are not confined to interpretation. For example, in the matter of the heavy custody area at Norfolk, allegedly set up in early 1934, Gill's position is that there was no such area, as Rothman reconstructs it, certainly no "hole"[75] For Rothman, the existence of the "hole" is of considerable symbolic importance: "once [Norfolk] had the hole, the experiment was over.[76]

In his zeal to establish certain general propositions, the case that Rothman presents against Gill is overdrawn at best. While ignoring several living witnesses, including Gill himself, Rothman compiles his evidence and draws his conclusions essentially from one source, the Norfolk Diary. The real point of contention derives from differing outlooks on the potentialities of men and institutions. Rothman, preoccupied with the contradiction between custody and treatment—and the oppressive features of treatment itself—is convinced that Gill's type of experiment must inevitably degenerate into some kind of tyranny over inmates. Gill, from an optimistic perspective of an earlier generation, set out to build a community prison and succeeded, in the time he had, in broadening the base of the prison polity to a modest extent. Simultaneously he was treading the uncertain path of individualized treatment. Gill's pragmatic achievement, widely admired and emulated at the time, was to create a notably humane institutional regime.

Retrospect and Prospect on Prison Democracy

The concept of the collaborative institution, which would stimulate inmate participation through shared decision making, was strongly endorsed by the 1967 President's Commission on Law Enforcement and Administration of Justice:

> From a rehabilitation standpoint, such inmate involvement with staff is not so important for its practical contribution to the efficiency of institution management as for its social function in *bringing inmates and staff into collaborative interaction.* . . . [It is] still another mechanism . . . for reducing the extent to which prison social structure alienates inmates from non-criminal persons and increases their identification with other offenders.[77]

As recently as 1973 and even while harsh criticism of the treatment model was building, the National Advisory Commission on Criminal Justice Standards and Goals again urged that

> correctional agencies should adopt immediately a *program of participatory management* in which everyone involved—manager, staff, and offenders— shares in identifying problems, finding mutually agreeable solutions, setting goals and objectives, defining new roles for participants, and evaluating effectiveness of these processes.[78]

In speaking of the value of *participatory management* and *collaborative interaction,* it is clear that these federal commissions are not merely aiming for improved communications. They are pointing toward a new type of regime in which the prison inmates share responsibility and share in making decisions—in short, power. The earlier experiences of Thomas Mott Osborne and of Howard B. Gill surely qualify as particularly noteworthy efforts in this direction. But Osborne and Gill were not alone in such experimentation with inmate participation.[79] Alexander Maconochie, Zebulon Brockway, and Hiram Hatch are among the nineteenth-century predecessors of Osborn, and Kenyon Scudder, Thomas Murton, and William Conte are representative of more contemporary efforts.[80]

Many of these experiments have been short-lived and the outcomes mixed. Also among the myriad inmate councils, most have served little purpose other than facilitating management objectives.[81] Here we focus, rather, on whether inmates are actually drawn into the system—into a genuine and legitimate role in "running the joint."

It is undeniable that there have been serious internal problems with all of the inmate participation models. In the cases of both Osborne and Gill critics have focused on the incompatibility of custody and treatment and on the personal leadership factor of the reforming warden. Both Osborne and Gill were certainly commanding figures, which led to the weakening of their reforms after their departures. However, many of the problems of Osborne's and Gill's innovations, inasmuch as they survived their originators, derived less from the issue of the coexistence of custody and treatment than from the trends toward an expanding and less selective inmate population, a scarcity of resouces and a declining public enthusiasm for reform.[82]

But it was not the internal contradictions alone that were decisive. It was mainly external political factors that led to the removal of both Osborne and Gill from their superintendencies. Yet despite intensive controversy swirling around Osborne and Gill to this day, they stand secure as the leading American pioneers of inmate self-government and of shared responsibility in the prison setting. Their reforms continue to be studied and emulated.

David Fogel, whose "justice model" for corrections has been much discussed since its appearance in the mid-1970s, describes the first element of his model as being patterned after Gill's ideas:

> The first element of the prison justice model is self-governance, but not in the historical sense of the "inmate council" or the "gimme group." Rather we suggest *the joint venture model* closer to Gill's idea of an inmate-staff governance group. . . . The linkage of the inmates and staff is crucial to the sense of fairness.[83]

In Fogel's model, the joint council would function as a mechanism for dealing with grievances and for program planning, while veto power remains in the hands of the top administration.[84] The aim would be to maximize the advantages of inmate participation in prison governance, while eliminating presumed "negative features." Fogel is impressed by "mounting evidence" that an atomized inmate body and "weak inmate organization" may actually increase the probability of riots. The opening of channels for negotiation may obviate the need for violent acts to get the prisoner's "political message . . . beyond the prison walls."[85]

Other proponents of inmate councils take a more conservative approach. J.E. Baker would confine the "proper functions" largely to a strictly advis-

ory one of providing "a free-flow channel of communication." But Fred E.
Haynes, who spent a summer in the early 1930s visiting Gill's Norfolk
Prison, became convinced that inmates were more knowledgeable than anybody else about how the system works; to take advantage of that knowledge, an efficient prison administration must offer its inmates a genuine
partnership. Criminologist Haynes, a strong admirer of Howard Gill, was
advocating the advanced position for his day that inmates should be the
beneficiaries of a redistribution of power leading to a recognized share in
governance.[86]

Beyond the partnership idea lies the conception of a bargaining arena
within which the various actors in the prison polity would each make their
just claims. Many of the inmate council schemes, including the Osborne and
Gill experiments, exemplify elements of this bargaining-arena model. The
most straight-forward recognition of such a concept would doubtless be to
legitimize prisoners' trade unions, juxtaposed to guards' unions and to the
prison administration as representative of state authority. Unions of prisoners, "one of the most revolutionary proposals," are viewed by criminologist Benedict S. Alper as likely soon to become "an accepted and established feature within penal institutions." Despite its radical connotations,
Alper sees such a development as democratizing and regularizing relationships that in their traditional subcultural underground form are marked by
violence and strong-arm methods. Thus, "a union of prisoners is . . . a salutary move."[87]

In sharp contrast with this perception of the route of progress is the one
articulated by political scientist James Q. Wilson. In the preface to his 1975
Thinking about Crime, he derides developments that others had viewed as
promising:

> I regard as a major barrier to effective change in criminal justice the
> tendency for decisions in this field to be unduly influenced by the organized
> interests of those whose behavior is to be changed. . . . The *reductio ad
> absurdum* of this process has been the emergence of prisoner unions which
> insist on participating in decisions as to whether any changes are to be made
> in the purposes and methods of prisons.[88]

What is the alternative? There is no guarantee of success, of course, in a
bargaining arena such as the one favored by Alper or the ones actually constructed by Osborne, Gill, and others. If it proves impossible to combine
participation with orderly process in a civic arena, the political battle is
thrown right back into an arena of violence. Then the probability goes up of
such disruptive events as hostage taking, an outcome that represents a last-
ditch bid by prisoners to alter their bargaining position.

Utilizing collaborative institutions and processes to restructure prison
polities is certainly no panacea. As experience has demonstrated, the diffi-

culties are truly formidable, especially in a fortress prison, and successes are often short-lived. The pitfalls and built-in limitations impede and ultimately may frustrate even the most promising democratization projects. One factor, which is often given insufficient weight, is that any formal change in a prison regime has to be undertaken within the larger legal-institutional system that embraces corrections. State legislatures and executive agencies can, if they so wish, give direction or create opportunities for inmate participation in the prison regime. But the prison polity is not a law unto itself, and the higher state authority, especially in the contemporary era, takes precedence. A hospitable legal-political framework would seem to be a prerequisite for proceeding with the reconstruction of the prison polity.

A second limiting element is the deep conservatism of the correctional system and the correctional establishment. Innovation and experimentation are, virtually without exception, perceived as threatening. These generalizations may be criticized as too sweeping in that more than a few of today's penal administrators are skilled and sophisticated practitioners. Nevertheless the nature of their job and of the pressures upon them has strong tendencies to reaffirm their support of an authoritarian status quo. Reformers are invariably stamped as mavericks, which places them "outside," even if they are not already there. Osborne was an outsider who was able to enter and eventually dominate his first prison because of the fortuitous circumstance that he was a leading personality in the town of Auburn, New York. Gill, too, was an outsider, but he was offered an opportunity to build an important social institution from the ground up. Thus the outsider, free of the restraining commitments of the professional penologist, may initially have a clearer road toward meaningful reform goals, if he can get in and stay in long enough.

Finally there are intrinsic limitations on democratic reforms, given the nature of a prison and the society in which it exists. It is certainly arguable that any effort to make over the prison, consistent with humane values, remains an exercise in futility. There is nothing else to do but abolish it, many have concluded.[89]

Reformers like Gill and Osborne simply went ahead with the work they felt they had to do, although they were usually aware of limits. Osborne pushed the limits, taking the maximum risk, to metamorphose Auburn and Sing Sing into adult replicas of the George Junior Republic. Gill's conception was not one of pure democracy but something more akin to a guided democracy. The warden is at the apex, holding an absolute veto, with a degree of devolution of power aimed at achieving community objectives. And the dominating social objective became, as formulated by Gill himself, the approximation of a "normal" community, but one that was "under wraps."[90]

There is much to be learned from such experiences, though it would make little sense to try to repeat them today. Important changes have occurred in the prison world, as well as outside it, since Osborne and Gill carried out their experiments. Part II of this study focuses on one contemporary experiment, which tried to bring democracy into the prison. The scene is Washington State Penitentiary at Walla Walla, a prison with its own peculiar history and environment, another set of reformers, and a "new breed" of prisoners.[91]

Notes

1. Norman S. Hayner, "The Prison as a Community," *American Sociological Review* 5 (August 1940):580.

2. Ibid., p. 582.

3. For discussion of some nineteenth-century predecessors, see Harold M. Helfman, "Antecedents of Thomas Mott Osborne's 'Mutual Welfare League' in Michigan," *Journal of Criminal Law and Criminology* 40 (May–April, 1949-1950):597–600. *Inmate self-government* is the label most often applied to the projects initiated by Osborne. Gill, however, objects to the term as a misnomer. He prefers the designation *joint participation* or *shared responsibility,* a system of collaborative management joining inmates with staff.

4. Conversations with Howard B. Gill, 1980–1981.

5. David J. Rothman, *Conscience and Convenience: The Asylum and Its Alternative in Progressive America* (Boston: Little, Brown, 1980), p. 122.

6. See Joseph Hickey and Peter Scharf, *Toward a Just Correctional System: Experiments in Implementing Democracy in Prisons* (San Francisco: Jossey-Bass, 1980), pp. 3–4. See also Hickey and Scharf, "Thomas Mott Osborne and the Limits of Democratic Prison Reform," *Prison Journal* 57 (Autumn–Winter 1977):3–15. According to Osborne, "The sole aim of the Mutual Welfare League is to prepare men for real life in the free society of the world outside." Osborne, "Self-Government by the Prisoner," in *The Prison and the Prisoner: A Symposium,* ed. Julia K. Jaffray (Boston: Little, Brown, 1917), p. 105.

7. Thomas Mott Osborne, *Society and Prisons: Some Suggestions for a New Penology* (New Haven: Yale University Press, 1916), p. 154. On the origins of the idea of community responsibility for inmates and its development by Osborne, see Fred E. Haynes, *The American Prison System* (New York: McGraw-Hill, 1939), chap. 13.

8. See Osborne, *Society and Prisons,* pp. 152–153; Haynes, *American Prison System,* pp. 295–296. The George Junior Republic in Freeport, N.Y. has been in operation down to the present day.

9. Haynes, *American Prison System,* p. 296; Osborne, *Society and Prisons,* p. 120.

10. Osborne's personal account is *Within Prison Walls* (New York: D. Appleton & Co., 1914). See also Osborne, *Society and Prisons,* pp. 119–138. Osborne's biographer, Frank Tannenbaum, stresses that Osborne was aiming at establishing credibility among the inmates. See Tannenbaum, *Osborne of Sing Sing* (Chapel Hill: University of North Carolina Press, 1933), p. 65.

11. Osborne, *Society and Prisons,* p. 159. See also Osborne's speech of September 1915 to the Efficiency Society, in Corinne Bacon, ed., *Prison Reform* (White Plains, N.Y.: H.W. Wilson Co., 1917), pp. 135–137.

12. Thomas Mott Osborne, *Prisons and Common Sense* (Philadelphia: J.B. Lippincott, 1924), p. 20.

13. Ibid., pp. 34–35.

14. Haynes, *American Prison System,* p. 299. See also Thomas O. Murton, *The Dilemma of Prison Reform* (New York: Holt, Rinehart and Winston, 1976), p. 201.

15. Rudolph W. Chamberlain, *There Is No Truce: A Life of Thomas Mott Osborne* (New York: Macmillan, 1935), pp. 265–266.

16. Quoted in ibid., p. 266.

17. Osborne, *Society and Prisons,* p. 230. See also Osborne's statement in Bacon, ed., *Prison Reform,* p. 130.

18. See Haynes, *American Prison System,* pp. 298–301.

19. For a succinct summary of Osborne's experiments in three prisons see J.E. Baker, *The Right to Participate: Inmate Involvement in Prison Administration* (Metuchin, N.J.: Scarecrow Press, 1974), pp. 49–55, 64–69. See also Harry Elmer Barnes and Negley K. Teeters, *New Horizons in Criminology,* 2d ed. (Englewood Cliffs, N.J.: Prentice Hall, 1951), pp. 691–695.

20. Osborne, *Prisons and Common Sense,* p. 71.

21. The categories of major offenses were assault upon a guard, deadly assault upon another inmate, refusal to work, strike, and escape attempt. See Osborne, *Society and Prisons,* pp. 173–174. See also Chamberlain, *There Is No Truce,* pp. 274–275.

22. An account of this episode appears in numerous places. See, for example, Osborne, *Society and Prisons,* pp. 205–206.

23. On Osborne's period at Sing Sing, see the detailed account in Tannenbaum, *Osborne,* pp. 103–175. The best short account is Haynes, *American Prison System,* pp. 300–303. For an interesting collection of articles on Sing Sing under Osborne, see Bacon, ed., *Prison Reform,* pp. 109–145.

24. Osborne, *Society and Prisons,* pp. 206–207.

25. Frederick H. Wines, *Punishment and Reformation* (New York: Thomas Y. Crowell, 1923), pp. 397–398.

26. Tannenbaum, *Osborne,* p. 149.

27. Haynes, *American Prison System,* p. 302. See also Chamberlain, *There Is No Truce,* pp. 304–329.

28. The extent to which guards were alienated is one of the most controversial aspects of Osborne's regime at both Auburn and Sing Sing. Chamberlain and Tannenbaum provide evidence that Osborne retained strong staff support. There is little doubt that some of his top assistants were among his strongest backers. But Chamberlain also points to a letter of support for Warden Osborne sent to the governor of New York after the indictment and signed by ninety-nine keepers and guards. *There is No Truce,* pp. 348–349. Tannenbaum cites a letter from an Auburn guard stating that "it has never been so pleasant for me as it is now." See *Osborne,* pp. 94–96, 122–124.

29. Tannenbaum, *Osborne,* pp. 184–185. For detailed treatment of the attack on Osborne leading up to his indictment, see ibid., pp. 179–236.

30. Ibid., p. 185.

31. Ibid., p. 240. (Statement of Charles W. Eliot).

32. On the concluding stages of the ordeal, culminating in Osborne's resignation in October 1916, see ibid., pp. 246–257. See also Chamberlain, *There Is No Truce,* pp. 330–364, and Haynes, *American Prison System,* pp. 302–303. Baker, *Right to Participate,* pp. 64–69, briefly describes Osborne's final active position, as commandant of the Portsmouth Naval Prison, 1917–1920. He was assisted by Austin MacCormick, who was later to head the Osborne Association. Osborne, ever the innovator, set up a prisoners' organization comparable to the Mutual Welfare League at Auburn and Sing Sing, instituted a policy of return to active service of rehabilitated inmates, and weathered an investigation made under pressure from military critics but with the strong backing of Osborne by the then assistant secretary of the Navy, Franklin D. Roosevelt. This last of Osborne's three projects, the Portsmouth League, was the first to be dissolved—in 1921. Shortly after Osborne's departure, the commandant simply abolished the Mutual Welfare League, arguing that, "under the system, shrewd inmates managed to gain control . . . and manipulated it to their own advantage." The original Mutual Welfare League, the Auburn one, was swept away in a 1929 riot. And Sing Sing's MWL held out until 1950, although long since having been reduced to a "company union."

33. Lewis E. Lawes, *Twenty Thousand Years in Sing Sing* (New York: Ray Long and Richard R. Smith, 1932), pp. 113–114. Concerning Osborne's role: "The defect of Mr. Osborne's administration was in the overlapping of prisoner self-government with the warden's responsibility as an administrator. His intense desire to raise the prisoner to a normal plane led him to surrender his prerogatives. He became an advisor instead of a leader and ruler. The swing of the pendulum from severity to liberality was too wide. It resulted in chaos." Ibid., p. 107.

34. Ibid., pp. 116–120. A contemporary wrote: "Without Osborne there could have been no Lawes. . . . However much he has revised Osborne's program, . . . Lawes is building on Osborne [as is] practically every warden and penologist in the country." Chamberlain, *There Is No Truce,* p. 410.

35. Hickey and Scharf, *Toward a Just System,* p. 23. Roberto Michels, *Political Parties: A Sociological Study of the Oligarchical Tendencies of Modern Democracy* (1915; reprint ed., Glencoe, Ill.: Free Press, 1949).

36. Michels, *Political Parties,* pp. 400–402.

37. Hickey and Scharf, *Toward a Just System,* p. 23.

38. A.W. Gouldner, "Metaphysical Pathos and the Theory of Bureaucracy," *American Political Science Review* 49 (1955):496–507. Reprinted with permission.

39. Hickey and Scharf, *Toward a Just System,* pp. 23, 26.

40. For example, see ibid., and Elliott Studt et al., *C-Unit: Search for Community in Prison* (New York: Russell Sage Foundation, 1968).

41. See Barnes and Teeters, *New Horizons,* pp. 694–695.

42. Chamberlain, *There Is No Truce,* p. 352; John Jay Chapman, "Thomas Mott Osborne," *Harvard Graduate's Magazine,* March–June 1927.

43. For a detailed account of Norfolk up to 1934, see Thomas Yahkub, "A History of the State Prison Colony," in Carl R. Doering, ed., *A Report on the Development of Penological Treatment at Norfolk Prison Colony in Massachusetts* (New York: Bureau of Social Hygiene, 1940), pp. 71–206. See also Haynes, *American Prison System,* chap. 4.

44. Howard B. Gill, "The Norfolk State Prison Colony at Massachusetts," *Journal of Criminal Law and Criminology* 22 (1931):107–112.

45. The discussion here is based on personal conversations with Howard B. Gill, 1980–1981, especially a lengthy interview taped in August 1980. All quotes are used with permission.

46. Dr. Hans Weiss, at one time a case worker at Norfolk, quoted in Albert Morris, review of Doering's *Report on Norfolk, Federal Probation* 6 (July–September 1942):51–52. Through joint participation of prisoners and guards Gill sought to transcend the traditional antagonism between the keepers and the kept, a central feature of traditional prison culture. What is most doubtful, according to one critic of such a concept, is whether there can be a "reformative idea" based on a "shared moral universe . . . [between] punisher and punished." Michael Ignatieff, *A Just Measure of Pain* (New York: Pantheon Books, 1978), p. 213.

47. Yahkub, "History," pp.83–84. See also Hans Toch, *Police, Prisons, and the Problem of Violence* (Rockville, Md.: National Institute of Mental Health, 1977), pp. 85–86.

48. Gill interview, August 1980.

49. See Yahkub, "History," pp. 84–85.

50. Gill Interview, August 1980.

51. Quoted in Yahkub, "History," p. 179.

52. *Brief* of Howard B. Gill, in March 1934 hearing of charges, before Massachusetts Commissioner of Corrections, pp. 27–28. The joint committees of the council were construction, home and employment, education and library, medical work, maintenance, store, entertainment, athletics, the *Colony* paper, food, and avocational work.

53. Yahkub, "History," p. 84. The sketch here of the history of inmate participation at Norfolk is adapted mainly from ibid., pp. 83–87, and from discussions with Gill.

54. Yahkub, "History," p. 85. The workings of the Norfolk council system were described by the British Commissioner of Prisons, Alexander Paterson, following a visit. In recounting a dramatic clash between Gill and an elected inmate council early in the development of the Norfolk system, Paterson shows the tension between traditional inmate solidarity based on anti-staff attitudes and the community concept which Gill was promoting: "On one occasion a Bolshevist Council refused to take responsibility for guarding the Camp. The warden [Gill] accordingly submitted the matter to the Houses (i.e. the inmate body at large), who had to vote whether to support the Council and in that case accept a restriction of privileges, or to appoint another Council." In the ensuing vote, the recalcitrant council was recalled. Alexander Paterson, *The Prison Problem of America* (Maidstone Prison, England, 1935), pp. 92–94.

55. Yahkub, "History," pp. 85–86.

56. Gill interview, August 1980.

57. See Yahkub, "History," pp. 86–87. Paterson, (*Prison Problem,* p. 94) regards Norfolk's "brave experiment" as having progressed "almost as far as any men's prison has been allowed to go in the direction of 'self-government.'"

58. Barnes and Teeters, *New Horizons,* p. 698. At the same time, these authors believe that Gill's ideas as exemplified in Norfolk had "permeated the field of progressive penology."

59. Doering, *Report on Norfolk,* pp. xiv, xxi. After Gill's final dismissal in April 1934, Doering was appointed by the Massachusetts Department of Corrections as research director for the last year of Norfolk's five-year research project. Doering was highly critical of Gill's experiment characterizing parts of it as the waving of "a blazing red flag to the public bull." Morris suggests Doering's hostility may be related to his ties to the corrections administration that had employed him. (See Morris, review of *Report on Norfolk,* p. 51).

60. Yahkub, "History," p. 198.

61. Hurley, Francis X., "Report on Norfolk Prison," Report by the

Office of the State Auditor, Boston, February 10, 1934, p. 103. (In volume of materials compiled on the Gill Hearing, Harvard Law Library).

62. Gill, Howard B., "Closing Statement," Hearing before Governor Joseph B. Ely and Commissioner Frederick J. Dillon, March, 1934. (See also the "Briefs," March, 1934, on behalf of Gill—in the compiled volume, Harvard Law Library.)

63. According to Barnes and Teeters, *New Horizons,* p. 692, "no keepers or guards were allowed in the shops, where discipline was wholly in the hands of the convicts." Decisions rendered by a five-man board of inmate judges were "carried out by the regular officers of the prison."

64. See Baker, *Right to Participate,* p. 246.

65. See the discussion in Gordon Hawkins, *The Prison: Policy and Practice* (Chicago: University of Chicago Press, 1976), pp. 88–95. Gill's formula called for house officers to be 90 percent "treatment" and watch officers 90 percent "custody." See also Donald R. Cressey,"Limitations on Organization of Treatment," in Cloward et al., *Theoretical Studies,* p. 103. If such collaborative schemes pose a conflict of interest for guards, there is in this community-prison concept an even greater conflict for the prisoners. The convict code was traditionally the most fundamental body of informal, but no less binding, rules within the society of captives. We have already noted the confrontation that occurred in 1929 over the inmate watch. The paramount law of the convict code is directed against informers, thereby affirming the solidarity of the kept against their keepers. Thus every reform attempt at inmate-staff collaboration has found itself sooner or later confronted with this problem.

The treatment staff is likewise confronted with role conflicts in any prison-community framework. So it was, for example, with the therapeutic-community experiment at the Dannemora Diagnostic Center in New York. Its director, Bruno Cormier, maintains that a therapeutic community must exclude the self-government principle that the community "could vote itself out of existence" (thereby calling a halt to the therapy). This is, of course, the key difference, philosophically, in the therapist as authoritative decision maker versus citizen rule. See Bruno M. Cormier, *The Watcher and The Watched* (Montreal and Plattsburgh, N.Y.: Tundra Books, 1975), pp. 17–19.

66. See C. Ronald Huff, "Prisoner Militancy and Politicization: The Ohio Prisoners' Union Movement," in David F. Greenberg, ed., *Corrections and Punishment* (Beverly Hills: Sage, 1977), pp. 262–263. See also Frank Browning, "Organizing Behind Bars," *Ramparts* (February 1972): 40–45.

67. Rothman, *Conscience and Convenience,* pp. 379, 380, 420.

68. Ibid., pp. 118–127.

69. For Rothman's assessment of the results of the "therapy"

approach, see ibid., pp. 132–135, 144. See also *Struggle for Justice*, Chapter 6: "The Crime of Treatment."

70. *Handbook of American Prisons and Reformatories, 1933,* 4th ed. (New York: Osborne Association, 1933), 1:419, 423.

71. Rothman, *Conscience and Convenience,* pp. 385–386.

72. See ibid., chap. 4. (esp. pp. 144–149). While Gill had attempted a pragmatic combination of both "community" and "hospital," Rothman sees Gill's efforts as being mainly aimed at implementing the "hospital treatment model." (Ibid., p. 395.)

73. Ibid., p. 407.

74. Personal discussions with Gill, 1980–1981. Gill refers to the "Diary" as a "wailing wall." An assessment based primarily on this single source raises serious questions, especially when Rothman did not consult Gill himself, who is still (in his nineties) active in the field of penology.

75. Personal discussions. Gill states that during his tenure Norfolk had no hole in any meaningful sense. New arrivals and a few others, usually those scheduled for return to Charlestown, were held in maximum security. In January 1934 (when Gill was already fighting the charges of coddling inmates), some of the prisoners being returned to Charlestown broke all of the windows on the top floor of the Receiving Building, which led to the boarding up of the windows and hence the legend of the hole.

76. Rothman, *Conscience and Convenience,* p. 418. For Rothman, this points up that "the critical elements [in Gill's downfall] . . . were the internal ones," even though he concedes that "Gill was finally a victim of state politics." His dismissal in these circumstances thus "helped to blur the genuine significance of the events, making it seem that reform had fallen victim to politics, not to its own dynamic." Ibid., pp. 418–419.

77. U.S. President's Commission on Law Enforcement and Administration of Justice, *Task Force Report: Corrections* (Washington, D.C.: U.S. Government Printing Office, 1967), p. 50. Emphasis added. See also U.S. President's Commission on Law Enforcement and Administration of Justice, *The Challenge of Crime in a Free Society* (New York: E.P. Dutton & Co., 1968), pp. 415–416. The commission's recommendation (p. 416) speaks of "joint responsibility of staff and inmates," a formulation that could have been taken directly from Gill.

78. U.S. National Advisory Commission on Criminal Justice Standards and Goals, *Task Force Report on Corrections* (Washington, D.C.: U.S. Government Printing Office, 1973), p. 485. Emphasis added. At another point, the task force states, "A priority in corrections must be participatory management sessions in which managers bring staff and inmates together to chart the future course for all of them." Ibid., p. 469.

79. A useful survey of the use of inmate councils has been compiled by Baker, *Right to Participate.* The bulk of this study relies on reports received

from correctional authorities, primarily on a state-by-state basis. Most of the councils described have a strictly advisory role.

80. On Maconochie, whose radical innovations took place at an island penal colony off the Australian coast, see John Vincent Barry, *Alexander Maconochie of Norfolk Island* (London: Oxford University Press, 1958). His own writings on "convict management" were published in 1839 and reissued in 1967. For Zebulon Brockway (Detroit House of Correction, 1860s, and Elmira Reformatory from 1876) and Hiram F. Hatch (Michigan State Prison, 1885–1891), see Harold M. Helfman, "Antecedents of Thomas Mott Osborne's 'Mutual Welfare League' in Michigan," *Journal of Criminal Law and Criminology* 40 (May–April 1949–1950): 597–600. On Kenyon J. Scudder (California Institution for Men, Chino, in the 1940s and 1950s), see his *Prisoners Are People* (Garden City, N.Y.: Doubleday, 1952); see also, Baker, *Right to Participate*, pp. 93–94. Thomas O. Murton (Arkansas, 1967–1968) provides the most authoritative short account of his own innovations in his *The Dilemma of Prison Reform* (New York: Holt, Rinehart, and Winston, 1976), pp. 213–220. See also Tom Murton and Joe Hyams, *Accomplices to the Crime: The Arkansas Prison Scandal* (New York: Grove Press, 1969); Murton, "Inmate Self-Government," *University of San Francisco Law Review* 6 (October 1971):87–102; Murton, *Shared Decision-Making as a Treatment Technique in Prison Management* (Minneapolis: Murton Foundation for Criminal Justice, 1975). The innovations of Dr. William R. Conte, a psychiatrist who headed Washington State's correctional system from 1966 to 1971, will be discussed in detail in chapters 5–8. For Conte's own account, see Conte, "Modern Day Reforms in Washington State Penal Programs," *American Journal of Corrections* (May–June, 1971): pp. 27–30. With the exception of Conte, all of these examples implemented their experiments from their positions as prison wardens.

81. See Baker, *Right to Participate*.

82. See, for example, Doering, *Report*, pp. xvi–xviii, xxi. Gill himself concluded that much of his progress toward a harmonious prison community was dependent upon having a relatively small, selected, and homogeneous inmate body.

83. David Fogel, *". . . We Are the Living Proof . . . ": The Justice Model for Corrections* (Cincinnati: W.H. Anderson, 1975), pp. 213–214.

84. Ibid., p. 214. Fogel sets down these points as guidelines but emphasizes the need for experimentation, as well as for adjustment to diverse conditions.

85. Ibid., pp. 213, 215–216. Fogel relies primarily on research carried out by Richard W. Wilsnack and Lloyd E. Ohlin, focusing on inmate unrest during an eighteen-month period in the early 1970s (the "Attica period"). The results were later reported in Wilsnack, "Explaining Collective Violence in Prisons: Problems and Possibilities," in *Prison Violence,* ed. Albert K. Cohen et al. (Lexington, Mass.: Lexington Books, D.C. Heath and Company, 1976), pp. 61–78.

86. Baker, *Right to Participate,* pp. 248, 22. Baker, a long-time warden himself, in advocating any sort of inmate council concept, occupies what was, in fact, a minority position among prison administrators: he indicates that in 1960 the Wardens' Association "went on record as being opposed to the idea of inmate self-government [advisory councils]." Ibid., p. 245.

87. Benedict S. Alper, *Prisons Inside-Out: Alternatives in Correctional Reform* (Cambridge, Mass.: Ballinger, 1974), pp. 92-93. Alper also perceives the earlier Mutual Welfare League—roughly paralleling the "company unions" of Osborne's time, which in the United States then gave way to authentic trade unions—as, in some sense, a forerunner of these current developments behind the walls.

88. James Q. Wilson, *Thinking about Crime,* (New York: Vintage, 1975), p. xix.

89. "There is only one answer to the question: 'What can be done to better this penal system?' Nothing. A prison cannot be improved . . . There is absolutely nothing to do but demolish it," wrote Kropotkin in 1877. Roger N. Baldwin ed., *Kropotkin's Revolutionary Pamphlets* (New York: Dover, 1970—first published by Vanguard Press in 1927), pp. 221-222. See also, for an account of recent abolitionist movements, Gordon Hawkins, *The Prison: Policy and Practice* (Chicago: University of Chicago Press, 1976) pp. vii-viii, 5-12.

90. Interview with Gill, August 1980. The "under wraps" metaphor suggests a species of restricted "sovereignty," within which certain democratizing tendencies may be at work. The rationale for restrictions lie primarily in the presumed security interests of the larger society living beyond the guarded periphery, together with the degree of conformity that these external forces insist upon.

91. The *new breed* label was given special prominence through the McKay Commission's report on the 1971 Attica uprising. See: New York State Special Commission, *Attica* (New York: Bantam, 1972), pp. 106-107; 116-118.

**Part II
Power and Politics in
an American Prison**

5

A Survey History of Washington State Penitentiary

The Early Years

When Washington State Penitentiary (WSP) was built at Walla Walla in 1886, Washington was still a territory, and Walla Walla, in its southeast corner, was among its largest towns. WSP was a typical nineteenth century prison designed on the Auburn system of silent communal labor. (For a model of WSP today, see figure 5-1.) A report to territorial Governor Eugene Semple in 1887 contains this description:

A stockade of stone, laid in cement enclosing three acres of a parallelogram. The wall is laid in a trench three feet deep and six feet wide, it is six feet wide at the base, and tapers to a width of 16 inches at the top, which is 15 feet above ground and is covered with cement. It is perpendicular on the inside and is provided with numerous heavy buttresses on the outside. A plank walk, protected by an iron railing, runs the entire length of the wall on the outside. Two brick guard houses are erected at opposite corners of the stockade and wooden sentry boxes at the other corners. The stockade wall is provided with two sets of gates set in stone walls of the same dimensions as the stockade walls, the outer gates being made of heavy iron bars, the inner gates of boiler iron and fitted with patent locks. The gateway is covered by a one story wooden building, 22 x 32 feet in size, used as an office and sleeping room by the Warden. Inside the stockade are the prison buildings and a small building used as a laundry, etc., both of brick. The main, or cell building is 34 x 100 feet inside with walls 22 inches thick and 26 feet high. It has numerous barred windows, a corrugated iron ceiling, cement floors and two entrances provided with double iron doors having patent locks. In this building are 84 iron cells placed back to back, in three tiers, 14 in a row, 28 in a tier, having a corridor fenced off by an iron grating. The cells are each 5 feet, 6 inches wide, 9 feet long and 7 feet high. Each cell has a ventilating shaft, and is designed for two prisoners who sleep on hammocks. Four of the cells are dark, the others have grated doors.[1]

The penitentiary at Walla Walla replaced the Territory's first central prison, Seatco, in Western Washington. Authorized by the territorial legislature in 1874, Seatco was operated by private contractors who made profitable use of unpaid prison labor combined with legislative subsidies. The two sheriffs who were awarded the contract combined forces with a landlord

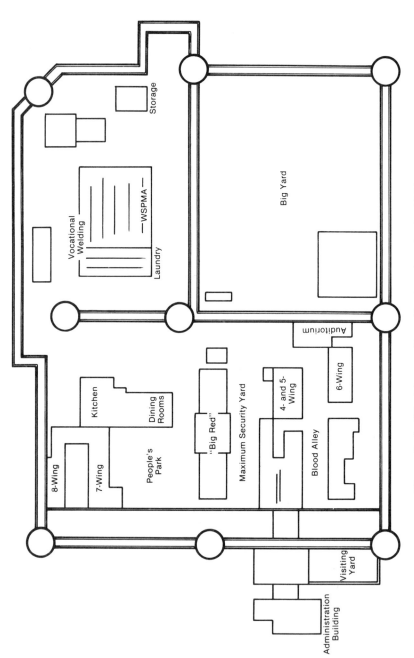

Figure 5–1. Washington State Penitentiary in the 1970s

to build the prison into a lucrative business. Convicts were employed in logging and coal mining, in a saw-mill and cooperage factory established near the prison site. Seatco soon acquired a reputation as the "worst prison in America."[2]

The proposal to build a territorially financed and controlled prison was bitterly opposed by the Seatco contractors, who undertook an intensive lobbying campaign against it in the state legislature. When they were unable to halt the legislation which authorized the penitentiary, they raised doubts as to its legality, and succeeded in blocking funds for the maintenance of prisoners scheduled to be moved to the new facility, thus delaying the transfers across the mountains for several months. At this point, the Walla Walla Board of Trade stepped in and organized a fund-raising campaign to support the institution until such time as the legislature made the appropriation.

The more than three-hundred mile move across the snow-covered Cascade Mountains, from the lush green forests of coastal Washington to the arid inlands, was a dramatic change. In the early days the greater concentration of population and even the state capital had been expected in eastern Washington. But by the twentieth century, this region was increasingly seen as a desert "Siberia," far from the growing cities of Puget Sound, which were home to most of the prisoners.

The change of prison regimen was almost as dramatic as the change of scenery. There was no more heavy labor in mines and mills: in fact, there was scarcely any work at all for the prisoners. This situation was a consequence of the Federal anticontract law, passed in 1887, banning the use of contract labor, thereby outlawing prisons such as Seatco.[3] What had been a thriving business utilizing prison labor came to a virtual standstill; and the opposite problem of idleness, which still plagues American prisons, soon made itself felt.

Even so, Warden J.H. Coblentz, who took office in 1893, was credited in those early years of the penitenitary with making "the most noteworthy advances" using inmate labor.[4] He added a new hospital, built a prison stockyard and packaging plant, improved the water supply, landscaped the grounds, doubled production in the prison jute mill, and in an unprecedented move, supplied the luxury of underwear to the members of the outside work gang. He also established a photo gallery operated by a convict photographer. But Coblentz's promising career at the new prison was cut short in 1894 when an investigating committee discovered that he had sold wheat sacks manufactured in the prison jute mill and pocketed the proceeds. Confronted with the evidence, Coblentz committed suicide.

Coblentz's successors seem to have done little to improve the quality of life at Walla Walla, as the prison became known throughout the state. A 1926 report based on a visit in 1925 from the National Society of Penal

Information (later to become the Osborne Association) showed that the number of acres enclosed by the wall had grown from three to twenty-three and the cell houses from one to five, with a total of 460 cells for over 900 inmates on three tiers. The dimensions of the cells had seemingly decreased since an 1887 official report and the two-men cells were filled to capacity, if not overfilled. The hammocks had given way to beds with straw-filled "ticks" for mattresses. There was no plumbing. A 160-acre farm had been added to the prison grounds. The report severely criticizes a "rigid and repressive" system of discipline and concludes by deploring "the overcrowding, lack of work and monotonous regime [which] cannot make good citizens. It is doubtful if it can even make good prisoners."[5]

In 1929, the National Society of Penal Information issued a second report on Washington State Penitentiary, based on a visit in the summer of 1928. Although the expanded farm operation was commended, the report was highly critical of the crowding of nearly 1100 prisoners into the same 460 cells.[6]

By the time of the appearance of the Osborne Society's sixth handbook in 1942, WSP had expanded from five to eight cell houses (the three additional ones being built between 1930 and 1940), with a total of 780 cells. As of January 1942, the population had reached 1630.

This team of observers visiting in the spring of 1940 still found much to criticize.[7] Overcrowding remained a problem and the Osborne Association visitors strongly recommended that single cells be built. Although they gave the penitentiary administration credit for the liberalization or abolition of some of the repressive and petty regulations, they urged the repeal of the silence rule for the mess hall which was not enforced anyway. And although they conceded a moderate advance in the introduction of a "rough appraisal" classificatory scheme (which was able to sort out the "normal" from the "feeble-minded" among the inmates), the team prescribed several additional steps, including a full-time psychologist and at least a part-time psychiatrist, before WSP would be able "to carry on the kind of individualized program that characterizes progressive prisons." They also suggested changes in staff recruitment policies and higher pay for employees, while deploring the weak educational program and recommending the organization of an inmate advisory council.

In an addendum to its critique, the association took favorable note of a key development that took place in Washington State's correctional system after the team visit but before the issuing of the 1942 *Handbook*. In late 1941, Richard A. McGee had been brought in as the top administrator of the state's public institutions. McGee, a respected administrator, had already appointed professionals to the positions of superintendent and assistant superintendent of WSP. The report calls McGee's appointment "of great significance."[8] However, McGee served fewer than three years in this post, before being hired by Governor Earl Warren of California to spearhead Warren's prison-reform program.[9] His departure probably delayed by a decade the transition to the remedial prison in Washington State and the limitation on the warden's autocratic authority by a rationalized state bureaucracy.

Years of Transition

Riot and Change

Beginning in 1953, a period of unrest, marked by sporadic outbreaks of violence and reaching its culmination in a costly and bloody riot in 1955, brought WSP forcefully to national attention.[10] In the period leading up to the big riot, events began with a two-day sitdown and hunger strike.[11] As a result, a governor's representative was dispatched from the state capital in Olympia to Walla Walla, with instructions to discuss the inmates' grievances. Fifty prisoners met with him and presented demands, which included replacement of the warden (Larry Delmore) and liberalization of the parole board policy.

When no official action followed this meeting, there was an outbreak of scattered violence. An explosion and fire in the "tag" (license plate) shop was followed by mattress burning and window breaking. Tear gas was used to restore order. The loss was estimated at between $2 milion and $3 million. The principal change that followed was that additional guards were hired.

It was in this tense atmosphere that the massive riot finally broke out. Hostages were taken, including the deputy warden, and for two days the prison was run by the riot leaders. There were some fights but no loss of life with the exception of an elderly guard who died of a heart attack two days later. The con bosses were in control; and their leader "Big Jim" Frazier—a lifer, described by Jack Griswold, an eye-witness, as "an intellectual killer"—organized a ball-bat-carrying convict "police force" with orders to control the violence.[12]

Negotiations with the penitentiary administration soon began. The chief negotiator for the state was Dr. Thomas Harris, a popular author (*I'm OK, You're OK*) and psychiatrist, who was then state director of institutions. The chief inmate negotiator was Big Jim Frazier. According to B.J. (Bobby) Rhay, who was to be superintendent from 1957 to 1977, Frazier was representative of the old breed of convict leaders, individualistic and stable as compared to the leaders Rhay was to deal with during the 1960s and 1970s. "They [the old breed] would look you in the eye and fight you toe to toe. The new breed was different, unpredictable."[13]

In April 1956 a new warden was appointed. This, in Griswold's account, was a direct outgrowth of promises made to end the riot, as were changes in parole board membership and procedures.[14] The new warden, Merle Schneckloth, was brought from California, but he returned there within a year. He was replaced by B.J. Rhay.

The Rhay Regime

When B.J. Rhay assumed the top position at WSP, he was, at the age of thirty-five, the youngest prison warden in the United States. When he left, twenty years later, he was the senior superintendent in the country. His long tenure at Walla Walla was sandwiched between notably unstable periods there. He had assumed the leadership of a traditional, poorly equipped, and antiquated warehouse prison; supervised its change into what was, at least in theory, a remedial prison; presided over its transformation into one of the most open maximum-security facilities in the nation; and finally led the return to a custody-oriented institution. His political-survival instincts and managerial flexibility were truly remarkable. A top Olympia official once described Rhay's approach as one of "determining which way the wind is blowing and rowing as fast as possible in that direction." Others, including some inmates, admired his adaptability, even when they opposed him on particular issues. The more militant prisoners of the 1960s and 1970s conceded Rhay's flexibility in less flattering ways, referring to him as "Oh-Promise-Me Bob".

Rhay found some of the conditions he inherited at the old territorial prison appalling and did not hesitate to say so. In the superintendent's report of 1958, his first year in that job, he complained:

> Cell blocks four and five at the Penitentiary were built in the 1880s. . . . There are no plumbing facilities in the cells [and] twice a day the inmates empty buckets into an open sewer outside the cell block building. . . . During the hot weather if the cells are kept closed the odor is unendurable.[15]

But by 1960 two new wings had been built, plumbing had been installed throughout the prison, and other improvements had been made in the conditions of confinement. What Rhay wanted from the legislature in those first years was, he recalled, "bricks and brains" to rebuild the antiquated human warehouse into a modern correctional facility.[16]

Walla Walla, the "company town" of the penitentiary, was Rhay's home town. He had begun as a night tower guard in 1945, left to complete his studies in sociology at Whitman College in Walla Walla, then returned to WSP briefly to work in classification. By this time he had become the son-in-law of the warden. A change in the governor's chair led to the removal of Tom Smith, his father-in-law, and for B.J. Rhay an interlude in New York as an investigator for Erle Stanley Gardner's "Court of Last Resort". In 1954, Rhay returned to WSP to organize the reception-guidance unit.

In 1957, B.J. Rhay reached the top post at WSP, promoted from associate superintendent for treatment. He soon made his reputation as a tough and fearless warden. An incident which took place two years after he assumed the superintendency in the penitentiary was to make him a hero in his home town. During an escape attempt by three inmates, the officer at the security booth "froze on the gun". Rhay snatched the weapon from the guard and shot two of the inmates. The third gave up.

In those days "B.J." was a warden in the classic custodial mold. Although he presided over a prison that was by the late 1950s called a correctional institution, WSP was still essentially a warehouse prison. He ruled his domain as if he were the all-powerful sovereign. Like the traditional authoritarian warden described by Tannenbaum, he was "legislator, judge and executioner."[17] In other words, he "ran" the joint.

For Rhay, this strong warden role extended through the 1960s. He was held in high esteem by correctional colleagues and fellow townsmen. But when he became the defender, however reluctantly, of the reforms of the early 1970s that aimed at transforming the penitentiary and his place in it, he found himself under attack from the local press and powers who had applauded him a few years earlier.

At this same juncture, his charisma seems also to have suffered in the eyes of his staff. Robert Freeman, who was associate superintendent for treatment at the time, feels that Rhay "dragged his feet at first, then he came back and told the staff 'this is how its going to be.'" Freeman, who spent twenty-seven years at the penitentiary, went along with the initiation of reform: "I've always been a company man," he said. "When the boss told me to do it, I did it."[18]

Rhay was a "good soldier," He obeyed the orders of his superior officer while harboring his own private, sometimes rather colorful, views about him. His superior in this instance was William R. Conte, the director of institutions. Although Conte was to resign less than a year after the reforms were launched at WSP, the entire reform era continued to bear his imprint.

The Conte Era

In 1966 when Conte was appointed Washington state director of institutions, he had been head of the state's mental health division for seven years, while Rhay had been ruling over "his" hill for nearly a decade. The dominant concern of B.J. Rhay and his administration was custody. He knew that an explosion such as occurred in 1955 could well lead to his own downfall.

William Conte, a psychiatrist, was an outsider to the correctional system. The Department of Institutions included supervision over thirty-two institutions, only a portion of which were prisons in the strict sense. From the time he joined the department in 1959 as supervisor of the division of mental health, Conte had worked closely with the director of institutions, Garrett Heyns.[19]

Heyns, who was strongly oriented to treatment and rehabilitation, found in Conte a kindred spirit. Together they developed a philosophy of administration designed to serve as a policy guide for the Department of Institutions. Its aim was to "create and maintain optimal treatment and educational services for inmates, patients, residents, students, members and their families," to promote and apply research and clinical experience, to "approach vigorously the problems of prevention," and to develop a congenial work environment that would promote staff cooperation.[20] Conte later summed up the approach embraced by the philosophy of administration as a form of participatory management in which "all parties, regardless of their rank, are welcome to express themselves and to be active participants in the development and implementation of state operated institutional services."[21]

Thus broad ideology and the administrative groundwork for the reforms that Conte was to implement had been formulated during Heyns's term of office. Heyns had been viewed as a correctional professional, albeit a treatment-oriented one, who did not move too fast and could understand staff problems. "He belonged to the old school," Rhay said approvingly; "he believed in a disciplinary based institution." By contrast, Conte, who became director of institutions in 1966, was from the beginning regarded as an outsider, one who, in Rhay's words, had "never walked the line."[22] "He simply came in, gave the job his best licks and then left," said Associate Superintendent for Treatment Robert Freeman.[23]

Conte was aware of the suspicion and hostility towards him and the values he represented. These attitudes were, in his view, largely responsible for his premature resignation and eventual failure of the reforms. He later recalled:

> When I raised questions about the reason for the strip cell and/or when I spoke about the human aspect of the treatment endeavor, . . . I was told by many staff at all levels of the organization that the men in prison were animals and that this was the only kind of treatment they could understand. Of course I was being told I did not know anything about prisons.[24]

Attitudes such as these had already handicapped Heyns, according to Conte, and undermined his own efforts when he succeeded him. Even among the professional staff of the institution, "the only place I felt there was an interest in what I was saying was in the educational directors." In 1967 Conte began to have regularly scheduled meetings with the superintendents of the various correctional institutions. Later, associate superintendents and other staff were drawn into these meetings. The minutes revealed to him "the extent of the resistance to change as well as the depth of the hostility that existed between staff and residents. Reflecting on adult correctional institutions of Washington State in the mid-1960s, he wrote, "There is no way I could have described the prison as an arena for treatment or rehabilitation. It was not even a place where a man might expect civil treatment."[25]

Nevertheless Conte considers his efforts with B.J. Rhay to have been successful. In the spring of 1970, Conte sent Rhay to Europe to visit institutions and correctional authorities in England, France, the Netherlands, Denmark, Norway and Sweden. When Rhay returned, he submitted a report on his travels to Conte. Rhay was impressed by such features as short sentences, small prison populations, high levels of staff training, intensive involvement of the parole officer with the prisoner throughout the term of incarceration, use of community sponsors and advisory groups, furloughs, and the role of the ombudsman. The ideas that he found most compelling were those related to democratization and decriminalization.[26]

But Rhay also expressed reservations in his report about the applicability of these ideas in the United States. "The European's inbred respect for authority and professionalism makes it easier to impose new ideas," he wrote. They also have a higher respect for persons and property, which may explain why crimes of violence are minimal . . . most of the institutions visited were comparable to our city and county jails rather than our state and federal institutions. The features in the European institutions that he felt would be most applicable to American corrections were those related to staff training and staff-to-inmate population ratios. Rhay concluded with praise for the "warm rapport between staff and inmate" that he found in the European institutions.[27]

Conte was pleased by what he interpreted as Rhay's "conversion."[28] "He learned much in regard to human dignity which is fundamental to good programming."[29] But Rhay felt that Conte failed to take into account his (Rhay's) reservations concerning the applicability of the European experiments to the Washington State situation.[30]

Rhay claims that he, as well as the rest of the staff, were caught by surprise when the reforms were announced at a press conference at Seattle's Civic Center.

> They just said on November 18th (1970) at the Civic Center—there was a press conference—bang! bang! bang! You've got four reforms. Now implement them. Nobody knew where we were coming from or where we

were going . . . and I think this is the reason we're getting the trauma. We simply didn't do it in the organized systematic way that we used to develop a program.[31]

This press conference was the occasion for Conte to unveil details of the reform program before a broader public. A series of liberalizing measures was to be implemented, including the abolition of censorship; the extension of telephone and visiting privileges; the easing of disciplinary methods (the final demise of the strip cell); and, the most far-reaching and controversial, the promise of forming a resident government council, to embody the principle of inmate self-government.[32] These internal reforms were to be accompanied by expanded work-training release programs, first authorized by the state legislature in 1967, and the legislating of new furlough programs. In addition, plans for a wide expansion of educational opportunities for inmates, both inside the facility and outside, were announced.

In Conte's view the groundwork for acceptance of the reforms by prison administrators had been developing over the previous decade. Yet their actual introduction into a penitentiary such as WSP would require time and genuine initiative at the grass-roots level.[33] Although the policies were mandated, the mode and the details for bringing them into effect was not.

Conte believed that the years of intensive discussions among institutional administrators and other staff members that had preceded the reforms should have smoothed the path. He sensed Rhay's resistance and attributed it partly to his personal history,[34] partly to the conservative staff culture in which he had lived for so long, and partly to his fear of losing control.

But the administrators and staff whose responsibility it was to implement the new program had a different perspective. They blamed the reforms, characterized by them as the ill-conceived and naive scheme of a "liberal-in-a-hurry," for the demoralization, violence, and confusion which followed.[35]

Such a difference in perspective could scarcely fail to express itself in conflict over particular changes and over the broader objectives of the penal system. Conte thought these aims were clearly outlined in his philosophy of corrections, elaborated a full year before the actual reforms were announced in late 1970.[36] He believed that his therapeutic approach to corrections was clearly sanctioned by the laws that created his administrative agency.[37] The criminal justice professionals who worked under him continued to see their work in terms derived from traditional custodial models of incarceration. They considered that they had been ill-prepared, ill-informed and ill-served by what they came to identify as the "Conte-Horowitz Team."

The other half of this team was a Seattle attorney, Donald J. Horowitz, who was appointed in June 1970 to head the legal staff of the newly created "umbrella" agency, the Department of Social and Health Services (DSHS). Although this reorganization was strongly opposed by Conte, Horowitz became Conte's intimate associate in carrying through the reforms. In people's minds, including most administrators, Horowitz became as closely tied to the reforms as Conte himself. "Horowitz dictated a lot of stuff that came out of Conte's mouth." said WSP's former Associate Superintendent for Treatment Robert Freeman.[38] Simon Dinitz and John Conrad, who later worked with Freeman on research projects, characterized the reforms as the product of Conte-Horowitz "teamwork," a "two-pronged program of rehabilitation and due process."[39]

Horowitz, who later became a Superior Court judge, had denied dictating anything to Conte. Horowitz summed up the era and the roles of the principal actors in this way: "Conte dreamed up some rules changes. I enforced them. Rhay resisted them."[40]

Self-Government in Action

Laying the Foundations

The event that triggered the implementation of Conte's reforms at WSP was a protest action typical of the 1960s, a strike over hair regulations:[41]

> Prior to December 22, 1970, a few radical youths had spoken from the prison auditorium stage encouraging the population to join them in a protest move to obtain permission to grow long hair . . . Older, more experienced convicts had countered that a protest should concern more serious grievances. Nevertheless, a motto developed "If you care, grow hair." An agreement was made among a large number of inmates that if one more prisoner was placed in the isolation unit . . . the entire population would strike and refuse to come out of their cells. At approximately 10 A.M. on December 22, word was circulated via the prison grapevine that a young prisoner had been sentenced to isolation for growing a beard. In less than one hour, [almost] every inmate . . . had come off their assigned jobs and were in their cells. On the morning of December 23, 1970, all 1,345 inmates of the Maximum Security except the [Control Center] clerk, remained in their cells and a peaceful strike was under way, one that was to have far-reaching effects and which would result in a revolutionary new concept in penal treatment.[42]

The "sit-down" strike triggered by the "hair revolt" shut down the penitentiary for ten days.

Meantime a series of meetings took place between the superintendent with his staff and the Inmate Advisory Council, a "traditional" liaison group of inmates, established in 1956 to handle minor grievances but with no power to make decisions.

The strike ended on New Year's Day of 1971, with agreement to implement most of the reforms (except self-government) that Conte had announced. This ushered in a "transitional" phase of great uncertainty on all sides. The old rules were suspended until new, more liberal ones could be formulated. This left the guards no longer sure of the extent of their authority, while the inmates, "having tasted a measure of victory over the administration, tested their new freedoms by taunting the custody officers . . . "[43]

Over the following weeks, tensions mounted, leading up to a dramatic series of events that were to precipitate the formation of "self-government" at WSP:

> On March 22, 1971, an incident occurred which nearly ended in a racial bloodbath and defeat for the new program before the concept could be implemented . . . Racial conflicts had been frequent in the past, but with the coming of the new liberal philosophy, the races were on the verge of a race war, needing only an untimely incident to set the tinder-box of feelings off. On the day in question, a group of whites and blacks were viewing a television program in the prison auditorium. . . . At the end of one program when the inmates customarily would vote on the choice of the next one, a young white inmate demanded that the elderly black assigned to change channels on the T.V. set, tune in on a certain program that wasn't scheduled or voted on. When the elderly black responded that he couldn't do it without a vote being taken, the young white struck the older black . . . Soon a melee ensued with members of both races.[44]

Throughout the night and into the next day, numerous racial clashes erupted, bringing the penitentiary to such a pitch of tension that a race war seemed imminent. Black inmates, who constituted little more than 20 percent of the population, felt the most threatened in this volatile situation. That evening hundreds of angry white prisoners, armed with homemade weapons, assembled in the auditorium. The guards hastily retreated, leaving the grounds to the inmates.[45] Then the following events were recorded by the inmate chronicler:

> Several inmates, blacks and whites alike, mounted the stage of the theatre and acted as a catalyst, and managed to calm the confused and hostile crowd of would-be combatants. Appeals were made by several inmate leaders not to proceed with the hostilities but to unite and combine the strength of the races against the system which had encouraged and fostered racial distance and which had tacitly sanctioned a near-massacre. The crowd who only a moment before were ready to kill each other responded with a spontaneous sigh of relief, weapons were discarded, and thus began a racial unity and harmony that continues to baffle the most cynical observer of prison behavior.[46]

The day after this incident, the Race Relations Committee (RRC) was formed by the inmates. Described as an "outlaw [extralegal] but obviously necessary control group," it became for a time the dominant leadership force inside the walls. It developed its own distinctive mechanisms for settling disputes and avoiding interracial violence.

> First, members of the RRC would approach the two adversaries and seek to effect a settling of differences without physical encounter. If this approach failed, the two parties were taken to the Prison Gym where large shower stalls were situated, into which the two discordant inmates were placed and told to settle their differences under the referee eyes of members of the RRC. Fists, feet or baseball bats were allowed but most men chose to fight bare-fisted. This frontier style of settling personal differences soon reduced encounters of a serious nature, and a welcome peace settled upon the troubled prison.[47]

In retrospect, both keepers and kept would agree that the RRC experience was a kind of "dress rehearsal" for full-scale self-government. At this juncture, the superintendent, key members of the administration, and inmate leaders began the process of creating the Resident Government Council (RGC). It required no fewer than fourteen drafts of a constitution plus two rounds of voting before formal ratification (including approval of the administration) was completed on April 14, 1971. The eleven council members, to be elected by the inside population, would represent the prisoners to the administration and the public. (The minimum-security building would have a similar but separate representative body.)

The first RGC elections were held on April 24 and 25, 1971, thus formally initiating the new era in Washington State Corrections. B.J. Rhay, without expressing any hard judgment on its long-range viability, described the new concept as "a fifty-fifty partnership": "the guards were to pull back 50 percent and the inmates were supposed to come forward 50 percent in responsibility."[48] Meanwhile, Conte had announced his resignation, effective July 1, 1971.[49]

The series of events leading up to the election and installation of the first RGC impressed those on all sides as remarkable. Even given the trends generated by the pressures for change in America's warehouse prisons, which had been accumulating over recent decades, WSP had appeared to lag behind. It was a typically tough maximum-security custodial fortress, operating in a plant nearly a century old, when suddenly it was transformed. Inmate organizations and clubs ranging from the ethnic native American, Chicano, and black formations to the "Lifers with Hope" sprang up and received formal recognition. And the tough convicts became legislators, policy makers, with a government of their own, the Resident Government Council (RGC), representing the inmate body as a whole.

Inevitably responses to such a sweeping change varied drastically. Most inmates compared the RGC favorably with the former Inmate Advisory Council, which had lacked power.[50] A black inmate who was president of the first RGC, saw the merits of the new regime in broad terms:

> We feel more like human beings for one thing. And this is being allowed to be able to think for ourselves. We believe that people in the institution under self-government will be able to make it much better in society. Because the way it was under supercustody you was not allowed to think for yourself. If you wanted to get in trouble just start thinking for yourself.[51]

A long-time guard, president of the officers' union, felt that under the new order the inmates had turned the tables:

> Now this program was dropped in, just dropped in. The residents and staff didn't know exactly what to do with it. As it happened the residents organized first and better. They took advantage of the staff and the staff found themselves backed into a wall. The residents could call them names for just doing their job, you know, as it was done before.[52]

An inmate leader concurred that relationships had been drastically upset—that when prisoners felt they were able to participate in decisions affecting their lives they "stood up to the hacks" as never before.[53] The guards, in their turn, sensed they were losing control. They could no longer punish the defiant prisoner at times and in ways of their own choosing. All infractions now had to be written up; much verbal abuse had to be ignored. They began to feel the inmates had better access to the administration than they had.

Superintendent Rhay had remained publically noncommittal, even supportive, of the reforms in the early days. Later, however, he openly expressed his dismay at the changes that were "suddenly kind of cast down on us," particularly self-government, which "philosophy-wise [was] a complete change."[54]

William A. Hunter, a psychologist, was WSP's only full-time psychotherapist. He regretted the passing of the authoritarian era and criticized the state authorities who "came in and turned the population loose to do its own thing," comparing their "surrender" to that of Neville Chamberlain at Munich.[55]

Thus, while radically different attitudes towards the reforms could be found within the prison community, it was generally agreed that a significant degree of power redistribution had taken place. For better or for worse, the old patterns of control had been drastically shaken by the theory and practice of "self-government" as introduced by the reformers in Olympia.

The Hopeful Years, 1971–1973

Under the residents' new constitutional structure, each RGC was to serve for six months, and then be succeeded by a new council, chosen through regular election by secret ballot. Just after the first changeover of elected representatives a long article on the Walla Walla program appeared in the *New York Times*. Barely a month earlier, the bloody events at Attica prison had shocked the nation and WSP was seen as an example of an effort to steer in another direction. The *Times* story described the fortress prison in the far Northwest as seemingly headed toward the removal of its guards and the eventual demolition of its walls. Thus WSP was suddenly thrust into the national spotlight.[56]

This was a heady atmosphere for the inmates. A few months earlier they had narrowly avoided a full-scale race riot. Now they had their own government. By the time of the New York reporter's visit, they had held two orderly elections, had designated officers and committee heads, and had made a creditable record of working "to improve the institutional environment through participating in short- and long-range planning and . . . communications," as prescribed by the RGC's constitution.[57]

Behind the scenes, however, the path was anything but smooth, most notably in terms of the response of the line staff. A top-level evaluation team, headed by Richard A. McGee, visited Washington State in June 1971, midway through WSP's first RGC.[58] Speaking broadly of the state's corrections system, McGee reported marked progress in moving the program forward consistent with the Conte philosophy, but the team's recommendations on resident government contained the warning that as long as "many of the staff see themselves as being short-circuited out of the action," the program had "little chance" in the long run. Nonetheless, McGee cautioned: "To retreat from these advances now could well be disastrous. The gains must be solidified."[59] The team perceived "resident participative management" in Washington State as embodying a concept that was not new but that had never been as successful in practice as it should be. Yet although staff-inmate relations might prove to be the Achilles' heel, the report held that the constitutions and electoral systems were basically sound; and it endorsed the objectives of resident government in opening up communication channels and democratizing prison relationships.

From the inmates' point of view, the early councils appeared in retrospect as the high point of the self-government experience. They believed that they now had a role to play within the prison polity. Toward the end of the 1970s, a former RGC officer reflected on his feelings at that earlier time:

> The RGC had distinctive voting rights and privileges, we could call Olympia [the state capital], we could set up our own press conferences. We could

call in reporters when we wanted to. We could take pictures, we could, you know, write out what we wanted to write out, we could send out, we could write out our own newspaper. We had all those discretionary situations that the former [advisory] councils never had. We even made decisions on the budget for awhile.[60]

The credibility of the initial councils was attributed by inmates to the following accomplishments: the establishment of·an image of substantial power especially when contrasted with the kind of weak inmate liaison committees that had been a long-time feature of the institution; the achieving of various inmate requests that had been made repeatedly over a number of years, which thus accrued to the RGC's credit; and the implementation of proposals for the council members to sit in on classification and adjustment committees and "to get a vote and be able to support some of the men who had a good claim."[61]

In those areas where Conte's directives mandated reforms, the RGC had the task of designing a proposal to implement the reform. This included, for example, the telephone-use policy. "Everything that Conte had given us, supposedly, had to be restructured and put through the administration for their consent." Thus, even though "they took out what they didn't want us to have," the council was able to take credit for what was allowed and then implemented as policy.[62]

Although at first the RGC tended to be the dominant inmate body, the reform era saw the blossoming of a large number of inmate groups. In many cases, these inmate organizations had prereform origins, often of a semilegal character. But the new prison regime brought open recognition to these groups, although in some cases they had to be given a less provocative name.[63] They would be set up with written constitutions, election of officers, and a defined scope for their activities. This broad legitimation of group life, a hallmark of the new open regime at Walla Walla, signaled WSP's entry into the world of the interactive prison.

In the initial RGC constitution, the scheme envisaged no formal inclusion of organized groups. Nonetheless, in practice, the important clubs played the role of something like a political party system:

> The original council came from two persons from each one of the major groups. It was selected and then it was voted in. The Race Relations Committee was actually two people from each club inside here, representatives, that [later] went to the RGC. . . . There had to be a representative of each one of the groups. So you had so many ballots for the BPFU [black] bloc, so many ballots for regular [unaffiliated] population bloc, so many ballots for the Bikers [motorcycle club], so many ballots for everybody that was there . . . that's the way we could avoid the thing becoming all black, or all white, or all anything.[64]

Thus the operative self-government system of the early 1970s at WSP was leading to the breakup of an undifferentiated prisonized mass and its transformation into a pluralistic multiethnic political culture.

The period of the first three RGCs—from spring 1971 to fall 1972—was, on balance, a constructive one. In the face of unremitting criticism from outside, stubborn guard hostility, and persistent sources of frustration, the inmates' morale remained high, and the overall quality of leadership was maintained at an encouraging level. Although the summer of 1972 featured a work boycott organized by the Black Prisoners' Forum Unlimited, the standing of the RGC as the central organ of self-government remained reasonably intact in the inmates' eyes.[65]

Even during these hopeful days, however, the portents were not all positive. A prisoner on furlough from Walla Walla in early February 1972 was accused of shooting to death a state trooper. WSP's furlough program was very much valued by the inmates in spite of the complaints about its inadequacies. It now appeared to be in serious jeopardy. The RGC convened an emergency general assembly of the 1300 residents to get the backing of the population for expression of condolences to the family of the state trooper and for the RGC-sponsored plan to tighten the furlough selection process. After getting a confidence vote from the population, RGC leaders called a press conference to air their view that the bad record on furloughs reflected the lack of genuine inmate involvement in the screening. Within a few days, the governor had issued an order restricting the WSP program to those with minimum-custody status, which included some within the walls as well as in the minimum-security building. The RGC spokesman hailed this action, taking the view that this curtailment of the furlough program had saved it from total extinction.[66] This was not the only setback. The Lifers with Hope club had instituted, with Rhay's approval, the "Take a Lifer to Dinner" project, in which lifers took short-term outings in the company of staff members.[67] In May 1972 an inmate out for dinner on this program escaped and subsequently was charged with the murder of a pawnbroker. This incident not only brought cancellation of this morale-building program but put considerable strain on the whole self-government structure.[68] Some inmates grumbled that this affair had been provoked by Warden Rhay as a first step in scuttling the reforms.

Accusations of this sort were given further currency by a member of the third RGC in a lengthy article entitled "Walla Walla, Myth and Reality." The author charged in a national prisoners' journal that the Reform programs were "designed to fail" by Rhay and his administrative staff, and he complained that, while the first two RGCs had been able "to establish a foothold for Self Government," the third council was being thwarted by Rhay's "divide and conquer" methods, which aimed at "breeding distrust and contempt" between members of the RGC and their constituents.[69]

WSP's inmates were not hesitant in using the media to air their views and their grievances. Publication of an inmate newspaper, *Voice of Prison*

(VOP) began during the first council. One early issue included an article by Warden Rhay on his 1970 tour of European prisons as well as other stories on the variety of tour groups coming inside WSP and on residents' speaking tours on the outside.[70]

By the summer of 1972, however, the self-government system was clearly under strain. Blacks were particularly disgruntled over what they viewed as discriminatory treatment and "tokenism" on rehabilitation programs, parole eligibility, work release, and numerous other matters. The BPFU issued a "Black Manifesto" (July 1972) containing twenty-two demands, following this up with a three-day work boycott.[71] This platform of the black prisoners had gained wide support among the general prison population and led to concessions that went well beyond black interests to include a successful bid for direct inmate negotiation with responsible state officials.[72]

What was evidenced by the events surrounding the Black Manifesto and the boycott was that the politics of self-government had not excluded the politics of confrontation or, at the same time, the politics of negotiation. Emboldened by these gains, the inmate paper entered state politics through giving explicit editorial endorsement to the incumbent governor for reelection in the fall elections. The *Voice of Prison* in a long editorial reviewed the prison-reform record of Governor Dan Evans and contrasted it unfavorably with the positions of his opponent, declaring that "the *Voice* as a free press cannot and will not straddle the fence in this all important election."[73]

Almost at once after its installation, the fourth RGC had to face the problem of preventing further slippage in the standing of the self-government system. In the belief that the inmate body now possessed some political capital at the gubernatorial level and increasingly frustrated by what they considered a custodially minded penitentiary administration, the members of the RGC made the startling decision to resign *en masse* at the end of November 1972.[74] In a letter sent directly to Governor Dan Evans, they charged that the councils were being denied the authoritative role that had been promised when self-government was instituted. With the prodding of state officials, Rhay, together with DSHS Assistant Secretary Gerald Thomas and the state's new ombudsman, John Henry Brown, met with the representatives of the RGCs who had resigned. A first result of these negotiations was an agreement that the RGC members would resume their offices. The significant result was that a joint resident-staff committee was to be set up, with the task of rewriting the RGC constitution in order to clarify the scope of the RGC's authority and define the rights and responsibilities of inmates, staff, and administration.[75]

Then began a period of some four months of staff-inmate collaborative work. The committee consisted of inside inmates, minimum-security building (MSB) residents, and line officers. The new constitution, which did not alter the structure in any fundamental way, was ratified, rather unenthusiastically, by an inmate vote in March 1973, simultaneously with the election of the fifth RGC.

The rewriting of the constitution was a kind of symbolic renewal of the basic mandate for the self-government system. When the revised constitution was unveiled, a code of ethics for members of the RGC had been added, together with the provision that the RGC "will seek through legal and socially acceptable channels to expand the area of its responsibilities . . . and to implement programs of rehabilitation." The staff was enjoined to carry out its responsibilities "accurately and truthfully . . . to the best of their abilities," and the superintendent was made responsible for "the implementation of meaningful programs."

Inmate reactions to the remodeled constitution varied but tended toward the negative, particularly among blacks (BPFU), who viewed their participation in redesigning the system as insufficient: Interviewed on the eve of this amended constitution being put into effect, a black spokesman denounced the results:

> It's lousy, it ain't worth two dead flies. No, we reject that totally. . . . It
> don't represent ethnic groups whatsoever and we didn't have any input into
> it. They went ahead, and proceeded to draw it up and we were too big a
> group in this penitentiary not to have input into it.

A white inmate, who resigned as an officer of the first RGC, wanted to return to some degree of "regimentation": "I don't believe in anarchy and that's what you've got in this penitentiary."[76]

Thus by the mid-point of the four-year experiment in self-government, the flaws in the machinery had created problems sufficient to undermine the optimism even of its supporters. Nevertheless a basic commitment to the reform system remained and attempts were made to cope with its deficiencies. But this renovation process did not succeed in regaining public confidence in the RGC.

The Decline, 1973–1975

In the final two years of the RGC a decided turn in the public mood took place. Whereas an atmosphere of expectancy and hope had buoyed the initial effort, the pendulum began by 1973 to swing away from reform. The once-heralded model of inmate governance began to lose ground rapidly. The change in the political atmosphere was observable at all levels, from a sulky and frustrated inmate polity to the exasperated state correctional administration. Over the next few years, along with a marked resurgence in concern for security and custody, came the mounting conviction that the

WSP-type fortress prison was essentially unsalvagable as a means to rehabilitation. Crowding and idleness intensified, further aggravating a deteriorating situation.

A new Division of Adult Corrections was created in 1973 out of two
divisions within the DSHS. It was to give direction in the corrections area,
which had largely lacked identifiable leadership since the departure of
Conte two years earlier. A highly respected California correctional expert,
Milton Burdman, was installed as deputy secretary of DSHS.[77] A California
prison superintendent, L.N. Patterson, was hired to direct the administrative reorganization of adult corrections. Patterson took a dim view of Conte's reforms, concluding that they had been imposed too precipitately and
had wrecked morale. He was particularly critical of the governance experiments:

> The idea has created a lot of interest all over the country, but it's a farce, in
> that there is a lot of interchange but very little communication between
> staff and residents. I would like to be clear-cut, honest, and either say this
> is an advisory council, which has no part in government, or find a way to
> make it work with inmate participation. . . . Maybe there is some thera-
> peutic value in it, but we're using a lot of staff time to give a few prisoners
> some fancy therapy.[78]

The permanent director arrived at the beginning of 1974. He was Harold Bradley, also coming from long service in the California correctional
system. Concerning the RGC, the new director stated:

> If it means self-rule, that's an unreasonable expectation. I don't want to
> mislead the residents into thinking that decisions of institutional manage-
> ment will be made by majority vote. But if it means effective input by those
> affected by the decisions, then we encourage it. They can become partic-
> ipants in decisions, involved in the same sense that one's staff subordinates
> participate in decisions. That's very feasible within clearly understood
> boundaries.[79]

The Burdman-Bradley team at the state administrative level did not
identify with advocates of repression.[80] Rather, as moderate reformers
schooled in the California correctional system, they believed the reform
thrust that Conte had initiated was threatening to exceed feasible bounds
and public tolerance, and therefore restrains must be applied. The dilemma
that this posed was how to pull in the reins without precipitating an explosion. At the end of his first year as head of the state's prison system,
Bradley was to face this dilemma in acute form at WSP.

At the Walla Walla institution, the RGC system, although on insecure
grounds, had not yet been played out. The installation banquet for the fifth
RGC in March 1973 was elaborate, attended by a large number of outside

visitors and featuring optimistic oratory. A black inmate leader gave the keynote address:

> This is not a penitentiary. . . . The concept of penitentiary is gone here, when I can walk by an officer and say, "How ya doing baby?" The attitude that we express is what creates the penitentiary. . . . I would hope that the men that are coming into the [residents'] government would see it that way. . . . We have a self-government inside of this institution that cannot be destroyed in spite of anything that happens.[81]

Inmate groups outside the RGC or loosely associated with it were becoming increasingly active at this time. The BPFU's Black Manifesto, with its twenty-two demands, led to the hiring of a minority affairs administrator, newly established as a staff position.[82] An inmate self-help group called the Family had launched an upholstering business in the former women's prison building outside the walls; now known as the Bridge, it had proved highly successful as a work-therapy project and had won federal grant money to pay its staff and for its investment in machinery and materials.[83]

Another federal grant led to the establishment of an ambitious self-help group called SAM (Social Adjustment for Minorities), which hired a former Walla Walla inmate as its first director and manged to weather a drug-smuggling scandal involving its second-level leadership.[84] Projects such as SAM and the Bridge demonstrated that grant moneys were not inaccessible to inmates. As an inmate observed: "Regardless of what the program came out like, they got a program. The administration, once the money was granted, went along with it."[85] As the first program to receive such funding, the Bridge acquired considerable prestige. Walla Walla also boasted of its educational program, which in May 1973 graduated fifty-eight inmates with a two-year college degree, a national record, according to Governor Dan Evans.[86]

At this time, a major struggle developed over the leadership role of the RGC. In June 1973, a series of eleven demands were drafted by the RGC. These included due-process reforms in disciplinary hearings, introduction of a drug-rehabilitation program, and removal of an unpopular hospital physician. After a late-night "informal poll" of the inmates, a work stoppage was called. Rhay questioned the authenticity of the poll, put the penitentiary on "deadlock"—keeping the inmates locked in their cells for ten days— and then proceeded to conduct his own poll in an effort to demonstrate the shallowness of the support for the RGC's current leadership.[87] Also, Rhay was able to exploit divisions among the inmate clubs and their leaders, some of whom disapproved the work-stoppage strategy. The RGC president resigned, announcing that only a faction of the Council backed the strike.[88]

While the lockdown did not extend to the MSB outside the walls, the special status of the separate MSB-RGC did come into play. The administration pressed this outside council to act as the mediator in breaking the stalemate on the demands, but the MSB-RGC balked at playing this role. Instead, at a crucial point, the MSB appeared ready to join the inside in the work stoppage:

> We [the MSB] threatened them [the administration] to strike. We told them that there were five demands . . . or else we would sit down. . . . Before we could have a sit-down, they came out here the first night: they agreed to the five negotiable points, but we wanted to negotiate then and get some answers on them and not later on. So the next morning, bright and early, the riot squad showed up. And they just picked out sixty of [our] so-called ring-leaders, and ran us all in [to the penitentiary].[89]

Sixty was a spectacularly large number for such a mass transfer from minimum to maximum; and the MSB group was returned shortly thereafter to the Building. Rhay, having succeeded in demonstrating the weakness of the RGC, proceeded to negotiate with the club leaders, treating the RGC as simply one among the clubs. At the end of June, the lockdown was lifted and agreement on three points was announced.[90]

In retrospect, it is clear that the RGC never regained the ground it lost in those tension-filled June days. In effect the RGC was relegated to the status of another special-interest group, no longer functioning as the real leader in the inmate participation experiment. From then on, it became increasingly difficult to recruit an adequate number of candidates for council elections or to stem the tide of resignations from council positions once the elected members had been installed in office. In the fall of 1974, there was a delay of more than a month in holding the elections while a revised constitution was put to a vote of the population and inmates were induced to enter the electoral lists for the eighth RGC, which proved to be the last one.

On Friday, December 13, 1974, the eighth RGC was finally installed. Rhay, who sought to dispel widespread rumors that he was planning to dissolve the RGC, pledged his support to the new council. He assured its members that he was "looking forward to a close association with you."[91]

On December 30, 1974, a small group of WSP inmates invaded the hospital, grabbed all the narcotics they could find, seized thirteen hostages, stabbed two women employees, and, in a separate incident, took over one wing of the prison.[92] In another wing just at that moment, members of the RGC were holding a scheduled agenda meeting with Rhay. Their discussion of a list of demands and grievances, contained in an eight-page reorganization agenda, was abruptly terminated when news of the outbreak reached the warden.

The previous day, the RGC and the heads of major inmate clubs had met with their Citizens' Advisory Committee (CAC) in an effort to get support for this agenda and also for their charges that the penitentiary's administration was not complying with state law in administering the prison. After a stormy discussion, the CAC agreed, with reservations, to endorse the Agenda and to help in getting "the convicts side of the story" to the public.

The incident at the hospital and in 8-Wing was soon ended through the rapid action of the superintendent's riot squad with some help from inmate leaders. Officers of the RGC assumed mediating roles and helped to quiet the disturbance and restore order to the institution.

The superintendent was convinced, however, that one or more RGC leaders were involved in instigating the incident, in part so that they could later pose as playing a key role in its resolution and thus regain some measure of credibility with the inmate population and with the public. An unidentified WSP inmate was quoted at length in a Seattle newspaper to the effect that the council had given up on negotiations and wanted to force the administration to yield on the key issues: "The idea was that the people will only listen to violence. The plan and the only plan was riot."[93] But another inmate, in a personal interview, strongly argued the spontaneity of these events:

> Some couple of guys who were drug users, who have been abused by the system, primarily, went to the hospital and flipped out, went to get their stuff. Spontaneous as all get out. You know, two spontaneously, totally isolated incidences, which connected together make it seem as though Walla Walla's going to explode.[94]

Regardless of the full truth of the matter, Warden Rhay reached the conclusion, shared by the guards, that the disturbance had been planned and that at least some RGC members had been "in the heart and core of this—and probably more than I have locked up for it right now."[95] Rhay noted that the state's corrections director, Harold Bradley, had hastened over to Walla Walla at the time and in confronting the RGC had told them flatly that this was the end of self-government.[96] The guards saw the events of December 30 as the product of the "permissiveness" brought in by the reforms. The president of the officers' union, Steve Chadek, believed WSP's prison regime had grown "so loose this doesn't even look like a penitentiary."[97]

The publicity was not favorable to the inmates. The fact that two nurses had been injured gave a particularly ugly flavor to the outburst. The RGC president was quoted as saying, "Everything we worked to accomplish went down the drain with that one incident."[98] What was the RGC's loss may, however, have been the club system's gain, particularly the Bikers'. Rhay was inclined to give to the latter much of the credit for helping to quell the outburst. In the prison newspaper, the over-all impression is that the leaders of the WSP Motorcycle Association —(WSPMA) were the unsung heroes of the crisis and had then helped to fill the vacuum of power in the aftermath—a vacuum created by guard absenteeism and resignations.[99]

The RGC continued to lose ground, despite certain recovery measures that its leadership instituted. In the belief that "lack of communication" had "spurred the population into a general state of confusion" at the time of the "December 30" incident, a daily bulletin, the *RGC Daily News,* was initiated. This bulletin, through its daily reports, attempted to prepare the way for the situation that would be created by a threatened guards' strike, stressing the need to maintain communication during the resultant lockdown.[100]

But the turnout for the RGC primary elections in early March had been so low that the general election was canceled and the primaries were rescheduled for April 10. Meantime plans were underway to rewrite the RGC's constitution yet again.[101]

On April 1 Superintendent Rhay, to nobody's surprise, announced that the RGC had been dissolved. According to the press release, this action had been taken by Rhay "at the request of the inmate population" and announced jointly by the RGC president and Warden Rhay following a "decisional meeting."[102] It was clear, however, that the final decision was Rhay's.

Simultaneously it was indicated that plans were being made to form a new council. But this council would not attempt to reestablish a partnership between residents and administration, which, in Rhay's view, had proved unworkable, chiefly because "RGC leaders have used this office for their personal gain." The People's Action Committee (PAC), which had functioned as the RGC's liaison in dealing with the population, was to act on behalf of the inmates while the new structure was being formed; and a revived Race Relations Committee (RRC) would supplement the PAC.[103] In the meantime, a revision committee, called the Resident Restructural and Implementation Committee (RRIC), was set up, with the task of designing the new structure over a ninety-day period.[104]

Some inmates expressed agreement with the administration's implication that WSP's inmates had made a botch of democratic self-rule. According to a young, politically active white inmate:

> They were untrained, unskilled in what they were doing, they had absolutely no concept at all of what a government should run like. . . . So they just took everything they could get, and their eyes were a hell of a lot bigger than their stomach, and slowly but surely . . . the administration started taking the bone back, you know, a piece at a time.[105]

Other inmates, however, blamed administration intransigence and subversion for the failure of the RGC to function as it was designed. An older white inmate put it this way:

> The administration just sort of divorced theirselves from the whole situation because it was forced on them, so they indirectly uncooperated from the whole thing, if there's such a word, and they just sort of sat back and had a non-active resistance to it, you know. They doubted it would work . . . so sure enough, it didn't work.[106]

With the demise of RGC, an era in the reform experiment in inmate self-government had come to an end. When, three months later, a restructured Residents Council (RC) was inaugurated, significantly the "G" for "government" had been dropped, and the constitution was designated as "guidelines." Rhay had laid down that "the final authority is and will be the Superintendent."

Thus what remained of inmate participation at Walla Walla after the abolition of the RGC was a restricted advisory council, structurally similar to the RGC but functionally quite distinct. The role of the special interest groups, especially the Bikers, grew stronger and more direct. The liberalized rules and other popular features of the reform period remained more or less intact for a time. But the inmates government, the centerpiece of the reform era, had been swept into history.

Aftermath of Reform

In many ways the years since the dissolution of the RGC have been lived in the shadow of that earlier period. In this perspective the second half of the 1970s featured a prolonged *post mortem* on the meaning and consequences of the reform era.[107] It is in this sense also that one can speak of this stormy period (1975–1981) as the aftermath. In the course of the brief history of the RGC two dramatic episodes had stood out: at its beginning the narrowly escaped race riot, which led to the introduction of self-government and the December 30, 1974 outbreak that brought about its downfall.

These incidents became legendary and lived on into the post-RGC era, as did the spirit of the open prison, in which a politicized prisoner body is accorded a role in decision making. After 1975 the inmate role in the WSP polity increasingly narrowed and the classic ills of crowding and idleness steadily worsened. And the reforms become everybody's favorite scapegoat.

Three features stand out in the aftermath of the reforms at WSP: violence and its suppression, rapid turnover in the higher administrative staff, including the superintendent, and judicial intervention, principally on behalf of the inmates.

The first of these, violence, was pervasive. The final days of the RGC were marked by a violent eruption. After the RGC's demise, violence continued to escalate, bursting out especially in 1977 and 1979. Two salient reasons, often noted in relation to this increase in violence, were the flooding of the penitentiary with drugs and the expanding power position of the Bikers, who reputedly controlled much of the drug trade inside the walls. More basically, there was the overcrowding, joined with idleness, which, in turn, was related to the shift to toughness in public attitudes and in sentencing philosophy.[108] These developments were accompanied by a rapid rise in the collective power of the guards during the second half of the decade, leading to further polarization and retaliatory violence. Inmate power, concentrated in one or two of the major clubs, lacked a strong and legitimate focus such as the RGC and often acted out its rivalries in violent ways. Inmate politics were chaotic and only occasionally was the polity brought together in a show of solidarity against the administration.

Certainly among the most significant features in the Walla Walla story of these years was Rhay's departure in 1977 after twenty years in office and the rapid changes of superintendent which followed: two wardens Douglas Vinzant and Nicolas Genakos, in a single year, 1977–1978; James Spalding, a former guard at WSP in 1978–1981; and, finally, Bob Kastama, appointed under the aegis of a new governor and a new corrections director, Amos Reed, in May 1981.[109] If there was a single thread running through these various regimes, and especially pronounced in the case of Superintendent Spalding, it was the determination of the administration to reclaim its authority, as against both inmates and guards.

The last of the three factors—the intrusion of the courts as overseer in the penitentiary—involves essentially one major federal court decision in 1980 that branded WSP's treatment of its inmates as constituting "cruel and unusual punishment."[110] The most direct result of this exertion of judicial power was to apply pressure to reduce the inmate population behind the walls at Walla Walla. But the full impact of the court's action and its longer-range effects on the power configuration of this interactive prison have yet to be assessed.

Last Years of the Rhay Regime, 1975–1977

In the closing hours of the 1975 legislative session, Washington State's House of Representatives passed a resolution pointing to the upsurge of homicides, rapes, and drug abuse behind the penitentiary walls and expressing the view that the warden, not the state capital, should have complete operational and administrative control so that steps could be taken to restore order and safety.[111] The recipient of this vote of confidence was Walla Walla's veteran superintendent of eighteen years, B.J. Rhay.

Rhay's task of maintaining a balance of forces, and controlling the violence, was becoming increasingly difficult. There were five inmate murders in the year 1975 alone.[112] The inmate groups were struggling among themselves for power. The BPFU, once the dominant organization, was challenged by the growing power of the mostly white, crypto-fascist Bikers, who were rapidly acquiring a monopoly over the drug trade in the penitentiary. Yet the warden's attitude toward the Bikers seemed fairly tolerant. He described them as "role models for young boys who do not like to wash" and felt they were ignorant of the meaning of the swastikas with which they decorated themselves.[113] Rhay at various times implied that the very fearsomeness of the Bikers could act as a stabilizing influence, as in the December 30 incident. Thus the Bikers assumed somewhat the role of the warden's unofficial trusties, without compromising their power as the new con bosses.[114]

Rhay's stock was not particularly high with the guards, a development that was partly a function of the growth of guard unionism and in part reflected a carry-over of resentment from the self-government era. The guard force welcomed the end of the RGC system but was not confident about the future. One disaffected guard was quoted as saying, "The prison lost its control over five years and it's going to take us five more years to get it back.[115] Meanwhile the rising tide of violence spread fear through the prison and made the pursuit of tighter security of paramount concern, especially to the guards, who felt themselves in continual danger. The turnover among guards reached astronomical proportions; in 1976, it was reported as running at an annual rate of 70 percent.[116]

In early April 1977, a homemade bomb, booby-trapped in a cigarette lighter, exploded and blew four fingers off a guard's hand. Then a few days later on April 10, Easter Sunday, about three hundred inmates looted the inmate store and set the prison chapel afire. Just a week earlier, the prison had come off of an eight-day lockdown that followed a demonstration by fifty black inmates.[117]

The week leading up to the Easter events had seen the development of a highly explosive situation. The guards were enraged by the maiming incident and were determined to locate the source of the bomb manufacture, thought to be in the isolation wing.[118] During their shakedown of cells, the guards beat some prisoners and used mace on them. Rhay agreed to the request of the RC for a right of access to segregation, which apparently led to confirmation of the guards' excesses. On Saturday the RC called the major club leaders together and agreement was reached that they would call an inmate strike in thirty days unless their grievances were redressed and the guards disciplined for the beatings.

The council now had an issue that could solidify the inmates. On Sunday morning, the RC phoned Rhay and James Harvey, associate superintendent for custody, for an urgent meeting, but neither prison official would agree to come to "the walls." It was then—after the RC leaders dropped the thirty-day waiting period and called for an immediate strike— that the Easter riot erupted. The inmates fully expected a deadlock to follow their announcement of a strike, since in past WSP history the two had always gone together. Thus even in this volatile situation, the bulk of the inmates headed for their cells in what they termed a voluntary lockdown. Some angry inmates looted the prison store so they would have supplies during the coming lockup; and a few inmates fire-bombed the prison chapel, while still others then helped the guards put out the fire.[119] Thus began a grueling forty-six-day lockdown, the longest and most highly publicized that WSP had ever had.

The lengthy stalemate that marked the next six weeks resulted primarily from the polarization between guards and inmates, with Rhay nearly help- less to break the deadlock. Guards proceeded to shake down cells for con- traband, taking the opportunity to strip the cells of licit as well as illicit inmate property.[120] The inmate leaders, meantime, were allowed to come together to draw up their grievances, which were not limited to the confis- catory and sometimes brutal shakedowns. Refusing to meet with Warden Rhay, the RC went over his head to the recently inaugurated governor, Dixy Lee Ray, with a request for an investigation.

The state capital responded with the appointment by the governor of a blue-ribbon commission headed by the new head of DSHS, Harlan P. McNutt. Of its five members, two were those proposed by the inmates. The Institutions Committee of the House of Representatives considered opening its own probe. It was chaired by a young legislator, Ron Hanna, sympa- thetic to the inmates' side, and it included a former Walla Walla inmate as a staff member. The ex-inmate charged in a legislative hearing, held imme- diately after the Easter events, that the prison administration "has lost com- munication with the inmates." Bradley, speaking for the administration, conceded some of the criticism but insisted it was the environment—above all, the oppressive crowding—that precipitated such outbursts, rather than a malign prison administration.[121]

The McNutt commission came to Walla Walla in late April, took testi- mony and gathered documents from the RC, and proposed that the lock- down be ended. The RC indicated it could not call off its voluntary lock- down until there was some response to the grievances. After two more visits, the committee recommended some interim measures, most notably a proposal to transfer the deputy for custody, Harvey. Rhay, anticipating strong resistance from the guard force, balked at this proposal; and the president of the guards' union said, "I'm afraid if they told Mr. Harvey or Mr. Rhay to leave, we'd just leave with them."[122]

The objections to Harvey's transfer were undercut by his confirma- tion that he was requesting it. The guards' fears regarding other proposals of the McNutt panel, were allayed by finding that they were not intended as a new reform program. Most of the measures, such as the transfer of inmate "mental cases," were acceptable to both guards and inmates. But aside from Harvey's departure, the inmates did not feel they had made the sort of gains that would allow them to end their strike. However, the strike was essentially played out, although it took the inmates themselves two more long weeks to admit it.

The guards, as the end approached, protested strenuously against unlocking the cells, going so far as to apply for a court injunction to block the release of the inmates from their cells.[123] The conflict between Rhay and the guards was serious and painful. Rhay termed the guards' actions "a rebellion, which I never had to deal with before." Steve Chadek, the guards' union president replied, "management talks to the residents first and the guards are at the bottom of the totempole."[124]

On May 25, after forty-six days, the deadlock was finally lifted.[125] None of the basic problems of the penitentiary had been resolved. Quite the contrary; despite a deceptive calm the polarization of inmates and guards undoubtedly was intensified. Although the RC played a leading role during the lockup, having momentarily won solidarity out of the intense antiguard sentiment fueled by the April shakedowns, the fissures that soon reappeared in the inmate polity made the RC's power role ephemeral. Rhay had depended on some degree of accommodation with the RC and the club leaders in order to bring the strike-lockup to a conclusion; subsequently he did not permit the RC president to participate in his dialogue with the inmates. And the very length of the shutdown had been debilitating to any hopes of a tolerable relationship among the warring elements in the prison polity.

Rhay had originally been expected to retire from his superintendency in January 1977, leaving the incoming governor with the choice of a successor. Earlier he had stated that this was his intention. Instead he decided to stay on, at least for a while, in order to assist an inexperienced state administration. Some believe that the Easter riot and its forty-six day sequel had shown that Rhay's command of the situation had diminished and had confirmed the need to make a change. Others would say that the admitted ungovernability of Rhay's "old dinosaur," as he often called the penitentiary, had finally caught up with this scarred veteran. On June 26, a month after the lifting of the deadlock, Rhay's long superintendency ended with the announcement of his reassignment to a corrections-planning position in Olympia.[126]

On the Brink, 1977–1978

Douglas Vinzant became the first new warden of the state penitentiary in two decades. Vinzant, a corrections professional and former Methodist minister, had been in Olympia for three years, first developing the small prison ("miniprison") concept for the Evans administration's long-range plans and then running the Juvenile Bureau. Prior to coming to Washington State, he had been warden at Massachusetts' Walpole and Concord prisons. Although he was somewhat dismayed over the "powder-keg" he inherited, he expressed guarded optimism on WSP's future. He maintained that changes could be made, but not without the help of the rest of the corrections system.[127] First he intended to press for moving those inmates not requiring maximum security into alternate facilities, eventually reducing the population by half. His other announced priority was an attack on inmate idleness, through a revived industries program. But the hidden agenda was the critical need to stabilize the relationship between inmates and guards, which was becoming visibly more polarized at each crisis point. The new warden cautiously indicated that he wanted to establish credibility with both, saying he could work with the inmates, "but there is no way we'll negotiate with them."[128]

Yet within a month Vinzant was caught in a political crossfire over the extent to which he was gaining control over the WSP situation. Both the guards and the RC testified formally before a visiting legislative subcommittee, with the inmates clearly more encouraged by the trend of inside developments than the guards, who complained that the administration was not backing them up. The representatives for opposite positions on the House Institutions Committee were Alex Deccio, a hard-line subcommittee chairman, versus Ron Hanna, the liberal chairman of the full committee, who was sympathetic to the inmates. They expressed their views on the new course upon which Vinzant had embarked. Deccio was deeply disappointed that the new warden had not broken with the philosophy of allowing the inmates "too much control"; Hanna, on the other hand, was convinced that "the appointment of Mr. Vinzant was the best possible thing that could have been done for Walla Walla."[129]

Meantime Governor Ray, who had been in office only a half-year, had yet to indicate any clear policy direction in the correctional field. While the little she had said on the subject appeared more in line with a custodial approach—and her four-year administration was to confirm this—a main object at this stage seems to have been to replace personnel (including wardens) carried over from the previous administration.[130] In September 1977 both Milton Burdman and Harold Bradley were ousted and it was announced that Vinzant would replace Bradley as director of adult corrections. Vinzant was to take up the position in Olympia on November 1; meanwhile, he brought in a new assistant superintendent for custody, Nicholas Genakos, who, it was assumed, would be in line for the superintendency.[131]. Vinzant, however, was permitted to occupy both posts: half-time at Walla Walla and commuting to Olympia to administer the state's prison system.

Many questioned the wisdom of this decision to hold two jobs. In any event, the Vinzant era, both at Walla Walla and at state level, was not to be a long one.

Genakos finally took over as warden in July 1978. His top priorities remained the reduction of crowding and of idleness.[132] On overpopulation, Vinzant, as state director, wanted to press forward with a revised version of his miniprison plan, while Governor Ray frugally looked for ways to renovate existing state facilities. One of Vinzant's key objectives was one man one cell, but as warden of Walla Walla even a double-celling goal (with WSP's typical four-bed cells) proved elusive. WSP's population had stabilized to some degree, with a lower rate of increase, but it was still edging upward.[133]. On the issue of idleness, Vinzant was more successful. The numbers in industries had doubled by spring 1978, and the school enrollments had tripled. In addition, Vinzant was developing a project to "bring private industry in to utilize the labor force." Still two-thirds of the inmates were idle.[134]

A new eruption of violence brought the removal of Vinzant and Genakos from Walla Walla. The tone of Vinzant's regime favored an open prison with a wide range of inmate organizations and activities and improved inmate–staff communication. This "permissiveness" reminded the guards and the hard-liners, in the legislature and elsewhere, of the earlier reform era. Meanwhile in May 1978 Governor Ray, accompanied by Vinzant, toured the penitentiary for the first and only time, vowing she would relieve the crowding if the legislature would provide the money.[135] Then in August a pipe-bomb exploded in the hands of a guard who was attempting to dismantle it, fatally injuring the guard (he died three weeks later) and seriously wounding two other guards.[136] The war between guards and inmates, never far beneath the surface, was back in full force. Corrections director Vinzant, who had in fact given up the WSP superintendency the month before, could not survive the storm generated by the incident. Within a week of the pipe-bomb incident, Vinzant resigned with an angry response to the criticism of his policies by Governor Ray and the newly appointed DSHS secretary, Gerald Thompson.[137]

The governor pointed to Vinzant as the representative of a correctional philosophy that has "dominated the prison's administration for years" and had brought on the present unstable conditions. But state representative Hanna defended Vinzant, protesting he was being made the scapegoat for problems created by the crowding. It was Gerald Thompson, however, the DSHS head, who indicated in precise terms how he wanted the penitentiary run: security was to be tightened: he was launching a two-year program to that end; the inflow of drugs and weapons would be stopped; and inmates should have less voice in how the prison is administered. In short, he had dismissed Vinzant because he wanted "tighter control" and a more conservative approach, not a prison run by inmates.[138] Within a few days, WSP's warden, Nicholas Genakos, also resigned, and James Spalding, once a Walla Walla guard and the officers' representative to the RGC, was named to replace him. This paved the way for bringing the eighteen-day deadlock to a conclusion.[139]

Retaking the Penitentiary, 1978–1981

The appointment of James Spalding marked a sharp turn of direction at WSP. While there is some question concerning the extent to which Spalding's course may have been governed by stern guidelines from the state-level administration, there was little question that a mood of toughness had displaced Vinzant's liberalism. In attempting to "put the lid on," however, Spalding risked bringing on more outbreaks. In fact, he found himself fighting a two-front war: he was forced to confront prisoner violence while becoming locked in conflicts with the guards and their union. Toward the end of his three-year tenure, Superintendent Spalding commented ironically on the Conte reforms, which he and many others blamed for the troubles: "They [the reforms] may have got us through the 70s without a major riot. It only came when we tried to regain control."[140]

The tightening up of WSP began with such measures as restrictions on inmates' escorted leaves; 197 were permitted in July 1979 but only 14 in September, after Spalding took over. The new policies brought some inmate programs to an end and put strict limits on others. DSHS Secretary Thompson remarked that "the control of funds and placement of residents in jobs, by [other] prisoners, suggest a power structure I don't really like." Despite what many of the inmates considered the provocation of the new policies, there were only sporadic acts of violence (mostly inmate-on-inmate) during fall 1978. Inmate leaders passed the word that "the lid is on," which the president of the guards' union described as merely preliminary to a blackmail threat to take the lid off.[141] But the guards themselves conceded that their control of the institution was only on the periphery and that the inmates dominated the interior.

In mid-February 1979, Spalding transferred out of WSP eight inmates whom he viewed as troublemakers, including the president of the resurgent Lifers club. Then came a hostage-taking incident, an act of desperation to get the attention of the outside.[142] The penitentiary was approaching an explosive pitch in June, following the murder of an Indian by a Chicano inmate. Three days later, a young guard was caught in the crossfire of the Indian inmates' retaliatory trap and was stabbed to death, the first direct killing of a guard in WSP's history.[143]

The lockdown that resulted was to last for more than four months. On

June 15 WSP's inmates were locked into their cells. After some delay, the warden ordered a shakedown throughout the prison to cleanse it totally of contraband. Meantime a consultant team from the American Correctional Association (ACA) was brought into Washington State to investigate the crisis situation at WSP.[144] Simultaneously with the ACA team's visit in early July, the guards—some of whom had taken to calling themselves the Cross Revenge Squad (after their murdered comrade)—reached 8-Wing in their shakedown. They locked groups of inmates in a storage closet while the search squad made a shambles of their personal belongings. This triggered a riot in 8-Wing, in the course of which the prisoners completely demolished their cells. The inmates were then moved outside into the yard, where they were to remain for more than six weeks. WSP had coupled its most destructive inmate riot with a guard riot. The next day brought even worse. The 8-Wing inmate-guard riot had destroyed property in massive amounts. In the segregation unit the guards were accused of having brutally beaten several inmates, sodomizing a particularly disliked one with a night stick. The *Seattle Post Intelligencer* editorialized, "The get-tough policy . . . is not paying off, except in murders, riots and worsening tensions."[145]

In late August the ACA warden's report was made public, with its conclusion that conditions at WSP were "intolerable."[146] The report pointed to a conflict between "two competing management systems" in evidence at WSP, which was the cause of "major difficulty." The first of these systems was the "traditional approach . . . [where] staff runs the institution and inmates play a passive role." The second model was "participating management" or "shared decision-making," in which "the inmates have a high degree of participation in . . . decisions . . . along with the warden and his staff." "[I]mmediate steps . . . to alleviate the severe overcrowding and idleness" are top priority. After that, staff-inmate cooperation requires measures to "create an effective environment between the competing management systems." The report does not suggest a synthesis of the two models; rather the administration must reclaim the institution that the staff believes was "given" to the inmates in the early 1970s. Only after that has been achieved can the inmates be granted some elements of participation. According to the wardens' team, the first step towards this end was to disband the clubs and abolish their special areas within the prison.[147]

Since these were measures that Spalding was later to adopt, it is not surprising that he expressed his approval of the ACA report, as did spokesmen for the state corrections offices. But for WSP's young warden, the inmate organizations were only one of his problems. Equally serious were conflicts with the guards and the guard's union, which followed his dismissal of a group of forty-two who had walked off the job to protest the hazards of the working conditions during the long, hot, summer lockdown; these dismissals were in addition to those of the five accused of the brutalizing of prisoners.[148] And to add to Spalding's problems was a federal court suit filed in the closing days of the lockdown charging the prison with guard brutality and other constitutional violations. This raised a major challenge to the entire correctional administration of the state.

While this first year of Spalding's superintendency had been marked by extreme tensions and violence, the second year was to see the fight against the inmates' federal suit develop into a fierce struggle in the judicial arena. And Spalding's final year would be one in which the implementation of the court's directives became the first order of the day.

The events that had occurred in the segregation wing on July 7 and 8, 1979, opened the way to a major challenge to the lawfulness of this penitentiary regime. Critics could no longer be silenced by the dismissal of a few guards. And even before the lockdown had been terminated, medical evidence had confirmed at least one case of injury to an inmate, the rape apparently perpetrated by a guard's night stick. The prospective legal actions (*Hoptowit et al.* v. *Ray*) would encompass the whole penitentiary as well as the inmates of 8-Wing and of segregation. The director of the state's American Civil Liberties Union, one of the major participants in the litigation, announced, "We plan a joint lawsuit . . . for immediate injunctive relief from overcrowding and guard brutality, for damages for the beatings, and for damages for loss of personal property."[149]

Following on the heels of the medical report was a state investigative report, apparently leaked from Olympia, that confirmed the beatings of prisoners who were handcuffed.[150] In October suits were filed on behalf of the inmates by a coalition of forces, principally ACLU and Prison Legal Services. The case was assigned to U.S. district judge Jack Tanner who, shortly after taking over the case, requested that the Justice Department enter the case as a friend of the court.[151]

In December Judge Tanner made a finding that "excessive physical force" had in fact been used and issued a preliminary injunction against the WSP administration that it should stop. DSHS Secretary Thompson responded by issuing a statement strongly defending the penitentiary's staff from top to bottom.[152] Although these moves were essentially preliminary skirmishing, they had repercussions at the prison. It was claimed that "guard resentment" over the court order was exacerbating an already tense situation. Meanwhile the state administration pressed its drive to have Judge Tanner removed from the case, and the ACLU charged the state's officials with "ineptitude" and "cover-up."[153]

While these maneuvers were taking place in the public arena, inside Walla Walla penitentiary the clubs in losing their own clubhouse areas had been deprived of their "turf," the RC had been effectively abolished, and a small square of green know as Lifer's Park was now, after being paved over, referred to as "Spalding's Slab." In making quite explicit his intention to return to a tighter regime, Spalding underlined his belief that "people function better" within a controlled environment; and this is especially what the older cons prefer: "Its safer—they don't have to watch their backside so much."[154]

The turmoil and violence of 1979, doubtless the most tumultuous year in WSP's history, had clearly strengthened Superintendent Spalding's determination to "retake" the prison. In his later court testimony he argued that, at the time he took over in August 1978, the inmates "had total control of the facility." In a written statement to the Federal Court, he blamed the club system as the main source of trouble, with many of these groups dominated by strong-arm cliques "who advocated violence and were quite radical and devious." Spalding specified that the main purpose of the summer lockdown, aside from disarming the prisoner body, was to deprive inmate clubs of their power and influence. Thus the lengthy deadlock had offered the opportunity to "change the entire philosophy of the WSP."[155]

It appeared obvious to the defenders of the Walla Walla regime, that they would have an uphill battle in Judge Tanner's court. This was especially so when Tanner brought the federal government in as *amicus curiae* and followed by issuing his preliminary injunction barring continued mistreatment of inmates. Against the state's objections that it would take longer than six months to prepare properly, he set trial for May 5, 1980 and required that written submissions be made of all testimony. The trial testimony was to be limited to witnesses who would be cross-examined by the opposition. Spalding complained about the tensions and burdens caused by the dozens of lawyers and prison experts swarming over WSP:

> My top administrators are, unfortunately, spending about 40% of their time directly related to the lawsuit. . . . We're operating on the assumption that running the facility is secondary to responding to the law case. It's been extremely detrimental to the program and our day-to-day functions.[156]

The bulk of the "experts' visited WSP on behalf of the U.S. Justice Department. A mountain of reports concerning conditions inside WSP were delivered to Judge Tanner prior to the May trial. For its part, the state had asked Anthony P. Travisano, executive director of the ACA, to reexamine the prison and compare it with what he and his warden's team had found in July 1979. After this second tour, Travisano, judging that WSP was implementing many of his team's recommendations, concluded that WSP was now "slightly above average."[157]

On the first day of the four-day trial, the lawyers for the inmates produced two former guards who testified concerning the socialization process they had experienced at WSP. This testimony pictured the guards' orientation as presenting the theory that rehabilitation depended on sufficient beatings of the inmate so he would want to stay out of prison thereafter. These witnesses also claimed that there existed a particularly tough guard clique, which encouraged confrontations with inmates.[158]

The core of the state's defense was the contention that, guided by the recommendations in the ACA report, there was a process of steady improvement underway at WSP in such areas as prison crowding, medical care, and guard training. And in his opening statement, assistant attorney general Bill Collins reflected the prevailing philosophy of retaking the prison: "We think the evidence will demonstrate that the administration has reasserted control of the institution. . . . Security has been increased and, with that, safety has increased and tension has, contrary to testimony, been reduced."[159]

In Olympia, meantime, DSHS Secretary Thompson flung down the gauntlet to Judge Tanner challenging him to decide the case against the state. He called upon the public to be skeptical of the "expert" testimony and to take account of the fact that those who were suing were "depending on the testimony of convicted felons and disgruntled former employees [guards]." He then lashed out at Judge Tanner, though without naming him: "The thrust of judicial actions in recent months demonstrates a propensity to move back to the early and mid-70s, when inmates wielded considerable power in the operations of adult correctional facilities. That would be a step backward in the department's efforts to run a system the way the public wants it run."[160]

The fourth and final day of the trial brought Superintendent Spalding to the stand. Tanner, quoting from a press report of Thompson's statement that the inmates would take back the prison if the state were to lose, asked Spalding if this would happen. Spalding said he did not know, but his testimony reflected apprehension that the steps he had taken toward changing the philosophy of the institution could be undone. At the end Tanner asked the warden if he thought Walla Walla should be closed, to which Spalding replied in the affirmative. Later, however, outside the courtroom, he indicated he would not favor closing WSP unless there were alternatives available.[161] The warden clearly believed that the right direction had been taken even through the disastrous summer of 1979.

In closing arguments for the inmates' side, attorney Steve Scott expressed the heart of the plaintiff's case: "The prisoners of the penitentiary at Walla Walla came to this court to show that the defendants [the state officials] have subjected the prisoners to even below the basic minimum of human decency.[162]

After the trial concluded, state officials quite openly expected the worst. Secretary Thompson charged that Tanner had denied the state a fair trial; and both he and Warden Spalding predicted that they would lose.[163] On May 24 Tanner announced his decision orally: "The totality of conditions at Walla Walla is cruel and unusual punishment beyond any reasonable doubt.'' In his verbal order, to be spelled out a month later in full written order, Tanner announced he would be appointing a special master to oversee the implementation of the court's orders, that he did not "intend to interfere with the administration of the prison," and that important changes would have to be made in such areas as crowding, idleness, and guard brutality in order to bring the operation of the prison within constitutional standards.[164] The state of Washington indicated it would appeal after it had received the full written ruling. All legal fees and costs were assessed against the state, only the beginning of a process that, in bringing WSP up to court-mandated standards, was sure to be a charge upon the taxpayers for a long time into the future.

The court gave the state sixty days to produce its plan for raising Walla Walla to constitutional standards. In the spotlight was the issue of inmate population, for which the goal at WSP had been set at 750 (inside the walls) by the end of 1981. The inmates held a press conference, with the chairman of the Inmate Advisory Council (IAC) claiming conditions had worsened and were pushing WSP to the edge of another explosion.

Meantime the court's special master had been appointed. He was Michael Lewis of the Center for Community Justice, Washington, D.C., who cautioned that the prisoners would have to be patient.[165] In preparing his own comprehensive plan for presentation to Judge Tanner, Lewis held nine days of special hearings in Seattle, one feature of which was expert testimony on mental health care and what Tanner had termed WSP's "pervasive racism." A psychiatrist who had worked at the penitentiary suggested that the scope of the needs at WSP required five full-time psychiatrists; other witnesses derided the state's "abominable" plan for guard's racial-sensitivity training as inadequate and deplored the widespread belief among guards that prisoners (especially minorities) are "less than fully human."[166]

At the end of these hearings, Lewis announced his conclusion that transfers of five activist WSP inmates—just a month before the Spokane trial in which all five were plaintiffs—had been essentially retaliatory. According to Lewis, the evidence presented by the state to justify the transfers into solitary at Shelton was completely unconvincing and should be expunged from the files. In branding the state's cases against the five as trumped up, Lewis suggested that political motivation rather then a genuine security interest had determined these actions.[167]

At Walla Walla, while superintendent Spalding was pointing to the "tremendous strides" made in response to (or quite aside from) the federal court's order, the IAC chairman, a young black inmate, asserted the opposite. Spalding interpreted these "strides" as having been a function of 1979's "big lockdown," the climactic chapter in the retaking of the prison from the inmates. Although there was no suggestion that the federal judiciary would be defied, the warden made clear his feeling that the claims of guard racism and brutality made at the trial had been highly exaggerated and led to the mistaken conclusion that the conditions at WSP were "intolerable." The IAC chairman, while deriving some long-term optimism from the federal court's decision, found no evidence of improvement in any sector. From the inmates' perspective, the dangerous tensions promised to build up again unless they felt some short-term progress was being made on the problems of crowding, idleness, racism, and the rest. Spalding, however, forecast "some real periods of calm over the next several years."[168]

This reported calm was ruptured that same month, on December 29. An inmate-guard scuffle had broken out when the guards attempted to take an inmate from the visiting room to segregation. The IAC chairman intervened and was then himself hauled away to isolation. This incident sparked a rampage of fires and window breaking reminiscent of the Easter riot of 1977 on a smaller scale.[169] As Spalding himself later described the events: "The population said they would riot if I didn't let him [the IAC chairman] out. I didn't, they did."[170] Inmate leaders aired their views at a press conference a week later, disputing the prison administration's version of the December 29 outburst and contradicting Spalding's reported claim that Tanner's order was creating tension and confusion among inmates. "In all likelihood it [the federal court's action] has prevented trouble. It gives us hope."[171]

The day after the inmates' press conference, a strike was called, with the demand that Spalding be dismissed as warden. In previous work stoppages, the administration had uniformly ordered a lockdown; but in this case, Spalding said he would not do so unless he judged that the situation had gotten out of hand. A new governor was to take office within a week. The inmates had announced that they would end their strike simultaneously with John Spellman's inauguration. But claiming to have picked up rumors of an incipient riot, Spalding ordered the inmates deadlocked on that very day. Five days later, the lockdown was lifted.[172]

By spring 1981 some apparent improvements had been made in WSP's living conditions. The population has been brought down below 900; almost all the inmates were occupied in jobs or education; the prison staff had been enlarged; mental cases had been moved to another facility; and violence had nearly dropped from the statistics. Superintendent Spalding, still in command, now expressed the mellower view that the court's decision gave a helpful boost to WSP's reforms, though he expressed apprehension about further confrontation with the Tanner Court through refusal of the legislature to provide the necessary money or through failure to meet the court's timetable on reduction of the population. However, for Spalding, the all-important "reform" was the retaking of the penitentiary: "They [the inmate leaders and their groups] don't have turf anymore. That belongs to me."[173]

On May 7, 1981, major appointments were announced by Amos Reed, the head of state corrections. Spalding was to leave Walla Walla on July 1 to assume the position of deputy director of the new Department of Adult Corrections, of which Reed would be the first secretary. The new superintendent would be Bob Kastama, a professional with experience in several types of correctional setting. Kastama gave assurances that he did not intend to depart from the philosophy that Spalding had stamped on Walla Walla: "Everyone has to understand from the bottom on up that the prison has to be managed by the administration." Kastama had studied prisons in Scandinavian countries and conjectured that some time in the future our society might similarly choose small institutions that favor rehabilitation over warehousing. In the meantime, however, the U.S. was simply not going to abandon large prisons. Kastama commented on the institution that he had inherited: "I . . . realize this [WSP] is the ultimate challenge . . . the Mount Everest of corrections in the state of Washington."[174]

Notes

1. "State Prison," *Perspective* (Washington State Dept. of Institutions—Spring–Summer 1966): 7–8.

2. Blake McKelvey, *American Prisons: A History of Good Intentions* (Montclair, N.J.: Patterson Smith, 1977), p. 229. Heavy irons called "Rinquist boots," after the local blacksmith who forged them, were riveted to the prisoners' ankles and not removed until release or death. This first Washington prison became know as the "Seatco Dungeon." ("State Prison," pp. 6–7.)

3. McKelvey, *American Prison,* p. 229.

4. "State Prison," p. 11. The following discussion of WSP in the late nineteenth and early twentieth centuries is based primarily on this source.

5. Paul W. Garret and Austin H. MacCormick, eds., *Handbook of American Prisons,* 2 (New York: Putman & Sons, National Society of Penal Information, 1926), pp. 563, 571–573.

6. Paul W. Garrett and Austin H. MacCormick, eds., *Handbook of American Prison and Reformatories, 1929,* 3 (New York: National Society of Penal Information, 1929), p. 970.

7. See Austin H. MacCormick, ed. *Handbook of American Prisons and Reformatories, 1942* (New York: Osborne Association, 1942), 5, II:418–425 for a detailed critique.

8. Ibid., p. 425. See also p. xxiii and pp. 387–388.

9. *The Memoirs of Earl Warren* (New York: Doubleday, 1977), p. 194. See also: Richard A. McGee, *Prisons and Politics,* (Lexington, MA.: Lexington Books, D.C. Heath and Co., 1981.)

10. A listing of prison riots includes three WSP outbreaks during the

wave of the early 1950s: August 20, 1953 and July 5 and August 14, 1955. See Vernon Fox, *Violence Behind Bars* (Westport, Conn.: Greenwood Press, 1956), pp. 11–12.

11. H. Jack Griswold, Mike Misenheimer, Art Powers, and Ed Tromanhouser, *An Eye for an Eye* (New York: Pocket Books, 1971), pp. 150–158. The following discussion is largely based on this eyewitness account.

12. Ibid., p. 155.

13. Conversation with B.J. Rhay, March 12, 1981. All quotes are used with permission. These events also became the subject of a popular prison novel: Frank Elli, *The Riot* (New York: Coward-McCann, 1967). Elli, an ex-convict, was a WSP resident at the time.

14. Griswold et al., *Eye for an Eye,* p. 156. B.J. Rhay, who was appointed associate superintendent for treatment immediately following the riot, agrees that the changes came after it, but denies they were a result of this uprising. Conversation with B.J. Rhay, March 12, 1981.

15. "State Prison," p. 10.

16. This section is based on a conversation with B.J. Rhay, March 21, 1981.

17. Frank Tannenbaum, *Osborne of Sing Sing* (Chapel Hill: University of North Carolina Press, 1933), p. 14. Comparisons could be made with Warden Joseph Ragen of Illinois' Stateville (1935–1960), as described by James B. Jacobs, *Stateville* (Chicago: University of Chicago Press, 1977), pp. 28–51.

18. Conversations with Robert Freeman, July 13, 1980. Quoted with permission.

19. On Heyns's regime, see "Adult Corrections in Washington State," *American Journal of Corrections* (November–December 1962):5–7, 10, 17.

20. Garrett Heyns and William R. Conte, "A Philosophy of Administration" (1965), in William R. Conte, ed., *Selected Writings of Garrett Heyns* (Olympia, Wash.: Sherwood Press, 1975), pp. 75–80. Heyns, a Ph.D. in political science and history, became superintendent of the Michigan Reformatory in 1937, following twenty years as a professional educator. In 1945 he became president of the American Prison Association. In 1957, already in retirement, he assumed the post in Washington State.

21. William R. Conte, "Some Perspectives on the Reform Program: Washington Correctional System, 1960s" (unpublished manuscript, 1980), p. 2. All quotes are used with permission.

22. Conversation with Rhay, March 21, 1981.

23. Conversation with Freeman, July 13, 1980.

24. William R. Conte, "Comments on the Administration of Healing Services in Governmental Operations (with Special Reference to Correctional Programs" (unpublished manuscript, 1978) pp. 13–14.

25. Ibid., pp. 19–22.

26. B.J. Rhay, "Observations on European Correctional Systems," in "Planning Prospectus" (Washington: State Department of Institutions, 1970), p. 88. Rhay's perception of democratization centered on the staff training process, which led to "excellent rapport . . . between staff and inmates," to "real feelings of humanity on the part of prison staff towards their charges," and to the easing of the task of administrators in selling "staff and inmates on the democratic ideal." Rhay called decriminalization "one of the most important movements in Western Europe" and noted that in all the countries he had observed it was an ongoing process of reviewing the criminal code in relation to changing social needs and norms. Ibid., p. 84.

27. Ibid., pp. 89, 90.

28. Rhay did not interpret the results of his European trip or his subsequent cooperation with the program as signs of any conversion. He insists that his early misgivings about many aspects of the reform programs, particularly self-government, never disappeared. Moreover, Conte and Rhay had very different interpretations concerning the aims of Conte's travel proposal: Conte believed this could broaden Rhay's perspective and introduce him to penal innovations abroad; Rhay, on the other hand, took the position that his trip was a fact-finding mission and a service to Conte, whom he still viewed as a newcomer to the corrections field. See Rhay's speech to Resident Government Council, Institute I: "A Search for the Prison of Tomorrow," Washington State Penitentiary at Walla Walla, (January 10, 1972), p. 32.

29. Conte, "Comments on the Healing Services," p. 22.

30. Conversations and interviews with B.J. Rhay.

31. "Walla Walla," KING (Seattle), television documentary (1971), produced by Emory Bundy. Reprinted with permission.

32. *Seattle Times,* Nov. 18, 1970. The newspaper articles outlined a general scheme for prisoner participation, including grievance mechanisms and other elements of due process.

33. See Conte, "Comments on Healing Services," pp. 9–22.

34. "The superintendent . . . had been an employee at Walla Walla when his future father-in-law was the warden. . . . A background such as this made it virtually impossible for him to cast off easily the traditional position which correctional officers held toward men who were in their charge." Quoted in Gabrielle Tyrnauer, "What Went Wrong at Walla Walla?" *Corrections Magazine,* June 1981:40.

35. In one article of a nine-part series (1979) on Walla Walla, Conte was described as a "free-thinking, liberal social psychiatrist." The theme was the familiar one of the prison as a "Pandora's box," which Conte allegedly opened, leading to the later difficulties. The two top WSP admin-

istrators of the Reform era, now-retired, are quoted: "He [Conte] created the chaos we're suffering today" (Rhay); "it was just mass confusion and I don't think it has settled down yet—its still confusion" (Freeman). *Spokane Spokesman—Review,* November 22, 1979. This series, under the title, "Walla Walla: Fury in the Soul," appeared November 18–26.

36. A "Philosophy of Corrections," which had been formulated over the years 1966–1969 by Conte and his state-level staff, had been released publicly on December 10, 1969. *Seattle Times,* Dec. 10, 1969. There was national television coverage on NBC news. See also William R. Conte, "Modern Day Reforms in Washington State Penal Programs," *American Journal of Corrections* (May–June 1971):28–29. Full text, with Conte's commentary appears in the *Bulletin* (Washington State Department of Institutions) (March 1970):3–15. It became a manifesto for the reforms and continued to be quoted by prisoners in informal conversation as well as banquet speeches and newspaper articles long after Conte's departure. It was appended, as a kind of Bill of Rights, to the Resident Government Council (RGC) constitution.

37. Conte's philosophy of corrections held out rehabilitation, not punishment, as the central focus of incarceration. "Its [confinement's] primary purpose [must be] the successful return of that individual [inmate] to productive and responsible citizenship." Further, the prison experience "should encourage each individual to exercise judgment and behave responsibly rather than to rely . . . upon rules." This is to be accomplished by developing staff skills and providing inmates with a variety of work, training, treatment, and social programs in order to "avoid or overcome the disabling effects of institutionalization." Conte, "Modern Day Reforms," p. 28.

38. Personal conversation, February, 1981. The two state-level administrators actually served together for just one year: Conte left his position as deputy secretary of DSHS (with responsibility for corrections) in mid-1971. Horowitz served until the end of 1973.

39. John P. Conrad and Simon Dinitz, "Position Paper for the Seminar on the Isolated Prisoner," presented at the Academy for Contemporary Problems (Columbus, Ohio) and sponsored by the National Institute of Corrections, 8–9 December 1977, p. 33.

40. Quoted in Tyrnauer, "What Went Wrong," p. 39.

41. See Lloyd Allen Weeks, "The Background of Penal Democratization," in Resident Government Council (WSP), Institute I.: "A Search for the Prison of Tomorrow" (January 10, 1972), pp. vi–xvii. Weeks was a WSP inmate at the time.

42. Ibid., pp. ix–x. *Maximum security* refers to the prisoner population within the walls, excluding the two-to-three hundred housed outside the walls in the Minimum-Security Building (MSB).

43. Ibid., p. xi.

44. Ibid., p. xi–xii.

45. Ibid., p. xiii. Later, Superintendent Rhay reportedly stated: "I think it would have been a mistake for the custody officers to have intervened at this point. If they had busted it up, self-government would never have come about as spontaneously as it did. This was something the inmates had to work out between themselves."

46. Ibid., pp. xii–xiii.

47. Ibid., p. xiii.

48. Ibid., pp. xiii–xiv. In 1975 Rhay openly rejected this fifty-fifty concept as unworkable and undesirable.

49. Conte later attributed his decision to retire to two principal factors: he believed his reform program was blocked and professionalism undermined by the new administrative structure in the Department of Social and Health Services (DSHS); and that power was being excessively concentrated in the hands of the unions. Conte viewed the public employees' union, now for the first time enabled to bargain at the state level for the prison guards, as having thereby acquired decisive power over prison policy and administration. Personal communication to the authors. See also Conte, "Reorganization for What?" p. 137.

50. Interviews, August 1972, March 1973, October 1974.

51. "Walla Walla," KING (Seattle) television documentary (1971), produced by Emory Bundy. Reprinted with permission.

52. Ibid. Sgt. Robin Moses.

53. Interview, April 1978. Inmates and guards to a large extent understood the changes the same way. A black lifer, active in self-government from its inception, reflected in the late 1970s that the more obvious changes, such as the relaxed hair and dress codes, were less significant than self-government, even though they more readily triggered the wrath of the guards. "It's because of the attitude which came out of it [self-government]," he said.

54. Interview, March 1973.

55. Quoted in "State Penitentiary 'A People Eater'?" *Seattle Times Magazine,* May 5, 1974, p. 9. Dr. William A. Hunter.

56. *New York Times,* October 18, 1971, p. 24. Over the next year, Walla Walla received a great deal of exposure in the media, including an article in the *New York Post,* November 1, 1971, p. 35, and stories in *Newsweek,* November 1, 1971, and *Life,* September 8, 1972. The author of the *Life* article, Barry Farrell, "A New Way to Run the Big House," termed WSP "the leading edge of a nation-wide movement to overhaul U.S. prisons." This attention may itself have skewed the experiment in that both prisoners and staff were made more self-conscious by the bright spotlight.

57. The summary evaluations made in this study grow out of personal visits and interviews conducted by the authors, beginning in 1972.

58. This was the team's second visit. Following a request to McGee

from Conte that Washington State's correctional programs be examined in the light of his philosophy of corrections, the team had been formed and made an initial visit (early 1970). McGee assembled a team that included sociologist Clarence Schrag of the University of Washington; Milton Burdman, California's head of parole; and Russell Oswald, New York State commissioner of corrections. Conte indicated to McGee that he wanted to assess the current situation with a view to realizing his philosophy of corrections. He voiced particular concern about staff "attitudes and philosophies," urging the survey team to provide him with "any observations and suggestions . . . [on] staff development."

59. Richard A. McGee, "Review of State of Washington Adult Corrections System." Report to William R. Conte, Director of Adult Corrections. (1971) Mimeographed.

60. Interview, April 1978. This statement is surely one of the more expansive on inmate power during the early councils. The claim to budgetary power is doubtless exaggerated, "decisions" translating more nearly as "participation."

61. Interview, October 1974. The inmate "vote" on these committees was, in a formal sense, advisory. This former inmate leader rated the first two councils as especially productive in being able to push through much of the backlog of requests that had been made repeatedly over the years for such items as free-world clothing, . . . cassettes, . . . TV sets." The same inmate leader pointed to "our greatest accomplishment" (on the first RGC) as the resignation of Associate Superintendent of Custody William P. Macklin, which accrued to the Councils' credit even though it had not actually proposed his retirement. "We gave him ulcers that caused him to resign." For the inmates, this event apparently underlined, more than any other single event, the spirit of the times. Macklin symbolized the "custodial" character of WSP—and his departure marked, hopefully, its burial.

62. Ibid.

63. See pp. 158, chapter 7.

64. Interview, April 1978. One of the principal structural problems with WSP's inmate government was the coordination between the "inside the walls" RGC and the council in the Minimum Security Building (the RGC-MSB). The Building, as it is called, houses roughly one-fifth of the inmate population outside the walls. The RGC-MSB held its own elections and had separate membership, but the two sectors were to work as one. Effective coordination proved extremely difficult, primarily because the interests of the two populations were different, with respect to types of programs and work, length of time until scheduled release, and so on.

65. In January 1972 the second RGC sponsored an ambitious institute involving inmates, administrators, representatives of the guards, outside professionals, the press. (See RGC, "Prison of Tomorrow,"). Superinten-

dent Rhay praised Conte's role as reformer and extolled the meeting as a sign that the RGC was "coming of age." Dr. Conte himself did not attend but sent taped remarks emphasizing the continuity of the various reform activities with his "Philosophy of Corrections." Finally, representing the correctional officers, Lieutenant James Spalding (who was to become the tough superintendent of 1978) foresaw guards becoming more and more involved with the inmates as the hallmark of the future.

66. RGC, "Weekly Report," February 6–February 12, 1972. See also "Washington State Tightens Administration of Furlough Programs," *Prison Law Reporter* 1 (March 1972):203.

67. A guard leader commented on the irony that formerly any kind of fraternization had been discouraged. "How close are we supposed to get?" *New York Times,* October 18, 1971.

68. See Farrell, "A New Way To Run the Big House," pp. 34–35; *Seattle Times,* May 23, 1973.

69. "Doc" Metzger, "Walla Walla, Myth and Reality," *Penal Digest International* 2 (August 1972). The most serious of Metzger's charges was that RGC members were being systematically barred from inmate areas when a resident asked to see one of them in order to register a complaint.

70. The warden's article was "From Walla Walla to Wormwood Scrubs," *Voice of Prison,* October 6, 1971, pp. 4–5. For the news items on WSP's "interactive" prison life, see ibid., pp. 20–21.

71. See "Diary of Two Strikers," *Voice of Prison* (August 1972).

72. See the BPFU's publication, *Uhuru* (August 1972?):4, which contains the full text of the Black Manifesto. This document, despite its radical appearance, contained essentially reformist demands, starting off with requests for more and better treatment programs, broadened work release, and parole reform. The two top DSHS administrators came to WSP to negotiate with the inmates. The immediate result of the Manifesto was the creation of a new position of minority affairs administrator.

73. *Voice of Prison* (October 1972):1, 3, 5. The following month, the *VOP* editorialized that, "with the elections behind us, we find ourselves with our chosen candidate in the Governor's office"—and the time had arrived to make a big push for prison reform in the state legislative arena. *VOP,* November 17, 1972, pp. 1, 11.

74. See "Prison Inmate Councils Resign," *Seattle Post Intelligencer,* November 28, 1972. Prior to the residents' elections of fall 1972, the two councils—the one inside the walls and the one outside, in the MSB—had been combined within a unified organizational structure. Given their separate membership and competencies, however, this linkage fell short of a merger, even though it was described that way. Warden Rhay blamed the outside (MSB) council for the walkout.

75. On the restoration of the RGC system, see *Seattle Times,* Decem-

ber 1, 1972 and *Seattle Post Intelligencer,* December 2, 1972. See also *Voice of Prison,* December 22, 1972, in which the President of the "inside" RGC expresses considerable reserve about the prospects of "making our self-governing apparatus something more than a 'puppet government.'"

76. Interviews, March 1973.

77. "Super-Agency Deputy Named," *Seattle Post Intelligencer,* June 26, 1973. See also John Conrad, "Milton Burdman, 1920–1980," *Crime and Delinquency* 26 (July 1980):434–436.

78. R.V. Denenberg, "Profile: Washington," *Corrections Magazine* 1 (November–December 1974):33. Copyright 1974 by Criminal Justice Publications, Inc., and *Corrections Magazine,* 116 W. 32nd St., New York, N.Y. 10001. Reprinted with permission.

79. Quoted in ibid.

80. By the time Bradley and Burdman had taken over in Washington State, disillusionment with the rehabilitation model had become widespread in the field of corrections. The Conte reforms, especially self-government, represented the treatment motif. Linked closely to this trend was the growing attack on the indeterminate sentence, formerly an article of faith among progressive penologists. Discretion was increasingly viewed both as inequitable and as contributing to the kind of maneuvering for personal benefit that was subverting WSP's inmate polity.

81. Excerpts from a speech by the fourth RGC's executive secretary at the inaugural banquet of the fifth RGC, March 29, 1973.

82. The first occupant of this post, Vincent Lombard, served from January 1973 to November 1974. He was succeeded by a counselor, Ivan Bush, a few months later.

83. See "The Bridge, Inc.," *Corrections Magazine* (November–December):45–52. The Bridge was required to pay the salaries of custodial personnel serving a security role in the outside building that it occupied. This project lasted for about three years.

84. Discussion with SAM members, October 1974. On the drug scandal that broke in the spring of 1976 and its link to one of SAM's inmate assistant directors, see "Heroin Ring Linked to Prison Murders," *Seattle Times,* May 19, 1976. The following day, the *Times* editorialized with the rhetorical question, "To what extent have the so-called 'policies of enlightenment' established in 1971—the creation of inmate 'resident councils,' for example—contributed to problems within the inmate population?" Ibid., May 20, 1976. See also "Heroin Operation in Prison Bared," *Seattle Post Intelligencer,* May 20, 1976.

85. Discussion in MSB, March 1973.

86. *Seattle Times* May 2, 1973. For further data on prisoner education, as of 1972, see Michael V. Reagan and Donald M. Stoughton, eds., *A Descriptive Overview of Correctional Education in the American Prison System* (Metuchen, N.J.: Scarecrow, 1976), pp. 261–262.

87. See "Prisoners Strike at Walla Walla," *Seattle Post Intelligencer,* June 21, 1973.

88. See ibid., June 22, 1973; *Seattle Times,* June 25, 1973.

89. Discussion in MSB, October 1974.

90. Negotiations had centered on eleven inmate complaints. See *Seattle Post Intelligencer,* June 21, 1973. The crisis ended with this announcement of preliminary agreement on changes of policy regarding disciplinary procedures, the prison hospital, and the mail room. Ibid., June 30, 1973.

91. Quoted in the prisoner's newspaper, *"It's Happening at WSP" VOP* (December 1974):2.

92. See the account in "It's Happening at WSP" VOP, (January 1974). See also "Uprisings at State Prison," *Seattle Post Intelligencer,* December 31, 1973; "Terror at Walla Walla—A Nurse's Story," ibid., January 1, 1974.

93. Ibid., February 2, 1975.

94. Interview with a black inmate leader, March 1975. He also stated that "the majority of the guys in the joint wanted no part of it, especially when they found out who was involved." Other inmates interviewed on the matter also generally supported the belief that the December 30 eruption took the population by surprise. It does, however, appear to have been kicked off by the rumor—false or at least premature—that the agenda negotiations had broken down.

95. Interview, March 1975. The investigation of the incident was still going on at that time, but Rhay stated: "If I had known then what I know now, I probably would have made that decision [to disband the RGC]."

96. In a later comment on his discussion with the RGC, Bradley several years afterwards recalled that his main concern had been the limits of public tolerance. "I was being seen as much more coercive in my intent than was in fact the case." Bradley felt that popular support was rapidly evaporating and that events such as "December 30" were completing the process. Bradley expressed the fear that "Washington was on the brink of a radicalization of the prison system very similar to that which occurred in California in the sixties." Quoted in Gabrielle Tyrnauer and Charles Stastny. "Special Report on Washington State Penitentiary to the Prisoner Organization Research Project" (Sacramento: American Justice Institute, 1980), pp. 68–69.

97. *Seattle Times,* January 12, 1975. Chadek asserted that most guards felt that Walla Walla, as a "last stop" institution, should be "run tighter."

98. Unwritten Code Is Violated in Walla Walla Uprising," *Seattle Post Intelligencer,* February 2, 1975. Rhay asserted that this was the first time violence had been done to a woman.

99. *It's Happening at WSP" VOP* (January 1975):4. The leader of the

Bikers reportedly stated to an assembly of inmates: "We are doing now what RGC was intended to do. We are running the penitentiary. We are governing ourselves." It should be noted that the editor of the newspaper at the time was a member of the Bikers' club.

100. *RGC Daily News,* March 4, 1975.

101. Ibid., March 19, 22, 25, 28, 30, 1975.

102. *Seattle Times,* April 2, 1975. At the time of the dissolution, Rhay indicated his view that the inmates had "lost interest" in RGC long since and that he had ample evidence that they were in "total agreement" with the action. Ibid.

103. Ibid., April 11, 1975. See also *PAC Daily News,* April 7, 1975, and later issues. The RRC was to concentrate on what the inmates called "climate control," that is, the atmosphere in relations among groups.

104. *PAC Daily News,* April 3, 4, 1975.

105. Discussion, April 1976. It should be noted, however, that this inmate at that time held a high position in the successor Resident Council (RC) and was indicating in what ways RC, in his view, represented an improvement over RGC.

106. Discussion, October 1975.

107. Reference to the reform era has come to mean largely the self-government conception and its embodiment in the RGC. Other features of reform introduced by William R. Conte, such as the work-release and furlough programs and liberalized hair and dress codes, have become part of the landscape. Thus it is the effects of the four-year tenure of the RGC system, not the reform program in its entirety, that remained a matter of intense controversy.

108. In the early 1970s, the penitentiary's population was dropping; it reached an all-time low around 1973–1974 with under 800 on the inside. It started to rise steeply in 1975, soaring more than 50 percent in the two years following the RGC's dissolution. In the spring of 1977, at the time of the Easter day riot and the forty-six-day lockdown, the inside population was around 1,400. The figures are derived from the RGC/PAC/RC *Daily News,* which regularly printed the official daily count. See also the figures cited by B.J. Rhay, "Idle Inmates—Superintendent Wants Work for Prisoners," *Seattle Times,* February 8, 1977, and "Rhay Says Crowding, Idleness Plague State Prison," *Seattle Post Intelligencer,* February 24, 1977. In a comprehensive survey of the expanding prison population in *Corrections Magazine* (March 1976):9–10 the increase on a national scale in the year 1975–1976 was reported as 11 percent, with Washington State at 14 percent for all of its prisoners. However, the walled population at WSP actually grew about 25 percent in that one year.

109. For a recent perspective on Amos Reed, now Secretary of Wash-

ington's new Department of Adult Corrections, see Bruce Ramsey and Stephen Gettinger, "Washington State Seeks a Return to Normalcy," *Corrections Magazine,* June 1981, pp. 33–37.

110. *Hoptowit* v. *Ray* 79–359 (ED. Wash., 1980). This important decision, which will be discussed in detail in chapter 8, rests principally on the Eighth Amendment of the U.S. Constitution. It was handed down by federal district judge Jack Tanner in May 1980.

111. See "Drugs, Disorder, Violence Within Prison Walls," *Seattle Times,* June 13, 1975. This legislative resolution, doubtless reflecting the general trend of public opinion, concluded, "The so-called policies of 'enlightenment' adopted in recent years have worsened conditions instead of improving them." See also in ibid., the critical editorials of June 23 and 27, 1975.

112. "Inmate Deaths Stain Prison Records," Ibid., May 20, 1976.

113. Interview, March 1975.

114. For a description of the Bikers, see "Hell's Angels Big Wheels inside Walla Walla Walls," *Seattle Post Intelligencer,* June 9, 1975. In the spring of 1976, the associate superintendent for custody reported that, of the more then one hundred inmates in protective custody, 80 percent were there because of trouble with the Bikers, the reputed "enforcers and collectors" for the presumed heroin ring. "Prison Pendulum Swinging Back toward Tighter Rein," *Seattle Times,* May 21, 1976. But compare the report on Walla Walla, "Prison Cycle Club's Stabilizing Force," *New York Times,* November 6, 1977.

115. "Prison Pendulum Swinging."

116. *Seattle Times,* August 4, 1976; *Seattle Post Intelligencer,* September 25, 1976. In early 1977, Rhay stated in regard to the guards that the turnover rate was 30 to 35 percent per year. He blamed the 1970 reforms for the decline of morale leading to this result. *Seattle Times,* February 8, 1977.

117. See "Fury in the Soul: The Guard's View," *Spokane Spokesman Review,* November 20, 1979.

118. Much of the information on these events was aired in subsequent legislative and administrative investigations.

119. See "Strike Ends—Struggle Doesn't," *Northwest Passage* June 2–June 20, 1977, p. 5. This version accords with Bradley's statements quoted in the *Seattle Post Intelligencer,* April 23, 1977, including the concept of a voluntary lockup. Interpretation differs drastically, however, since *Northwest Passage* is a vehicle for radical opinion.

120. The guards' excesses in some cases amounted to illegal appropriation of the inmates' personal possessions and led to later investigations and claims. See *Seattle Post Intelligencer,* August 3, 1977.

121. Ibid., April 13, 1977.

122. *Seattle Times,* May 4 and 5, 1977. Harvey was labeled "heavy-handed" by some members of the McNutt commission. *Seattle Post Intelligencer,* May 6, 1977.

123. See *Seattle Post Intelligencer,* May 24, 1977; *Seattle Times,* May 25 and 26, 1977.

124. "Warden Besieged: Inmates Angry, Guards Afraid," *Seattle Post Intelligencer,* June 1, 1977.

125. See the two analytical articles by Paul O'Connor, in ibid., May 30, June 2, 1977.

126. "Transfer of Prison Chief 'Bona Fide' Reassignment," *Seattle Times,* June 28, 1977.

127. Ibid.

128. "Unknown Warden Gets Wait-and-See Responses," *Seattle Times,* June 24, 1977. The president of the guards' union said the various conflicts with the administration had created "the lowest morale ever"; but with the newly appointed warden, "we're just going to start all over." Ibid.

129. *Seattle Times,* July 29 and August 2, 1977.

130. Governor Ray was unresponsive to Hanna's efforts to get a program of prison reform moving and she had just vetoed appropriations for miniprison planning, precisely the area Vinzant had worked in under the Evans administration. See editorial in *Seattle Post Intelligencer,* July 18, 1977. On the veto, see ibid., July 1, 1977.

131. Genakos was a former associate of Vinzant's, having been his deputy superintendent at Walpole. See ibid., September 13, 1977.

132. See Duff Wilson, "Can the State Corrections System Be Rehabilitated?" *Argus,* 85 (April 14, 1978). Genakos became Walla Walla's superintendent on July 18, 1978.

133. A militant prisoner group at WSP publicized its view on this issue in: "Prisoners Get the Squeeze," *Northwest Passage,* May 22–June 12, 1978, p. 18.

134. Wilson, "Can Corrections Be Rehabilitated?" p. 6. This article also reviews the impediments to inmate industries due to federal and state legal restrictions.

135. "Prison Tour Is Eye-Opener: Ray," *Seattle Times,* May 24, 1978.

136. The incident is summed up after the guard's death in *Seattle Post Intelligencer,* September 2, 1978.

137. See ibid., August 17, 1978. Vinzant complained that he had been faced with the "fantasies of a nice little old lady" (the governor) and a "nice young chap" (Thompson) who was completely beyond his depth.

138. Ibid.

139. Ibid., August 28, 1978. On the appointment of Spalding, the guards' union president expressed the view that this was an improvement: "At least we're picking from staff, with qualified people from our own

state." But he indicated the guards would have to see what happens."
Quoted in ibid., August 25, 1978.

140. Quoted in Tyrnauer, "What Went Wrong?" p. 41.

141. Eric Nalder, "The Trouble Brewing at State Prison," *Seattle Post
Intelligencer,* November 19, 1978, the first of a five-part series on WSP.

142. On May 9, 1979, ten hostages were seized but soon released. This
was the first hostage-taking since December 1974. For a detailed description
of the incident, see *Spokane Spokesman-Review,* November 19, 1979. See
also *New York Times,* May 10, 1979, p. 24 and *Seattle Post Intelligencer,*
May 10, 1979.

143. The murder of this guard, William Cross, is described in detail in
"Fury in the Soul: The Decade of Violence," *Spokane Spokesman-Review,*
November 23, 1979. See also *Seattle Post Intelligencer,* June 16, 1979.

144. The panel consisted of ACA Executive Director, Anthony Travisano, plus three wardens—George Sumner (San Quentin), Vernon Housewright (Vienna, Ill.) and Carl Robinson (Somers, Conn.).

145. "Riot at Prison Is No Surprise," *Seattle Post Intelligencer,* July
11, 1979. See also the earlier editorial criticisms, "How to Rule a Lawless
Place," June 27, 1979. On the inmates' ordeal in the yard, see "The Inmates Organized to Survive the Yard," ibid., August 5, 1979; "190 Inmates
Come in from the Yard at Walla Walla," ibid., August 22, 1979. On the
issues stemming from the guards' behavior, see ibid., July 20, 1979; August
16 and 23, 1979; and ("Amnesty [International] Sought Probe of State
Prison Charges," ibid., April 5, 1981).

146. See "Visiting Wardens' Report: 'Intolerable' Crowding at Prison," *Seattle Post Intelligencer,* August 22, 1979. See also the editorial,
"Advice on Prison Must Be Heeded," August 26, 1979.

147. American Correctional Association," A Report of Conditions at
Washington State Penitentiary" (College Park, Md.: ACA), July, 1979, pp.
2–3, 8, 12–13.

148. On Spalding's problems with the guard force and their union, see
"Prison Lockdown Ends But Tensions 'Still Boil,'" *Seattle Post Intelligencer,* October 23, 1979. Twelve guards had been suspended in connection
with the July beatings in the security unit, five eventually being dismissed
after a state investigation.

149. "Medical Evidence of Inmate Injury," *Seattle Post Intelligencer,*
September 3, 1979.

150. Ibid., September 11, 1979.

151. The U.S. Attorney's office would first conduct an investigation of
the brutality charges. See ibid., October 25, 1979. The now familiar "friend
of the court" (*amicus curiae*) role brings in interested parties who are not
formal litigants in the case.

152. Ibid., December 8, 1979. Thompson had formally moved to have

Judge Tanner disqualified for personal bias in the case. This was the first of several attempts to remove Tanner from the case.

153. Ibid., December 14, 1979; *Seattle Times,* December 15, 1979.

154. See "Fury in the Soul: What Lies Ahead," *Spokane Spokesman-Review,* November 26, 1979; "Guards in Charge Again at the Prison," *Seattle Post Intelligencer,* January 13, 1980; "'Prison Isn't a Fun Place,' Says Superintendent Spalding," ibid., January 18, 1980.

155. Ibid., May 9, 1980. In Spalding's view, the reforms of the early 1970s had caused staff to feel "excluded from the policy-making process," which did great damage to staff morale.

156. *Seattle Times,* April 14, 1980.

157. *Seattle Post Intelligencer,* May 4, 1980. Travisano's seems to have been the strongest statement that the state could produce from expert testimony.

158. *Seattle Times,* May 6, 1980. The reported rehabilitation theory seemingly follows that of Elam Lynds, 19th century builder of Sing Sing.

159. *Seattle Post Intelligencer,* May 8, 1980.

160. Ibid. Robert Tropp, Director of Adult Corrections under Thompson, had earlier expressed the view that the inmates had, in fact, acquired too much control in the early 1970s, but that it is difficult to turn everything around at once. Interview, December 1979.

161. *Seattle Post Intelligencer,* May 9, 1980.

162. Ibid.

163. Ibid., May 13, 16, 1980.

164. Ibid., May 24, 1980. The changes were to follow the new ACA prison standards. See *New York Times,* August 6, 1978, pp. 1, 40.

165. *Seattle Times,* August 22, 1980. It would be five months before Lewis could present his own plan, reporting to Tanner the faults he had found in the state plan. *Seattle Post Intelligencer,* January 31, 1981.

166. *Seattle Post Intelligencer,* December 6, 1980. Lewis himself suggested that the racial problem might be further exacerbated in the course of dealing with the crowding situation, since early-release programs for shorter-term prisoners would leave a higher ratio of minority inmates, who were carrying disproportionately longer sentences.

167. Ibid. The transfers had been carried out summarily without due process. The five had then been held in segregation for seven months. Lewis recommended that Tanner block any involuntary out-of-state transfers and that the state be ordered not to retaliate further against the five.

168. *Seattle Times,* December 8, 1980.

169. *Seattle Post Intelligencer,* January 5, 1981.

170. Quoted in Tyrnauer, "What Went Wrong?" *Corrections Magazine* (June 1981):41. The December 29 outbreak resulted in an estimated

$10,000 damage. Destruction in the summer months of 1979 had measured close to $1,000,000.

171. *Seattle Post Intelligencer,* January 5, 1981.

172. Ibid., January 9, 15, 20, 1981.

173. Timothy Egan, "The Prison is Calm—For Now," ibid., April 26, 1981. See also: Bruce Ramsey and Stephen Gettinger, "Washington State Seeks a Return to Normalcy," *Corrections Magazine,* June, 1981, p. 36.

174. *Seattle Post Intelligencer,* May 8, and June 28, 1981.

6

Society, Culture, and Politics in a Maximum-Security Prison

The Culture of American Prisons

Empirical studies of the prison community can be said to have begun with Hans Reimer's self-imposed incarceration in the mid-1930s.[1] A student of E.H. Sutherland, then chairman of the Department of Sociology at Indiana University, Reimer spent three months in a state penitentiary and two weeks in a county jail as an incognito participant-observer studying prisoners. The brief account of his experience to the American Prison Association set the tone and defined the framework of the more comprehensive studies that were to follow in the next three decades.[2]

Reimer's study was an ethnography of a microsociety, much in vogue among American sociologists of the time. He confined his observations to inmate life, describing an essentially autonomous community "outlined by traditions, a social hierarchy, mores, attitudes, and a mythology." He identified a community in perpetual conflict with "the prevailing order of society, personified by the institutional personnel," governed by a strict code of behavior, and organized into a hierarchical system of statuses and roles headed by the "right guy," a culture hero whose exploits of courage and "cool" were recounted to each succeeding generation of inmates. Escapes and riots could assume equally mythic proportions.[3]

The influence of the Chicago school of sociology and the ethnographic tradition that nourished it was as evident in Reimer's work as in Clemmer's classic, which followed. The prison was compared to a primitive society, isolated from the outside world, functionally integrated by a delicate system of mechanisms, which kept it precariously balanced between anarchy and accommodation. Despite periodic eruptions, the "society of captives" tended to return to its delicate balance. It was, paradoxically, a highly static model in a society filled with conflict and contradictions.

The culture concept was basic to these early prison studies and set the tone for later ones. Not only the sociologists, but others who wandered into the field from adjacent disciplines were captivated by it. Thus, McCleery, a political scientist working in Hawaii in the immediate postwar years, continued the tradition of comparing prisoners to primitives. Both lived in a society

131

confronted by a hostile and mysterious universe. Lacking any understanding of the forces that moved their world, prisoners, like primitives, invented
a class of devils, evil spirits, or *rats* to explain the appearance of arbitrary
forces. Accepting a "devil theory" to account for such forces, inmate
society, like its primitive counterpart, was easily dominated by a "priest-
hood" skilled in manipulating its concepts. . . . The "myths" of inmate
society attributed a certain dignity and freedom to the inmate class while
holding officials in contempt.[4]

Despite the early anthropological perspectives in criminology, few
anthropologists ventured into the field of prison studies. This may account
for the fact that while anthropological theory was becoming increasingly
interactionist, criminologists continued to utilize the early ethnographic
model of the "primitive isolate" in their studies of life inside the walls. In
a series of anthropological case studies, a monograph by Theodore Davidson appeared in 1974 comparing the society of prisoners in San Quentin to
"a small remote company town."[5] In making this analogy, Davidson,
an anthropologist, like Reimer, Clemmer, Sykes, and other sociologist
"ethnographers," emphasized the prison's isolation, its self-sufficiency,
and its unitary ruling power—in other words, its total character. By this
token, Davidson was also continuing the ecological tradition of the Chicago
school in prison literature.

But the company-town analogy could lend itself to a quite different
interpretation. Like most maximum-security prisons, a company town is an
urban institution in a rural setting within a larger urban industrial society.
Its apparent self-sufficiency is illusory. In reality, policies are made and
budgets are allocated in a distant head office by an urban administrator or
legislator. The decisions made in the head office are based on wider concerns that may be of regional, national, or even international importance.
The life of an individual prisoner, like that of a coal miner in a company
town, is affected by many of these forces—by the vagaries of state politics
and Supreme Court personalities and even international treaties on human
rights, as well as by the attitudes of the guards and the policies of the
warden.

From Culture to Subculture

The problems with the mircrosociety model of the prison had become
obvious well before Davidson began his study. Like small towns in a complex society, prisons were no longer autonomous sociocultural systems.
Multiple networks bound prisoner, as well as staff, to the society beyond
the walls. While the holistic approach of early anthropologists to isolated
tribal societies provided a fresh perspective for the study of institutions and
communities within a larger society, its use as a working model excluded
important segments of empirical reality.[6]

The first reaction against this early view came in the form of the debate over the *indigenous* theory of the origins of prison culture, credited to Clemmer, Sykes, and others. Irwin and Cressey argued in a 1962 article that convict culture was not a spontaneous response to the deprivations of incarceration but rather a cultural system imported from the streets.[7] This became known as the importation theory.

Other social scientists were developing the idea of *subculture,* a term that had come into use to designate cultural units of a complex society. In this area of research the general lack of anthropological presence found an exception in Walter B. Miller, whose development of the subculture theory of delinquency had a strong influence on prison studies in the 1950s and early 1960s.[8] It was the concept of subculture that helped to restore the relationship between the part and a larger whole.

Thus the microcosmic view of the American prison, like the American small town and other subcultures, was giving way to a more interactionist approach. This changing orientation was stimulated during the 1960s by ideological as well as strictly theoretical concerns.[9] The autonomous "prison community" of Clemmer was being replaced by James B. Jacob's "penitentiary in mass society," in which prison culture is related to all groups and institutions of mass society that impinge on the prisoners: the courts, the criminologists, the politicians, the administration, the custodial force, the press, and a variety of interest groups.

Contraculture, Prisonization, and the Convict Code

A variation of the subcultural concept, which seemed particularly applicable to the inmate culture described by Reimer, Clemmer, Sykes, and others, was that of *contraculture,* a term that stepped out of sociological jargon and into the general language in the turbulent 1960s as *counterculture.* In a 1960 article, Yinger defined contraculture as a species of subculture in which a theme of conflict with the values of the total society is central.[10]

The inmate contraculture, as embodied in the convict code, was strongly emphasized in the early studies. The code was a *charter* in that society, while *prisonization,* as described by Clemmer and others, was the process whereby the new prisoner—or "fish" in prison argot—was socialized and enculturated. The code, it seemed to prisoners and social scientists alike, expressed the fundamental character of convict society in the *warehouse prison* and survived with little change into the *remedial prison.*[11] It contained, on the surface at least, an inversion of conventional values and a call for solidarity against the keepers by the kept. In the code's terms the custodians of the prison were seen as standing in for a society that used its wealth and power to impose punishment for offenses the rich could commit with impunity.

In the 1950s McCleery, Grosser, Sykes, and others noted, with some surprise, that, despite the existence of this contraculture, prison inmates had a predominantly conservative orientation. Grosser compares the political culture of the prison to that of other oppositional groups who, beyond a certain point of frustration, tend to develop a revolutionary ideology. He asks rhetorically why no such movement is evident in American prisons, even though there is the belief in the widespread dishonesty of "so-called law-abiding society" and a lively interest in breaking its rules. Grosser then answers his own question in two ways: first, because of a conviction held by most prisoners that the prison system is stronger than any combination of inmates opposing it, and second, because the prisoners he observed seemed to have no cause beyond their immediate interests.[12]

When revolutionary ideologies did spread among prisoners in the late 1960s, they did not originate with the celebrated prison counterculture and its convict code but developed outside of it and partly in opposition to it. This provided practical confirmation of the theories regarding the basically accommodative nature of the traditional prisoner culture.

Empirical studies of this inmate subculture in the 1950s increasingly revealed areas of covert cooperation with the staff. To many observers it seemed that the convict code was something honored more in the breach than in the observance. By 1960 Grosser could observe, "It is generally agreed that the inmate social system contributes towards maintenance of the institution, despite the fact that the norms explicitly governing and justifying the inmate hierarchy are predominantly opposed to the aims of the administration."[13]

In recent writings the inmate contraculture has been labeled everything from a myth to a "sociological construct."[14] Our own fieldwork suggests that the code has become an ideology rather than a binding force in the lives of most prisoners. The rapidly rising incidence of intraprisoner violence and the accelerating demand for protective custody in nearly all American prisons suggests a reality other than that of a united convict culture in opposition to the system, as proclaimed by the convict code. And yet certain portions of the code persist, particularly the hatred of the *rat* or *snitch,* as prison informers are called. Many observers attributed the fury of the outburst at the New Mexico Penitentiary in February 1980 to revenge-seeking against informers.[15]

The Pluralization of American Prison Culture

Even as the debates over the nature and origins of prison culture or subculture continued well into the 1960s, profound changes were taking place in American society on both sides of the walls. Those walls themselves were growing increasingly permeable and the total institution of an earlier era was giving way to what we have called the *interactive prison*. It took social science a number of years to catch up with the developments that, by the time of the Attica uprising, were already being frequently debated in the media and by criminal-justice practitioners. The reasons for this scholarly culture lag could be sought in both the constrictions imposed by the long dominant functionalist theory and by the social background of the theorists.[16]

In a rare expression of candor on the part of an author, John Irwin confessed that, by the time he was completing his 1970 book *The Felon,* he had "the painful thought" that its principal argument was becoming obsolete. In this book Irwin elaborated the importation theory of prison culture, based on his own experience of incarceration during the 1950s. By 1977 he suggested substituting *interchange* for *importation* to account for new realities.[17] Thus the social movements of the 1960s, such as the civil rights and peace movements, also gave rise to the prisoners' movements, for the first time linking people whose preprison lives were spent in the insularity of the ghetto to the national movements centered on university campuses. This led to an unprecedented cultural exchange, striking to those who had known prisons in the days of the total institution.

It was no longer meaningful to speak of a single inmate culture or even subculture. By the time we began our field research at Washington State Penitentiary in the early 1970s, it was clear that the unified, oppositional convict culture, found in the sociological literature on prisons, no longer existed. It was still celebrated in idealized form by some of the "old cons," who were as upset over the rapid changes as were the older guards.

During our own research within WSP we found four distinguishable but overlapping political cultures or subcultures—an official one together with three distinctive inmate cultures. In table 6-1, an outline of these four cultures, with particular reference to WSP, is presented in terms of seven characteristics: legitimating *charter,* organizational structure, aims and goals, leaders and role models, ideological doctrines and slogans, channels to the external world, and action-motivating cultural themes.[18]

These four cultures functioned as political blocs, among which a variety of covert and overt types of interaction took place. The overt dimension (or *ideal* culture) was embodied in a code, an ideology, a rhetoric suitable for presentation to the outside and familiar to all members of that culture. The covert dimension (or *real* culture) more often expressed itself through actual behavior.[19] Lines of communication, both sanctioned and illicit, linked these cultures with particular segments of the outside "free world." This dynamic interactive pattern is shown schematically in figure 6-1.

Prison society, in WSP and elsewhere, has clearly become more complex, more pluralistic, than the traditional keepers-versus-kept dualistic

Table 6-1
The Four Political Cultures at WSP

	Official	Traditional	Reform	Revolutionary
Charter[a]	• Washington Administrative Code • handbooks for staff and inmates	• Convict Code	• "A Philosophy of Corrections" • RGC Constitution • Club constitutions	• Writings of Marx, Lenin, Mao and Black Power advocates
Organization	• formal hierarchical organization • bureaucratically defined roles	• informal organization • traditional roles	• voting blocs • interest groups • elected representatives	• informal/illicit • officially sanctioned "cover" groups
Objectives	• custody • treatment	• physical/psychological survival • fulfill economic/social/sexual needs	• participation • replace authoritarian model with democratic • promote welfare	• attain power within walls • link with outside revolutionary groups to change the system
Leadership	• administration • professionals	• "right guy"	• RGC representatives • club officers	• politicized inmates
Ideology	• punishment/deterrence • custodial model • rehabilitation • medical model	• solidarity against custodians	• participatory democracy • constitutionalism	• power to the the people • ethnic power • tear down the walls
Outside Communication	• bureaucratic channels • public relations	• illicit: visitors/contraband	• sanctioned access to media/citizens' groups	• uncensored literature/correspondence • visitors and contraband
Cultural Themes[b]	• hierarchy • authority • trade-offs • "just deserts"	• "do your own time" • don't snitch • solidarity with convict class	• participation • responsibility • cooperation	• prisoner power • ethnic power and pride

[a]Human groups . . . are bound together by a *charter* defining the purpose of their collaboration and its value. (Bronislaw Malinowski)

[b]A *cultural theme* is a postulate . . . controlling behavior or stimulating activity, which is tacitly approved or openly promoted in a society. (Morris E. Opler)

model of the warehouse prison. A closer look at these four cultures, with the important role now played by ethnic and political identities, can show how political culture functions in the definition and pursuit of group interests.

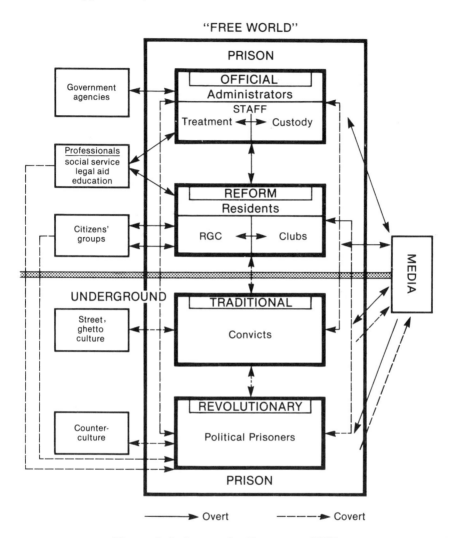

Figure 6-1. Interactive Patterns at WSP

The Four Political Cultures at Walla Walla

The McKay commission wrote in its report following the 1971 tragedy that Attica was every prison and every prison was Attica.[20] The same cannot be said of WSP, for this was just the time its liberal reform experiment had caused it to be singled out for national attention as the exception. Yet the setting was all too similar, and so were most of the conditions of confine-ment, as well as the infusion of new ideas from an American society in fer-ment. Nor did the rise of reform squeeze out the other political cultures. Thus, except for the reform culture, the other three WSP subcultures could be found in most American prisons at the time.

The *official culture,* deriving from the prison as a formal organization, was similar to official cultures in other prisons, with its regulations and rules, various staff hierarchies, collection of programs, and built-in con-flicts. Perhaps the most distinct feature at WSP was the long tenure of its warden, providing continuity of top administrative leadership throughout a period of drastic change. A second special characteristic was that, unlike many of the maximum-security prisons serving large metropolitan areas, the majority of WSP's inmate population was white. Blacks composed some 20 percent and other minorities (Indians, Chicanos) less than 10 percent.[21]

The *traditional inmate culture* was essentially the "prison community," which has been described by generations of penologists in prisons through-out the United States and many places in Europe.

The *revolutionary culture,* while recent in origin, could be found in many prisons, mostly underground. At Walla Walla, however, it was par-tially in the open, legitimized through the officially recognized ethnic clubs.

The *reform culture* alone was a special product of the time and place. It had historical antecedents, as we have seen, but when it was installed, WSP stood largely alone.

What these cultures had in common, above all, was instability. The old functionalist framework developed for analyzing systems in equilibrium was never adequate even for comprehending what we here designate as the traditional inmate culture. It is quite inappropriate for understanding these multiple and diverse cultures within a single prison polity.

Conflict has always been endemic and structural in the American max-imum-security prison. But as the older studies have shown, it could be con-tained through isolation, covert accommodation, and the use of centralized force. From one perspective, the convict code could be said to represent a safety valve for that conflict, embodying it in norms and values, tabus, and status hierarchies. The central conflict between the keepers and the kept has certainly nurtured, even if it did not create, the traditional prison culture. As the cohesiveness of that culture broke down and other competing cultures entered the prison, conflict became open and pervasive. It could no longer be confined to the institution but reached far beyond the walls.

The Official Culture

This is the culture of the prison as a formal organization, with its conflicting goals of punishment and rehabilitation. The prison, which operates through two or three staff hierarchies, has never succeeded in integrating their divergent purposes.[22] The inmates also have their officially sanctioned hierarchy, based on sentence length, "good time" toward early release, prison jobs, and organizational leadership, where officially sanctioned organizations thrive as they did at Walla Walla during the reform period. In the traditional custody-oriented official culture, a castelike relationship exists between the keepers and the kept.

In addition to the structurally determined conflict between these two castes, there are multiple lines of conflict among the various staff groups: custodial versus treatment staff, guards against the higher administrators who are their managers, and so forth. Where a legal staff exists as prisoner advocates, as was the case in recent years as WSP, they may well be in an adversary position against the institution. Educational and medical staff, often attached to the institution on less than a full-time basis, may also find themselves in conflict with other staff groups, the custodial in particular.

The conflicts between different sections of the staff became more open at WSP with the introduction of the reforms. One that has become particularly intense, partly as a response to the reforms, is that between higher administration and unionized guards.[23] During the reform period, the guards, while still having an official monopoly of power over the prisoners, began to perceive themselves as competitors with them for the attention and resources of the Division of Corrections and of the penitentiary administration. Conte blamed the growing power of the guards' union for both the failure of the reforms and his own resignation in 1971.

Undoubtedly Rhay's long tenure in office and his established reputation as a strong warden accounted in large part for his ability to maintain control. In his last years, (1975–1977), however, this control was badly shaken. His successors were still less able to dominate the situation. Neither the "permissive" Vinzant who followed Rhay, nor the "get tough" Spalding who succeeded Vinzant could restore the lost power to the warden's office. By the time Spalding—himself a former officer—became superintendent in 1978, the previously covert opposition of the guards had escalated into open warfare, manifested through threats of strikes and calls for Spalding's resignation. The covert culture was now overt: The correctional officers no longer pretended to represent the interests of either the institution or of their involuntary clients but rather those of their occupational group and, in a not clearly defined sense, the interest of their "class." Their adversaries were, variously, higher management, the Department of Institutions, the inmates, and the treatment personnel.

Thus in the process of change, latent elements are transformed into manifest ones, either through redefinition by a ruling group or through the "consciousness raising" of a politically organized interest group. As Rolf Dahrendorf has pointed out, conflict between interest groups leads to changes in social structure and power relationships.[24] At Walla Walla the covert oppositional culture of the custodial personnel, long held in check by the personal authority of a powerful warden and their own lack of organization, came into the open during the reform period.

In the case of the treatment staff, a similar process was at work, with very different results. While the overt culture of the treatment personnel was one of shared values and cooperation with other staff, the structural conflicts had led to the development of a covert culture of hostility toward both administration and custodial staff. Although all members of the official culture paid lip-service to the rehabilitative values, the allocation of resources and the marginal opportunities for the participation of treatment staff in policy decisions reinforced the professionals' feelings of low status and isolation within the organization. As Thomas and Peterson pointed out, rhetoric notwithstanding, the organization's principal goal, control, was never seriously challenged.[25]

During this period of change, the treatment staff did not choose the route of militant union activities. Instead they came to identify more openly with the prisoners, particularly the politicized ones. The reform period was a time when the efficacy and aims of rehabilitation were being questioned. Its latent function of social control was being made manifest by the Left, while the irrelevance of treatment to resocialization and crime rates was being loudly proclaimed from the Right. This ferment led to some soul-searching among the younger professional personnel in particular and, not infrequently, redefinition of identities and roles. Young veterans of the civil rights, student, and peace movements entered the ranks of treatment staff and brought their values with them. These values, in most cases, were much closer to those of the militant prisoners than to those of the older treatment personnel, not to speak of the custodians.

The *real* official culture, then, is one of continual conflict and competition, far from the ideal of a harmoniously integrated organization in which prisoners are "corrected" in a safe custodial environment by staff members with appropriate training and complementary roles. The contradictions and divisions are clearly perceptible, even across caste lines; inmates as well as staff have grown adept at manipulating them to their own advantage. In the fortress prison, "divide and rule" is a maxim that must take its place next to "accommodate and survive" as a universal precept of prison life.

Yet, as many observers have noted, there were accommodations and trade-offs that contained the conflict. But when that system was confronted by administratively sponsored reforms of any kind, the established cultural patterns were disrupted.[26] The conflict that emerged in the early 1970s between unionized guards and politically organized prisoners posed a new type of conflict. The inmates now saw the custodial functions of the prison as symbolic of the repression of the larger society; the guards, and administration in turn, saw the politicized prisoner as not simply a troublesome charge who must be punished for past transgressions and deterred from future ones but the vanguard of a movement that threatened their entire social universe. The peculiar vehemence with which penal officials of most nations have handled political prisoners, usually the least "prisonized" of inmates, reflects the dread with which they are regarded by the custodians. In Attica also, the violence of the official response to the prisoner uprising was heavily influenced by the militant rhetoric of the politicized leaders. Similarly radical inmates at Walla Walla claimed to have felt the fullest fury of the guards and administration following any disturbance.

The Traditional Inmate Culture

This is the sociocultural system that has been frequently described by observers of the prison scene and has been systematically studied by social scientists from Reimer and Clemmer down to the present. It is a system of values, norms, ideas, and behavior patterns deriving from the conditions of imprisonment and/or the prisoners' cultural antecedents, depending on what explanatory model is favored by the observer. While inmates bring various cultural ways to the situation, the conditions of imprisonment are highly uniform. The prisoners are initiated into their new existence by certain rituals of status degradation or mortification in which they are literally and symbolically stripped of their former identities:

> The acute sense of status degradation that prisoners experience generates powerful pressures to evolve means of restoring status. Principal among the mechanisms that emerge is an inmate culture—a system of social relationships that are largely at odds with those espoused by the officials and the conventional society.[27]

This suggestion of a causal relation between deprivation and the development of a covert counterculture is borne out by some empirical studies. Berk found a high correlation between inmate hostility toward institution and staff and the degree of custodial as against treatment orientation.[28] Since most American maximum-security institutions have traditionally been primarily custody oriented, generations of inmates have formalized these negative sentiments into the system of norms known as the convict code, with its emphasis on group cohesion and opposition to administrative rules and values. This long-standing normative system functioned to keep an uneasy order and stability in the potentially volatile society of captives. An older WSP inmate described the system in nostalgic terms:

> "The convict code . . . you didn't have nothing to do with a bull . . . a snitch was a snitch, a good convict was a good convict . . . your word meant

something [and] we had responsibility to one another, they had respect, now nobody's got respect for nobody, a word don't mean nothing.

Much of the convict code, as noted earlier, actually reinforces the values of the administration. In fact, the precept about "doing your own time" was often a central theme of the formal and informal orientation given by staff members to new inmates at WSP. Warden B.J. Rhay, at an installation banquet of the RGC—a body meant to symbolize a very different prison order—held up this same traditional model in an administrator's perspective: "Remember when all you had to do is come in here, put yourself in neutral, and leave the rest to us. We really took care of you. You had nothing to do but easy time, we did everything for you—you were happy as children and you were able to do a lot of time."

In the traditional maximum-security prison, inmate social organization and culture was officially ignored, discouraged, or both. Yet the inmates' role was tacitly recognized as essential to the successful operation of a prison where the involuntary clients outnumber the custodial personnel as much as ten to one. McCleery notes:

> There was substantial truth in the inmate claim that "the cons run the joint." However, the cons ran it in a way consistent with the dominant custodial values of peace and order. The hatred and contempt for "rats" which was shared by the guard force and inmate society rested on a valid sense of the fact that open communication constituted a serious threat to the traditional social order of the institution.[29]

The system of tacit collaboration between the keepers and the kept is reinforced by a variety of rewards and punishments on both sides. The guards may overlook small infractions of the rules; they might deliver letters, or favors on the outside or, in extreme cases, even smuggle in contraband. Negative sanctions may include assignment of unpleasant duties, isolation, and other kinds of disciplinary action. The cooperation of the inmates may take forms ranging from "not rocking the boat" to contraband payments. Negative actions may include mild forms of obstruction, noncooperation, verbal harassment, and ultimately riot. The system remains stable so long as these sanctions are merely threatened rather than being put into effect.

At WSP the stability of this traditional political culture was to be undermined by the emergence of two competing systems: one imposed by a reform-minded correctional leadership from above and the other filtering in from below, imported by the "new breed" of revolutionary convicts. Both of these systems contributed to the detotalization of the traditional custody-oriented prison with its characteristic political and social arrangements.

The Revolutionary Culture and the Ethnic Clubs

Another political culture had developed at WSP by the late 1960s. Like the traditional inmate political system, this new culture was largely covert and deeply hostile to the values of the prison administration. But unlike the traditional, which is oriented toward the status quo, its hostility extended to the entire society outside the walls. This was the revolutionary counterculture that emerged in prisons throughout the country, generating the "new breed" of inmate, who played so large a role in the 1971 Attica rebellion.

The world of the 1960s counter-culture, with its peace symbols, long hair, drugs, and militant political protest provided the primary source of nourishment for the prison's revolutionary underground. This underground, in turn, packaged and exported indigenous forms of prison protest to outside sympathizers. Black Muslims and Black Panthers, "peaceniks," and Marxists all exerted their influence on and were themselves affected by the prison's revolutionary culture. A link between two underground worlds of very different origins and ideology—ghetto and counter-culture—was provided by the drug culture, which left its imprint on all of the inmate cultures of the period.

In most prisons the revolutionaries, who had learned to regard themselves as political prisoners regardless of the offense for which they were incarcerated, lived a precariously underground existence. Within Walla Walla during the reform period, they achieved a quasi-recognition. The virtual abolition of censorship that came with the reforms led to the circulation of a variety of revolutionary literature ranging from Karl Marx to Malcolm X. The officially recognized ethnic clubs—the Black Prisoners' Forum Unlimited (BPFU), the Confederated Indian Tribes (CIT), and the United Chicanos (UC) were the main ones—became centers of revolutionary rhetoric and, in some cases, of radical activity.[30]

The first dramatic instance of this was the BPFU's boycott in the summer of 1972, which succeeded in shutting down a large part of the institution. One of the leaders of the boycott, a black militant who successively and simultaneously had participated as a leader in all the inmate political cultures, wrote a letter about the imminent boycott, outlined its strategy, and enclosed the "Black Manifesto," subsequently provided to the administration. The mere thought of such unfettered communication with the outside on the part of politicized felons could induce nightmares for most prison staff, but there was no evidence that outside groups were involved in any of this.

The ethnic clubs (later joined by occupational and special-interest clubs) thus acquired at least two latent functions: they became nerve centers and transmitters of radical ideology within the revolutionary culture, and they could form voting blocs and interest groups within the reformist culture.

The most prominent and powerful of the clubs in the early 1970s was the BPFU, which originally appears to have been the open organization linked to more radical groups that could not gain formal recognition. The official pamphlet that was printed by the organization in the early 1970s and distributed for public-relations purposes shows a picture of a giant clenched black fist emerging from a sea of sullen and angry faces, against the background of the wall patrolled by an armed white guard. On the one side there was a call to black unity for survival and the evocation of the martyrdom of George Jackson, whose name had become a red flag to prison administrators throughout the country. On the other side was a list of BPFU activities: black social therapy; development of vocational interest; improvement of educational interest; self-expression classes; and black workshops in drama; Swahili; and arts, crafts, and music. The two sides of this leaflet reflect the paradox of a self-professed revolutionary group officially recognized by the "system."

In 1973 BPFU originated an ambitious project, a therapy group entitled SAM (Social Adjustment for Minorities), which flourished during the 1974–1976 period. Some would regard this venture as a kind of caricature of cooptation. Under a government grant of more than $60,000, it had a paid director, a former "radical" black inmate and later student of business administration on a work-training release program. Its aims were stated in a pamphlet written by members of the program:

> The purpose of this project is to change the negative old habits, attitudes and behavior of a resident. For it is well known that anyone who enters an institution is negative: or else why would he be incarcerated. Within this program a resident learns to accept the reasons why he is in prison. He learns that he alone is responsible and that no one else can be blamed for putting him here.

The radicals doubtless recognized to some degree that the ongoing reform program would tend to channel political energies in a reformist direction. To pose a more radical alternative, revolutionaries frequently became advocates of prisoner unionization. A prisoners' union may well be less radical in theory than as symbol. Still the fact that Washington State's former governor, Daniel Evans, a strong supporter of prison reform, turned back all proposals for any such union supports the radicals in their belief that only such reforms will be officially sanctioned as do not interfere with the institutional power structure and status quo interests.

Later when the RGC was abolished in early spring 1975, the radical complement of the inmate political culture failed to mount any discernible protest. The Third World revolutionaries appeared to be substantially deradicalized, while the RGC no longer commanded much, if any, other constituency. The most powerful group in the penitentiary during the last days of the RGC was the Bikers, a group associated with symbols of violence. Their tight organization, Nazi symbols, readiness to resort to violence, together with the fear that they inspired among inmates, suggested a nihilistic Right radicalism. Such labeling must be used cautiously. What does *counterrevolutionary* mean in the context of a total institution? Contradictions abound. The Bikers were as firmly committed as any group to the convict code and on several occasions murdered suspected informers. Yet they formed a partnership with the prison administration to quell the December 1974 disturbance, the superintendent apparently entering this alliance with the aim of co-opting and thus "taming" them. Here again the interests of administration and inmate leaders came together within a closed system where both sides have a stake in stability. Thus although the Bikers (as most of the other clubs) came to the fore during the period of liberalization, they appeared to flourish best when the constitutional democracy of their setting was in decline.

The Reform Culture

The last of WSP's political cultures is the one that came to dominate the institution for the short period of the "self-government" experiment. As a creature of the prison reforms that had been promulgated by the central authority and lacking roots on the inside, the reform culture needed somehow to become assimilated to the prison polity in order to survive over the longer run.

This political culture was one of meetings, political campaigns, voting, and constitutional conventions. Elected representatives were allowed the free run of the prison and keep in personal contact with their constituents. There were weekly agenda meetings with Superintendent Rhay and frequent meetings with associate superintendents, educational and treatment staff, and club officers.

The RGC had an office, typewriters, and access to duplicating machines. It produced handbills and posters for its election campaigns. Its officers hosted outside visitors, including mayors and governors, organized semiannual banquets, and went on speaking tours outside the prison. They could be seen scurrying across the yard with attaché cases and would summon inmates from different parts of the institution for conferences and group discussions. They acted as mediators in conflicts between individual inmates or groups of them and the administration.

In the ideal culture of the reform movement, the ethic of maturity and responsibility was uppermost. But there was also the covert culture of manipulation, pressure and opportunistic uses of elective office, to which no political organization is immune. It was this side of the reform movement that was to be constantly cited by members of the offical culture as cause for failure of the RGC. Unlike the covert official and covert traditional inmate cultures, corruption in the reform culture was not given any credit for maintaining institutional stability.[31]

In practice, these four prison cultures existed within a single population, overlapping in their memberships and constantly interacting in the same arena. Only the last of these, the reform culture, was unique at Washington State Penitentiary. Its rapid emergence and precipitous fall during the first half of the 1970s will provide the focus of our analysis in the next chapter.

Notes

1. Hans Reimer, "Socialization in the Prison Community," *Proceedings of the American Prison Association, 1937* (New York: American Prison Association, 1937), pp. 151–155. "The study arose," Reimer wrote, "from an initial interest in the various plans and theories of inmate participation in the administration of penal institutions." Ibid., p. 151.

2. For example, Donald Clemmer, *The Prison Community* (New York: Rinehart, 1958); Clarence Schrag, "Social Role Types in a Prison Community" (Masters's thesis, University of Washington, 1944); Gresham Sykes, *The Society of Captives* (Princeton: Princeton University Press, 1958). Schrag's thesis grew out of fieldwork carried out at Washington State Penitentiary for an extensive statewide comparative study of prisons. The overall project is reported in Norman S. Hayner, "Washington State Correctional Institutions as Communities," *Social Forces* 21 (March 1943): 316–321. Earlier Hayner had collaborated with Ellis Ash in a participant-observer study of the state reformatory at Monroe, Ash having spent four months in 1936 as an inmate. Hayner and Ash, "The Prisoner Community as a Social Group," *American Sociological Review* 4 (June 1939):362–369. See also Hayner and Ash, "The Prison as Community," *American Sociological Review* 5 (August 1940):577–583. The contribution of University of Washington sociologists to the early study of prison culture is summarized in Lee H. Bowker, *Prisoner Subcultures* (Lexington, Mass.: Lexington Books, D.C. Heath and Company, 1977): pp. 2–3, 9–11.

3. Reimer, "Socialization," pp. 151–153.

4. Richard McCleery, "Communication Patterns as Bases of Systems of Authority and Power," in Richard Cloward et al., *Theoretical Studies in Social Organization of the Prison* (New York: Social Science Research Council, 1960), pp. 49–77.

5. Theodore Davidson, *Chicano Prisoners* (New York: Holt, Rinehart, and Winston, 1974).

6. In addition, as Laura Nader pointed out, the traditional ethnographic view of the primitive isolate applied to a community in a complex society is conducive to ideological bias, as has been frequently pointed out in the debate over the "culture of poverty" concept. By studying the powerless without reference to the people and institutions that control them and have a vested interest in keeping them that way, social scientists are loading their questions and skewing their answers. Nader, "Up the Anthropologist—Perspectives from Studying Up," in Dell Hymes, ed., *Reinventing Anthropology* (New York: Pantheon, 1972), pp. 284–311.

7. John Irwin and Donald R. Cressey, "Thieves, Convicts and the Inmate Culture," in David O. Arnold, ed., *The Sociology of Subculture* (Berkeley: Glendessary Press, 1970), pp. 64–80.

8. Walter B. Miller, "Lower Class Culture as a Generating Milieu of Gang Delinquency" in Arnold, *Sociology,* pp. 54–63. Miller's article first appeared in 1958.

9. See, for example, the contributions to Hymes, *Reinventing Anthropology,* and Ian Taylor, Paul Walton, and Jock Young, *The New Criminology* (New York: Harper and Row, 1973).

10. J. Milton Yinger, "Contraculture and Subculture," in Arnold, *Sociology,* p. 128.

11. For explanation of a "charter," see table 6-1 on p. 136. Sykes and Messinger, in summing up the chief tenets of the inmate code within five major categories, highlight the following: (1) *don't interfere with inmate interests . . . never rat on a con . . .* (2) *play it cool* and *do your own time . . .* (3) *don't exploit* [or] *. . . steal from the cons . . . don't welsh on debts . . .* (4) *don't weaken . . . whine . . . suck around . . .* (5) *don't be a sucker* [in trusting a guard]." Gresham M. Sykes and Sheldon L. Messinger, "The Inmate Social System," in Cloward et al., *Social Organization,* pp. 5–8.

12. George H. Grosser, "External Setting and Internal Relations of the Prison," in ibid., pp. 133–134.

13. Ibid., pp. 132–133.

14. A recent comprehensive review of the European as well as American literature on prison subcultures deals at length with the question of whether the convict code is myth or reality. Hilde Kaufmann, *Kriminologie* (Stuttgart: Verlag W. Kohlhammer, 1977), 3:27–30. Here German studies by Hoppensack, Hohmeier, and Reinert are cited. These attempted to verify empirically the existence and strength of the oppositional subculture and convict code. Hawkins also reviews the English-language writings on the subject and concludes that such "codes" are drafted by sociologists. Gordon Hawkins, *The Prison* (Chicago: University of Chicago Press, 1976), p. 73.

15. However, it has been reported that only thirteen of the thirty-three murdered inmates were identified as informers. *Corrections Magazine* (April 1980):8.

16. On this point, see John Irwin, *Prisons in Turmoil* (Boston: Little, Brown, 1980), pp. 30–32.

17. John Irwin, "The Changing Social Structure of the Men's Prison," in David F. Greenberg, ed., *Corrections and Punishment* (Beverly Hills: Sage, 1977), p. 24.

18. On the *charter* of a group, see Bronislaw Malinowski, "Man's Culture and Man's Behavior," *Sigma Xi Quarterly,* 29 (Autumn 1941):182–197 and 30 (Winter 1942):70–78. On cultural *themes,* see Morris E. Opler, "Themes as Dynamic Forces in Culture," *American Journal of Sociology,* 51 (1945):198–206. Brief definitions from these sources are quoted in table 6–1.

19. *Manifest* versus *latent* functions of social institutions was the terminology used by Robert K. Merton, *On Theoretical Sociology* (New York: Free Press, 1967), pp. 105, 115–127. The distinction between *ideal* and *real* culture was made by Ralph Linton, *The Study of Man* (New York: Appleton-Century-Crofts, 1936), pp. 299–303. Clyde Kluckhohn distinguishes *explicit* and *implicit* culture in *Culture and Behavior* (New York: Free Press, 1962), pp. 62–63. He also used the dichotomy between *overt* and *covert* culture; see, for example, "Covert Culture and Administrative Problems," *American Anthropologist* 45 (1945):213–227.

20. New York State Special Commission, *Attica* (New York: Bantam, 1972).

21. Hilda Bryant, "Inmates Agree, Walla Walla Is No Attica," *Seattle Post Intelligencer,* September 27, 1971.

22. See Lloyd Ohlin, "Conflicting Interests in Correctional Objectives," in Cloward et al., *Social Organization,* pp. 111–129.

23. But see James B. Jacobs and Norma M. Crotty, *Guard Unions and the Future of the Prisons* (Ithaca, N.Y.: School of Industrial and Labor Relations, 1978). These authors believe that guard unionization can have a salutary influence over the long run in leading guards, as they become "conscious of [their] rational self-interest, . . . to accept and even advocate many prison reforms they would [previously] have rejected." Ibid., p. 48.

24. H.J. Krysmanski, *Soziologie des Konfliktes* (Hamburg: Rowohlt, 1971), pp. 125, 138.

25. Charles W. Thomas and David M. Peterson, *Prison Organization and Inmate Subcultures* (Indianapolis,: Bobbs-Merrill, 1977).

26. McCleery, "Communications Patterns," p. 75. McCLeery emphasized in his study of a liberal treatment regime introduced into a custodial prison that social disorganization resulted from insufficiently prepared change regardless of the content of the change, communication being an essential element in orderly change.

27. Richard A. Cloward, "Social Control in the Prison," in Cloward et al., *Social Organization,* p. 21. See also Goffman, *Asylums.*

28. B.B. Berk, "Organizational Goals and Inmate Organization," *American Journal of Sociology* 71 (March 1966):522–534.

29. Richard McCleery, "Correctional Administration and Political Change," in Lawrence E. Hazelrigg, ed., *Prison Within Society* (Garden City, N.Y.: Doubleday, 1969), p. 126.

30. The political role during the reform era of these prisoner organizations will be discussed in detail in the next chapter.

31. Grosser, "External Setting," p. 138, points out that, through certain deviations from official norms becoming widely accepted, a new group of informal rules comes into existence. This constitutes the covert official culture. Donald Cressey notes that the lessening of tensions that follows normalized deviation from enforcing rules against inmates is seen by the treatment personnel as evidence of the accomplishment of rehabilitative goals, while in a custodial perspective it is viewed as evidence of disorganization and corruption. Cressey, "Limitations on Organization of Treatment," in Cloward et al., *Social Organization,* p. 110.

7

Prison Political Culture in a Reform Era: The Rise and Decline of Prison Democracy

The Arena

Located on a hill above Walla Walla, Washington State Penitentiary has barely changed in physical appearance since it was built as a territorial prison in the late 1880s. The massive walls, nineteen feet high and surrounding more than twenty acres; the nine watch towers, with their armed sentries; the multiple iron gates through which visitors, like prisoners and staff, must pass; the cramped cells with their two double bunks, containing at various times as many as 1750 prisoners—this was the setting of an institution wholly geared to its custodial task but ill-adapted to a reformative one. "The Walls" is kin to all the other nineteenth-century bastilles around the country that warehouse the rejects of American society.

Through a peculiar series of circumstances WSP became in the early 1970s a laboratory for one of the boldest experiments in recent penal history. Along with many other maximum-security prisons during the 1950s and 1960s, it had been evolving toward a type of prison we have called "interactive." This development was related to broad social trends which have undermined the absolutist character of the prison regime.[1] One of the most important of these is the bureaucratic model of correctional management, which, in the years following World War II, came to supplant the autocratic rule of the warden. This change took place at varying rates in different institutions. At Washington State Penitentiary, it did not overtake the Rhay regime until the early 1970s. The onset of this trend was usually marked by the creation of a Department of Corrections, which undermined the local and personalized rule of the warden. Neither humanitarian reforms nor commitment to rehabilitation and the introduction of a professional treatment staff had succeeded in eliminating prison absolutism at WSP. The preeminence of custody and the autocratic rule of the warden remained a reality until the early 1970s.

In their study of the uses of isolation and segregation at WSP, Dinitz, Conrad, and their associates use the year 1966 as a baseline. At that juncture the institution was, in their view, still a "traditional prison" under the "benevolent but conventional reign" of Garrett Heyns, a "respected prison director typifying the so-called 'correctional establishment'."[2]

By 1966, the year that William Conte replaced Heyns as director of institutions, the prison had long since been officially committed to rehabilitative treatment of offenders in addition to custody and punishment. But while a change in ideology had done little to change the power structure, the groundwork was being laid through the progressive "bureaucratization" of the entire corrections system—a move which leads to the transformation of the warden from "czar" to "manager."[3] Conte, for his part, saw this same period as one in which a measure of administrative reorganization was accomplished, "a spirit of communication and working-togetherness had been established, and the stage was set to move on to more reasonable and effective care and treatment of those incarcerated."[4]

Four years later, with the direct introduction of the reforms into the institutions, came a broad effort not only to renovate this custodial prison, but to rechannel the social forces which are inexorably diffusing power within the prison society. Whatever the prospects and the eventual outcome of this ambitious experiment to transform the prison polity, clearly there were deep-lying forces at work, reshaping the inmates' political culture together with the over-all social system of the prison. *Detotalization* is the label we have applied to this social and political process, that acts to "thaw" a total institution.

The Crisis of Legitimacy

The inmate culture, as we have seen, was becoming less homogeneous, splintering between those who accepted the values of the status quo and those who rejected the existent system. The prime issue was the extent to which the prison administration's exercise of authority within the prison polity continued to be recognized as legitimate. Traditional inmate political culture, however ambivalently, conceded that claim of legitimacy, while the "new breed" of prisoner increasingly questioned it.[5]

By the 1960s the prison regime was unquestionably approaching a crisis of legitimacy.[6] Forces of change were at work both within and outside prisons: the Civil Rights movement, the courts' abandonment of the hands-off doctrine, and the pluralization of the inmate population, reflecting the influx of this new breed of prisoners nurtured on urban streets. The resulting crisis of legitimacy, posing the most fundamental questions for governance of the prison polity, was linked directly to a sharp rise in prisoner politicization.

Some observers trace this trend, in part, to a growing disillusionment as early as the 1950s with the accepted treatment model.[7] But rejection of the legitimacy of the prison regime was much broader. This was a period of growing political consciousness throughout the whole society, witnessing especially the activation of blacks and other racial and ethnic minorities. Emerging in radical form in the 1960s and entering into the political consciousness of individual prisoners and prisoner groups, the ideology of the incipient prisoners movement included the following basic propositions: prison inmates have been victimized by society at every stage of their lives; they would not be in prison except for the racist, discriminatory, and wholly unjust criminal-justice system; it follows that prison inmates are political prisoners; moreover, prison inmates are deprived of even those reformist goals that were promised: a humane environment and rehabilitation; for all of these reasons, the prison regime has no supportable claim to legitimacy. Finally, what is to be done? Prisoners, constituting a victim class (a ''convicted class''), must achieve solidarity, linked with outside forces, and aiming at the goal of liberation.

But the group that took the initial steps in launching radical activism was not, as might have been expected, Marxist oriented. It was the Black Muslims, with their exclusionist and nationalist platform, who first coalesced organizationally in the 1950s, posing a basic challenge to the system. In attacking the racism and discriminatory practices of the prison through their religio-political ideology, the Muslims were actually reaching beyond the walls to assault the legitimacy of the repressive ''white government that ruled America.''[8] And while the Muslims were displaced as the vanguard force by the mid-1960s, the spark that they had provided was spreading an increasingly radical political consciousness inside the walls.[9] Revolutionary consciousness raising was given important dimensions in the careers and writings of such politically active prisoners as Malcolm X, George Jackson, and Eldridge Cleaver.[10] By the late 1960s these politicizing ideas and experiences were making themselves felt even in places not quite in the mainstream, such as Walla Walla, Washington.

The summer of 1972 saw the Black Manifesto and boycott at WSP. At the headquarters of the blacks' organization, the BPFU, shortly after the boycott, one of the leaders narrated his experiences in the 1960s:

I was in San Quentin and the political trend was the Muslim faith and certain people rejected the idea of the Muslim faith because the feeling wasn't there. They wanted to do something more emotional, like violence . . . and looking then at the movement of, say, Martin Luther King, the struggle was [to be] not violent. . . . Now, when I got out, blood was shed because I went back to Watts and the same kind of tension that was in the institution was in the community. . . . I think that anybody politically aware knows something's wrong . . . and this is where the renaissance of the 1960s brought all of it out to where all black people have become conscious . . . at different levels of awareness. If the whole black people were completely aware, then I think the whole system would have to change. Where it's just a few that is struggling and trying to hold up the others until they get ready to struggle—I think this is where we're at in this institution too.[11]

Later in this same exchange, another inmate pointed to the suppression of black literature (for example, *Soul on Ice*) and the ban on teaching black history in federal prisons during the 1960s. To his mind, there was a strong but unsuccessful effort by the authorities to prevent the development of black consciousness.

It was generally agreed, by members of all four of WSP's political cultures, that the growing political consciousness among black inmates (almost 20 percent) was a major factor in the crisis of legitimacy in the penitentiary. Yet by comparison with the situation in eastern prisons, Walla Walla had not achieved a high level of militancy by the late 1960s. One black leader observed that in WSP, the inmates were more concerned with immediate benefits, material advantages.[12] Nevertheless, important processes were underway, in Walla Walla as elsewhere, which were to lead to a less isolated and more interactive political culture.

Impact of the Reforms at Walla Walla

By the end of 1970, a far-reaching program of reforms was introduced into the political life of Walla Walla. The reform package was bestowed on the institution by Olympia. It was reformist, not revolutionary, and offered piecemeal remedies for gargantuan ills. Yet in a prison context, it contained a radical potential, particularly in its most celebrated plank: the mandate to form "governmental" inmate councils. It was this governance provision that attracted many of those committed to a full-scale renovation of the prison polity, while alarming those with an important stake in the established system. The official strategy underlying the reform mandate was aimed simultaneously at co-opting the radical and neutralizing the violent potential of the traditional politics.

The reform culture at WSP derived directly from the program being imported from the state capital, a "graft" applied by administrative "physicians" to the penitentiary's political culture. For such a graft to actually take at Walla Walla, heavy reliance would need to be placed on an organizational superstructure like the RGC. The inmates, in their newly politicized and pluralized state, seemed quite ready, even eager, to make the attempt.

Critics have raised serious questions about the extent to which real power was channeled into inmate hands. Frank Browning, an editor of *Ramparts,* saw little change of genuine prisoner power short of a strong prisoners' organization with bargaining power, in other words a prisoners' union. While conceding that WSP during its early reform stage appeared to be "far more humane than most," he put "little stock" in a situation in which the prison administration still controlled all the levers of power and could easily withdraw whatever concessions they had granted.[13] In other words, Walla Walla's RGC would amount to little more than a company union. Yet Warden Rhay, dubious as he was about inmate participation, believed that the shift of power was to be real and substantial.[14]

The head of the guards' union, Sergeant Robin Moses, maintained that "the residents organized first and better" to fill the power vacuum.[15] However, the opportunities for a genuine shift of forces within the prison polity may have appeared greater than they actually were. The exaggerated expectations on all sides arose from the term "self-government." In practice inmate self-government was necessarily limited by state law, by the terms of the administrative directives that established it, and by the inherently restrictive nature of a prison environment.[16]

Nevertheless, the term *government* became a symbolic representation of the prisoners' new status: that they were to be citizens and not merely subjects of the penitentiary and that they would have an active role in shaping prison policy.

Skepticism about self-government was more often expressed in the aftermath than when it was being set up. One of Walla Walla's long-time cons acknowledged in a 1975 post-mortem on the RGC that the term *self-government* has a "magic of its own," but he saw the RGC era largely as having lent respectability to the same "con bosses" in their use of traditional manipulatory methods:

Now, where before I was a leader of a negative nature, now I'm [regarded as] a leader of a positive nature, and I still have as much effect, if not more. . . . There has not been any change. Ten years ago, if this guy got busted and he went to the hole, and I was considered one of the leaders of the institution, and I decided that I wanted him out of the hole, . . . if Bob Rhay liked me, he would let him out—that's exactly what RGC [does].[17]

Another inmate observed with an equal measure of cynicism: "Whoever's in power runs the joint."

But at the beginning of the 1970s, the mood of the Walla Walla prisoners was ripe for new departures. One of the leading inmate politicians during this early stage described the new types of prisoners, that were coming into the penitentiary bringing new attitudes: "some of the kids from the streets, who went to college, a little more intellectual-type people," were coming into the penitentiary. "They were not regimented to this life and they were objecting strongly."[18]

Thus, the spirit of these times, combined with a green light from the highest administrator, opened up wide possibilities for change. Yet the reforms did not succeed in creating a lasting democracy inside the walls. Many reasons have been suggested for its failure. These were related to both preparation and implementation.

The most common criticism leveled against the reforms by the staff was that they were drawn up by a few liberal reformers in Olympia who lacked practical correctional experience; that this was done with inadequate input from the prison administration; and that it was imposed on the institution without warning. As we have seen, all these contentions were denied by Conte, who pointed to three years of staff preparation and consultation preceding the announcement of the reforms. In a 1973 interview, Rhay said that if the reforms had been "done the way we were used to it, it could have been done."[19] He meant by this, he explained, the working out of proposals in consultation with his staff to give them the feeling of participation. Yet judging by the strong resistance of both administration and staff to any redistribution of power, it is unlikely that such radical and far-reaching reforms could have emerged from below.

It can be argued that the reforms might have been more acceptable to the staff if they had been introduced piecemeal into the institutions. However, such an approach would have lacked the dramatic impact of a single package with the stamp of a new era upon it; and this would not have been consistent with Conte's philosophy of corrections.

The implementation of the reforms was essentially left up to the individual institutions, adding uncertainty and confusion to the staff's feelings of alienation. While the package was quite specific in prescribing certain basic rules changes, it failed to lay down clear guidelines for step-by-step institutional implementation of the self-government concept. This, combined with the in-built resistance to changes of the sort promised by this reform program, greatly impeded implementation. And with the premature departure of Conte, the reform era lacked the focus of strong and identifiable leadership at either the institutional level or in the state administration. Without the guidance of the key originator of the reforms, the responsibility for initiative and leadership now devolved on the inmates themselves.

How effectively would the inmates exploit their opportunity? First, it was crucial that inmate groups develop the RGC as the element of cohesion in the political arena. The place to begin would be through the electoral process and then through the effective functioning of the council itself. Second, the RGC, together with prison administration and staff, could have utilized its new-found scope for political development in developing some sort of *guided democracy.*

Was Walla Walla ready for this new course? Certainly there was a developing political consciousness among the inmates, but this was very uneven. At the same time, staff resistance to the reforms was strong, and not fully taken into account by the Olympia reformers. On balance the prospects were not particularly bright for the long-run success of this difficult social experiment. Nonetheless, an examination of the reform era's successes and failures may provide some useful insights into the political processes of a very peculiar type of institution, a maximum-security prison.

Political Pluralism

In practice it has been seen that the pluralization of a political system is a requisite of its democratization, despite the fact that classical democratic theory was hostile to a role for political groups.[20] Pluralism, first of all, describes the empirical reality of a society made up of a variety of relatively autonomous groups. Political pluralism follows from the formation of interest groups and political parties. It has as its goal the broadening of the political base of a polity and the realization of democratic participation. Historically egalitarian and democratic values have proved unrealizable without open competition of groups, typically through elections.[21]

What does this have to do with a prison? Starting from a Hobbesian state of nature an atomized inmate population, mired in the internecine battles of the powerless, then emerges into the social system of informal aggregated groups. At first these are underground groups, a form of political pluralism (in the empirical sense of the term) that is least likely to translate into egalitarianism and participatory democracy. Nor is the next step—the formalization and regularization of inmate groups—necessarily the route to democratization.

The prospects for the political development of inmate society in a democratic direction has been viewed pessimistically by most students of the subject. Korn and McCorkle, writing in the 1950s, underlined the extreme authoritarianism of the inmate social structure. Their observation was that if the prison regime were liberalized, "the rigid authoritarian patterns [were] transferred to a new and less stable center of gravity." They feared that giving power to inmate councils would lead only to "patterns of internal group coercion more punitive, more rigid, and incomparably more discriminatory."[22] Thus this view held that any devolution of power from the top plays into the hands of an inmate power elite, ruling over unprepared prisonized inmate masses.

The opposing position, represented by John Irwin, argues that this pattern of the prison polity (the Big House model) was focused on just one kind of relationship: "the corrupt arrangement between some prison bigshots and the administration." According to Irwin, this has long since ceased to reflect the reality in most prisons. The bulk of today's inmates bring their "pre-prison orientations" with them and are resistant to prisonization.[23] The cultural milieu, is frequently marked by an evolution toward a more open and interactive prison, creating opportunities for the renovation of the inmate polity.[24]

Prisoners' Organizations in WSP

Pluralism, in the sense of inmate groupings, predated the reform era at Walla Walla. Some of the informal (underground) groups, especially ethnic clubs, were given official recognition in the late 1960s. But when the reforms were formally introduced, inmate organizations came into their own.

The groups at WSP during the reform period fell into several categories: ethnic clubs, status clubs, community and self-help groups, religious or semi-religious organizations, and special interest clubs. The ethnic clubs, by far the most important category, included the authorized black organization, the Black Prisoners Forum Unlimited (BPFU); the United Chicanos (UC); and the Confederated Indian Tribes (CIT), which was the first ethnic group to achieve a recognized constitution at WSP. Lifers with Hope was clearly the most important status club. The Seekers, as well as Alcoholics Anonymous and Social Therapy, were early self-help groups, with others to follow. The Jaycees typified the community-group category, while the small group of Muslims were the most politicized religious group. Finally the Bikers, the Washington State Penitentiary Motorcycle Association (WSPMA), perhaps belong in a category of their own, although they may qualify as a special-interest club along with the Clipped Wings Club (model planes) and other avocational and hobby groups. The five most important of these open organizations were the three ethnic clubs plus the Lifers and the Bikers.

The BPFU was designed as an umbrella organization for the upwards of 20 percent black prison population. At the same time, there is evidence that underground and semi-underground black organizations continued to play an important role behind the scenes.

In fact, the BPFU, which gained official recognition at the end of the 1960s, seems to have been mainly a creation of activist blacks. These militants had close ties with the Black Panthers, and the Black Liberation Party (BLP) was also represented at Walla Walla. The BLP seems to have been used as a semi-open Panther front group and was the moving force in pushing for a formally authorized group.[25]

The BLP appears to have maintained its identity, acting as a pressure group within the black constituency. Members of BLP withdrew from BPFU when it periodically veered toward becoming merely a cultural and social club and then reaffiliated when it took a political turn.[26] The Liberators (BLP) dedicated themselves to politicizing black inmates in the direction of a vague kind of radical Marxist-Leninist Socialist consciousness:

> Our idea was to come with extremely radical insight to teach. Primarily the average dude inside the penitentiary, especially black, had no political awareness at all, nor any cultural awareness . . . [but] the "pen" is a naturally radical environment and usually the guys inside are [potentially] radical. . . . Liberators started holding meetings inside and the institution allowed us to have guests in, so we were training and training other brothers and we were strictly political, we didn't have anything to do with games.

. . . Most of us have understood Marx and Lenin, . . . this is primarily our platform. . . . Material wealth of every nation belongs to the people inside of it . . . [and] should be divided among the people equally.[27]

At Walla Walla, however, this was the era of reformism, even for the Liberators. The rhetoric was revolutionary, but BLP activists in practice concentrated on working for more and better treatment programs and expanded furloughs. Of the sixteen to eighteen Liberationists who passed through WSP during this early period, "every one of them [in 1975] is heading some kind of state program or he's into a state program." Their stated goal was not "to overthrow the state" but "to get into the working of the state, become some integral part of it to take our issue up and deal with it effectively."[28]

An important part of the reform political culture was participation in RGC elections and BLPers did not abstain. In fact diverse groups (such as the BLP and the Muslims) collaborated on the same political ticket:

OK, the BLP and the Muslims are literally, you know, talking about black equality, right? So they can both scream on that issue. Their [the Muslims'] problem was getting their dietary program together, right? So as a Lifer you could scream for their dietary program too, because that's all you talked about, using the kitchen, right? Whereas a member of the BPFU, he'd just scream about the Man was discriminating against your brothers, right? Because they were black. OK, as a Muslim he could scream, because he felt that they were dying, all the people in the institution were dying, and they were trying to set up a diet kitchen, but the institution wouldn't do it. You follow? So you had ways of getting interests [represented].[29]

Another means for bringing leaders into contact across party lines was the device of "honorary" membership in other organizations. One BLPer, for example, would become an honorary member of the Muslims, another of the Lifers, and still a third, even of the Bikers. Whatever the motive— whether collaboration or infiltration—there seems to have been a willingness at first to see the justice in the claims of other groups of cons. A black provided a surprisingly detached description of the Bikers' origins:

A group of whites—and rightfully so—felt that they were being let down, because they weren't Lifers, they weren't BPFU members, they weren't members of anything, so they formed a White Citizens' Council. . . . Now, out of the White Citizens' Council came the need for a bike shop . . . [and then, the Bikers]. And it became a political organization after that, . . . but originally the Bikers started as a protective group for most of the whites who felt they were getting trod on, by the Lifers, the BPFU, and everybody else.[30]

During the early period initiated by the Race Relations Council and then the RGC, there was cooperation on the councils, token cross-memberships in clubs, and serious efforts to negotiate differences between blacks and whites without resort to violence. But with increasing polarization, the potential for violence rose. A large part of the explanation lay in the drug traffic:

> The polarization—that came in primarily when the drugs came in the joint, because BPFU at one time was supposedly controlling the drugs. The Bikers got their end of the drugs, and said, "OK, look, we want a portion of it too." And then the Bikers, because of their affiliations outside with drugs really started bringing in loads of drugs, and then they became controllers of the drugs. Especially the lighter drugs. Then, in retaliation, in came the heroin, and then they got a taste of heroin, and that created the war between the two.[31]

Inmates generally link the corruption of the self-government system and its leadership, including the club system, to drugs and the drug traffic. From a slightly different angle, they described the struggle among WSP's inmate groups as an open power struggle:

> But the Bikers were polarized at one time from everybody; they didn't have anything to do with other clubs. Then they saw that that was going to get them snuffed, really, so they started getting affiliated with all the other clubs. Then they had a plan afoot at one time to put a Biker in office in every club that there was in the institution, with the exception of the BPFU, because they couldn't get one in, because by then the BPFU was anti-Biker, 100 percent anti-Biker. . . . Oh, God, yeah, we had wars with them, just really some nice wars. That didn't entail race at all. It entailed power. You know, "This is my property, this is my corner here, we won't bug you over there. If one of our members and one of your members gets in a beef, that's open season for everybody."[32]

Unity or Diversity?

The club system emphasized separatism and the particularism of group interests, whereas the RGC was premised upon some area of common inmate interest. The central unifying myth element of the system centered on the Race Relations Council and the dramatic circumstances of its formation at the beginning of 1971. In the early stages, this symbol of unity seems to have swept along Warden Rhay himself. In a 1972 interview with a *Life* reporter, he depicted the crisis as having been "one dirty look away from a race riot." Then the cooler heads among the inmates prevailed and the resulting truce "made [me] a true believer . . . real sudden-like."[33]

Superintendent Rhay seems throughout to have seen self-government in rather restrictive terms as primarily a communications device and secondarily for peacekeeping. He was persistently wary of the inmates' central organ, the RGC, and preferred dealing with the clubs individually. [34] Inmate leaders repeatedly attributed much of their difficulty in establishing a unified front on policy issues to what they characterized as divide and rule tactics by the administration. During the initial, optimistic stages, a BPFU top officer claimed to have confounded this tactic:

> One thing we have been able to do with the administration—I don't think they thought we could—[we] unified the population in the sense that you don't play one group against the other. . . . The administration in the past had been good at [that] . . . [but] we, the convicts themselves, formed a race relations group. [35]

Mutual suspicions were in the air, but the symbolism of the race riot that had been averted worked for a while. Inmate leaders quite clearly credited this early crisis with having cemented a unity against the administration as the oppressor. The rank and file had to be brought to the political consciousness that it was against their interest to fight among themselves. Some prisoner leaders, in supporting the guards' union in its push for higher pay, were seeking an even broader coalition against the administration. [36] Thus the politics of this era was essentially oriented to reform and united front, with some overlay of revolutionary rhetoric. And while a few of the militants might warn of the dangers of becoming overexposed and co-opted through a formalized reformist politics, the intoxicating spirit of a newly opened arena carried the population along for a period.

Yet the cement of unity was thin and the political culture was in large measure ill defined and immature. By 1976 a leader of the Resident Council conceded that the administration's divide and rule tactics had paid off. He lamented that, with the passing of the former penitentiary culture of convict solidarity, the new subcultures were isolated in "their own private little brotherhoods . . . [with] very little interaction between [them] . . . And then you wind up with a small rumble between clubs or whatever. So the old convict code is no more, . . . because of the individualistic-type trips." [37]

Division of the inmate body into ethnic organizations has been observed in many, perhaps most, American prisons. [38] And these groups, increasingly, are being given official recognition within prisons. At the same time the general principle has been to exclude openly political groups. To be approved, a group must be at least formally cultural and social in nature. The political group is forced underground or plays a covert role within a chartered group. This limitation to the nonpolitical, hard as it is to define, is not intended to be a mere formality but a strictly enforced standard. [39] WSP was somewhat exceptional in this regard. The line between political and nonpolitical does not appear to have been carefully laid down at any point. However, in the prereform days, when the Native American group and the other ethnics first organized and received recognition, the administration could withhold at its discretion approval from any group too obviously political. Thus the constitutions of all the groups formally confined them to cultural and educational purposes.

It seems reasonably clear, however, that the black prisoners' group—and to a lesser extent the others—undertook political education and pursued varied political goals under the guise of the cultural. With the coming of the reforms, the lines became even fuzzier. Few questions were raised when the groups actively entered the political arena—true, a reformist arena—with RGC electoral slates, and the BPFU did not lose its recognized status when it brought out its black manifesto, backed up by a nonviolent work boycott to force the issues to negotiations. The true test, of course, would have come if a group openly set up courses in Marxism-Leninism or linked up directly with an outside radical movement. However, even with these reservations, the WSP political arena in the early 1970s was remarkably lively and open. The prison administration sometimes seemed nervous about the situation, but on the whole, it did not try to depoliticize group life or to transfer activists out of WSP.

Overtly it was in this electoral arena that WSP's political life seemed to have taken on the characteristics of a quasi-democratic polity. Here, with the variety of political interests highlighted, is a brief description of the rounding up of candidates for an RGC election:

> There were enough blacks that there was always assured that there would be at least two blacks on the council, you see? We'd go to the club and we'd say, "OK, who did you want to put on?" "Well, we want L. on." "OK, L, you're on the council, you're representative for the Chicanos." So we had that power so we could go out and hit the guy and say, "OK, you're on the council," so that everybody was represented all the time. The administration would do the same thing; they'd say, "OK, we had a guy that we wanted on the council from the unattached population; his name is So-and-So, and would you look into that he gets on the council." Well, yeah, we'd put him on the council. And then we would feed him information to take to the administration, literally telling him, you know, "Look, take this back to Bob Rhay," and he would.[40]

But over the long run, representatives and leaders were not so easily recruited. Those who were thrust into leadership positions were easily compromised through their relationship with the prison administration. Numerous stories circulated concerning inmate politicians who had been trapped in compromising positions. And even in a maximum-security institution, with lengthy sentences, the population was not stable. The main scene of political action was the inside, from which inmates would move to the minimum-security building, a secondary scene. Prominent inmate leaders frequently made the move to MSB more rapidly than others. From there, work release (or parole) was the next step. The single most frequently mentioned factor in the decline of the self-government experiment was this draining off of top leaders.

The decline in the quality of group life observable during the four-year period from 1971 to 1975 reflected several important developments. Many of those with a belief in the self-government concept and a stake in that system became disillusioned. Leadership positions came to be occupied by inmates whose commitment was questionable or nonexistent. The cross-fertilization of leadership between the councils and the major clubs was attenuated. And with the weakening of the RGC as a centralizing and coordinating organ for the inmate polity, this council itself became essentially another club, competing alongside the others for position and talent.[41]

It was largely in this form that WSP's organizational pluralism was perpetuated into the later 1970s. Warden Rhay made no secret of his feeling more comfortable with the club system than with representative councils, which symbolized a politicized and participatory arena for the inmate body as a whole.[42] Even though the club system in its contemporary form had grown out of the social ferment of the 1960s, Rhay was evidently speculating on reestablishing some features of the kind of relationship that had prevailed under prison cliques and their con bosses.

The club system kept the political arena fragmented; and with the decline of ideologically oriented inmate politics and the departure of leaders attuned to radical rhetoric, it seemed to many observers that a depoliticization process was taking place. But the belief that these trends were in the administration's interest was largely illusory. The important groups were still intensely political, in the sense of being oriented toward power. And as ideological politics faded, the stage was more and more occupied by nihilistic politics, tinged with crypto-fascism, and raising the spectre of violence.[43]

The events of 1975 had led to the emergence of the Bikers as the most important inmate organization. Rhay believed that had this group not sided with order, WSP could have erupted into a full-scale riot. Two years later the Bikers' dominant status was reflected through the February 1977 issue of the prison newspaper in which the first ten of its twenty pages was devoted almost exclusively to the motorcycle club. The Bikers were depicted as essentially a self-help organization, and the club's vocational training activities were emphasized.

The Confederated Indian Tribes (CIT), WSP's oldest officially recognized ethnic club, were given a small front-page article in the same issue. On the inside page, the United Chicanos reported that they were in the process of rebuilding, with outside help, following a period of suspended operations due to a violent episode in 1975.[44]

About the time this issue of the prison paper appeared, Rhay made a complete tour of the clubs giving impromptu talks at each stop. The "Lifers With Hope" were chided for the decline in their credibility and Rhay remarked that "there was a time when I looked at this club as being the leading club in the institution." And he gave the following lecture:

> There's only one reason why clubs should exist—they give a resident the feeling of belonging to something and it provides a comfort to residents when they are with their kind. Clubs should be placed where people come together and feel good with each other and work to maintain a stable structure.[45]

This statement, which came shortly before the end of Rhay's twenty-year tenure, suggests once again the penitentiary administration's desire for low-key inmate pluralism—depoliticized, inmates grouped in culture blocs, controllable and self-controlled. Yet even in the periods of lull, WSP's pluralistic arena had been further balkanized into warring groups. Ethnic leaders continued to express deep suspicions concerning the administration's motives, while seeking to present a unified group front. It was a far cry from the original concept of representing prisoners' common interest through the medium of participatory and representative institutions. By mid-decade it was obvious that the hopes once placed in the clubs to function as quasi-parties[46] within a system of which an inmates' governance council would be the focal constitutional organ were not to be fulfilled.

Constitutionalism

Just as the responsiveness of a political system to its population presupposes an open political arena and an active political pluralism, so the system must have an effective constitutional structure in order to achieve responsible democratic government. The democratization of a prison is a highly unusual operation. Not only is the polity functioning under a tight bureaucratic structure but within an institution from which there is no voluntary egress. However great the amount of self-rule, autonomy, or participation that might be ceded, an inmate governance system will be restricted to what is sometimes called *guided democracy*. Superior force, power, and authority are concentrated at the apex of the institution and at the center of the state machine.

That does not necessarily turn any such inmate governance system into a rigged game. Much depends, for example, on whether a genuine bargaining arena has been created and on what real impact there turns out to be upon prison policy making. We would argue that a quasi-constitutional prison democracy needs to incorporate elements of both participatory democracy and a representative system.[47] The participatory aspect provides the civic education that was at the core of Osborne's conception. Certainly it is a kind of participation that can be identified as "co-optative." Its purpose is "to evoke the participant's interest, enthusiasm, and sense of identity with the goals of the enterprise in question."[48] In practice, this means that in the initial stages the participatory arena is manipulated by experts, who once they succeed in training the participants to act effectively, can hand over the reins to indigenous leaders. According to this analysis, co-optative participation (in a nonpejorative meaning of the term) can be an effective means of rehabilitating persons who lack the knowledge or the desire to help themselves.

While it is through the groups and committees, as well as through electoral and general political activity, that the *participatory* element is pursued, the *representative* aspect of a constitutional system is reflected by the apportioning of authority, the operating of representative institutions, and the provision for accountability to the citizenry. This does not exhaust the desiderata for such a system, but it does suggest criteria by which even such an unlikely experiment can be judged. (For a schematic representation of inmate governance patterns, see figure 7-1.)

Inmate Government and the RGC: Theory and Practice

For a four-year period, constitutionalism at WSP was embodied primarily in the RGC. The constitution for self-government, adopted in April 1971, was modified in March 1973 and again in October 1974. Although there was considerable dispute over these alterations at the time, they did not really represent any change in basic structure. Throughout, the key organ was an elected eleven-member council, having prescribed powers and responsibilities and treating directly with the superintendent, who could veto their decisions.[49] In fact, structurally and in terms of its formal functions, the successor RC was not very different on paper from its predecessor. The difference was largely in philosophy, spirit, and nomenclature. In place of a constitution for self-government, there would henceforth be guidelines for conduct and the term *government* would be expunged. The status of the RC was, at best, on par with other recognized inmate organizations—a far cry from the days of RGC gala inaugurations, frequent contacts with governmental luminaries, and national media attention.

Early in the reform period, there had been considerable theorizing by the inmates themselves about the self-government concepts. The prisoners were anxious to explore the relationships of the RGC to the prison population and to its other organizations. A three-page statement and diagram, entitled "Self-Government Structure," loosely derived from the treatment orientation of Conte's philosophy of corrections, sets forth the inmates'

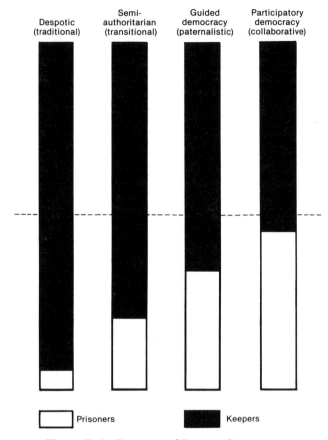

Figure 7-1. Patterns of Inmate Governance

conceptualization and conveys the flavor of their initial enthusiasm for the self-government ideal.[50] The new convict is viewed as entering a "plastic community," a state where "his mind . . . was kept in limbo." Prior to self-government, this is where inmate life would begin and end, nothing would touch the "inner man," any initiative would be stifled, and personal responsibility and growth would be nonexistent. The inmate's external behavior would be strictly controlled by rules and their enforcers. Now, proclaims this statement, the new inmate is at once introduced to a new set of alternatives: he is told on the day of his arrival of the many ethnic self-interest and therapy groups which are available to him. Thus after a period of examining this "range of expanded alternatives," the inmate moves "out of the plastic community, into a club or group which promises to satisfy one of his basic needs for growth or awareness."

By the time this statement was drawn up in 1972 an extraconstitutional body, the Clubs Action Council (CAC), had been established as the organizational coordinator. The CAC chairman was to be assisted in his task by a staff, which would provide liaison to the prison administration and to the outside. As the community and social activities of these groups expanded, the inmate would move out of the "plastic community" into something called the "near-actual society":

> This point of growth—this atmosphere—is the prime goal of the reform movement. To remove the artificial environment which existed under super-custody and to make it as near to actual society wherein the rights and opinions of the individual play a key part in the treatment used with his development—this is the paramount demand of our Bill of Rights.

The "near-actual society" has a "self-government" superstructure, the RGC, "superior to any previous prison structure in that the inmates play a vital role of participation in the procedure and policies which govern and treat them during their confinement." As "the first such government in prison history," the RGC ideally will closely cooperate with the prison administration, an ombudsman, and a citizens' advisory council. Taken together, this will be the instrumentality for linking the "near-actual society" inside and "free society" outside. (See figure 7-2 for a generalized picture of the RGC system, according to the inmates' own description.)

But in the "real world" of the penitentiary, as we have seen, the constitutional system of inmate representation faced nearly insurmountable obstacles. Structurally the nature and limits of self-rule were defined by the terms of the monthly (later weekly) "agenda meetings," at which the chosen inmate representatives met with the superintendent. The superintendent, through his possession of the veto, could grant or withhold approval.

For council members, there were heavy pressures toward turning the meetings into petty "gimme" sessions on behalf of their constituencies or themselves. It is difficult to conceive how such a system could attain a political equilibrium over the long run, lacking supportive and consistent leadership on both the side of the inmates and of the administration.

Oppositional voices within the prisoner polity were soon heard. A March 1972 newsletter by a dissident radical faction accused the RGC of being nothing but a "tool of the administration" and of settling for "tokenism" on rehabilitation projects and on work-release and furlough programs.[51] Following that summer's brief work boycott and black manifesto, a report prepared by a minimum-security building inmate-guard joint group (and including the chairman of the outside Citizens Advisory Council) that surveyed WSP's overall management was leaked to the press and given wide publicity. This document, presumably only a working paper (according to the DSHS deputy secretary, Jerry Thomas), contained concrete recommen-

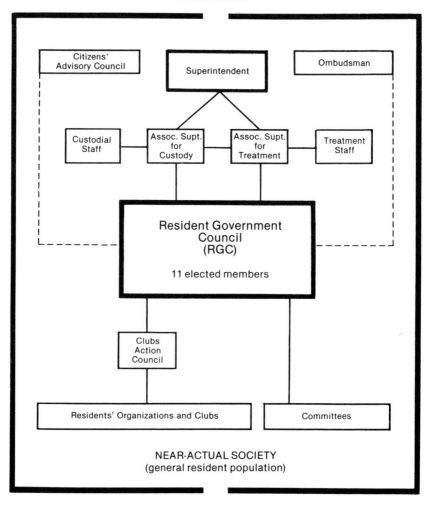

Figure 7-2. Residents' Government at WSP, 1972

dations on such matters as officer training, an ombudsman, and the classification committee; but the newspapers focused on its description of prisoners' conduct as often "uncivilized," the accusation that the prison
administration was "unresponsive to criticism."[52]

The accumulating strains within the prison polity doubtless fed into the fall 1972 crisis of confidence during which the fourth RGC resigned en masse and appealed to the state governor. From Warden Rhay's point of view, this mass resignation was an obvious power play. But from the perspective of the inmate politicians, it reflected their frustration with the rigidity of the system. Self-dissolution was in some ways an effective parliamentary means to express nonconfidence in the administration. After negotiations the body was reconstituted, and a joint staff-inmate committee was formed to reshape the constitution. The difficulty was that the problems deep within this prison polity would not yield to simple mechanical measures.[53]

Frustrations over the limits to self-government were building. A member of the reconstituted fourth RGC spoke for them all: "We should have the right to make decisions that affect the population and we don't. . . . It's pretty liberal for a prison, but . . . they keep the RGC's wings clipped, because actually what they are doing is stalling it in the effective arenas." Another spokesman elaborated: "We've submitted proposal after proposal, good ones, things that would help. And what do they do? They just keep putting it off, putting it off, until you just get so tired of pushing it that you drop it." As an example, this leader cited the council's attempt to introduce a drug treatment program.[54]

This theme is echoed by another councilman:

> We worked on a proposal for segregation that could really help some guys in there and the only thing they could come back was, oh, you will impair our security. . . . And he [Rhay] had the drug program we were talking about, just proposal after proposal stacked back there, and not once did they act on it, so that the warden says the other day, if this next [5th] RGC comes into office, if they don't get something down in a week or two he's going to really get on their case. All right, if he wants to do this, why don't he, then, get down and set up and start to implement some of those proposals?[55]

He continued:

> He [Rhay] seems to offer a lot of tokenism and in some of the things it's good . . . when I see the prison as what it is now, and what it was at one time, they could throw you in the hole for silent insolence, and I suppose they could do that now if they really wanted to. . . . But the thing is . . . they haven't moved one inch to try to help this population, they [the inmates] are not going to rehabilitate ourselves, they [the staff] are supposed to be trying to rehabilitate us, and for society. . . . We [the Fourth RGC] took and pooled all . . . [the past] proposals, and our own proposals and made up an agenda. . . . We went back in and it was a lot of hems and haws. . . . and nothing was ever done with all those proposals. . . . as far as self-government goes, we don't have anything to do with the policy made here in this institution.[56]

The long struggle over RGC participation in furlough decisions provides a striking illustration of these frustrations and of the persistent distrust between the keepers and the kept. A point of crisis came in early February 1972 with the killing of a state patrolman by a prisoner on temporary leave from WSP. The inmates insisted that they were effectively excluded (except for "tokenism") from the clearance process and that more direct RGC participation would make the system more selective. At a press conference held two days after the state trooper incident, the RGC presented statistics showing that 60 percent of those granted furloughs had prior escape records. At this meeting with the local media representatives, the RGC pressed for an enlarged role in the selection process. The RGC president argued that the "administration knows the man on paper, but we know the real man."[57]

There had been at least three separate RGC efforts at revising furlough and work-release selection criteria, including a proposal that had been rejected on a vote of the population. And at one point during this crisis over the furlough program, there was even a petition circulated among the inmates for recall of the RGC president. But at an emergency general assembly held immediately after the state trooper's shooting, the population gave a "98 percent vote of confidence" to the RGC's approach to the crisis.[58]

Collaborative management of screening mechanisms can create complex problems for inmate representatives and prison administration alike. In a report of a WSP staff meeting (with RGC observers in attendance), in March 1973, Rhay indicated that his staff felt that inmates "may have information we do not have about a man's chances for success in reduced custody." But since "we are sympathetic to the pressures such a [screening committee of inmates] will have" on it, the administration would want a simple "yes" or "no" recommendation, without asking for any of the reasoning.[59] This is only a sample of the involuted features of inmate participation at WSP.

The RGC's Decline

During the second year of self-government, there was growing unhappiness among the WSP population with the RGC system. The constitutional revision process (December 1972–March 1973) produced disappointingly meager results, but the attraction of constitutionalism was still compelling enough to spur the search for a way to make the concept a reality. The lead article of the WSP inmate newspaper of January 1973 featured an elaborate proposal to convert WSP into an incorporated city under the name Rhayville. While not taken very seriously, this project did advance some interesting ideas, especially in projecting a financially self-sufficient municipal enterprise, with minimum wages for labor and full-scale civic responsibility for the inhabitants of Rhayville.[60] But to the extent that the scheme represented a search for alternatives in developing an effective self-government, it reflected declining support for RGC-type representative government.

Inmate leaders were predicting the demise of the RGC at the very time the revised constitution was unveiled. Several believed that the fifth RGC, to be installed in the spring of 1973, could be that last one. According to one inmate, "The responsible people are not running for the Council. . . . They don't want no more of the garbage . . . and the tramps are running for the Council. . . . These are the people who have been controlling this penitentiary, politcally." But these same inmate critics argued that the realization of a responsible system, in concert with the administration, required reciprocity: "If the administration will say to the population we're going to do something here and we want the responsible leaders to step up . . . then the other guys that are coming out of the population say 'all right, now you're ready to work, we are too.'" Nevertheless these inmate leaders placed the principal onus on their fellow prisoners: "The convicts know who are the right ones . . . [and] the right ones are just not putting their names on the ballot."[61]

Interestingly Rhay himself attempted to structure a vote of confidence to demonstrate the decline of the RGC in the context of the inmate work-stoppage and subsequent lockdown ordered in June 1973. The warden then claimed to have received back 98 percent of the some seven hundred ballots distributed within the walls, recording the following results. A narrow majority (52 percent) opposed the work-stoppage that the RGC had called following a late-night informal poll. In answer to the question, "Do you have confidence in the present RGC to properly represent you?" less than a majority (49 percent) voted yes. On the longer-range issue of whether the RGC system should be retained, the population was given three choices; slightly more than one out of eight opted to abandon it outright, three out of eight voted to modify it in unspecified ways, and just under half (49 percent) wanted to support it.[62]

Another sign of the state of parliamentary "confidence" can perhaps be discerned in a bit of doggerel that was circulating at WSP about the time of Rhay's poll:

TO OUR ESTEEMED RGC

You quietly crept from north to south,
While noisily working both sides of your mouth.
Whatever the issue, you claimed expertise;
Your deepest convictions you changed with the breeze.
So, please won't you spare us anymore of your pap?
It's obvious to all that you're full of crap!
Want something for free? Please take our advice:
A swell case of lock-jaw would really be nice!

Subsequent efforts to revitalize the RGC system as a parliamentary arena were ultimately unsuccessful. Further attempts at constitutional revisionism, the favored route, failed to stem a growing inmate apathy toward the RGC and its politics. It was more and more difficult to get qualified candidates to run in the elections. The activists were increasingly occupied in other organizations or involved in therapy group or educational pursuits. This is not to say that the politicization process had necessarily run its course, but its impact was now more diffuse as the era of intensive radicalization had passed. Inmates showed a marked indifference toward being drawn into the RGC's activities and few were the potential leaders among the inmates who would any longer be attracted to the idea of staking their political career on identification primarily with the RGC and its activities.

Yet within the WSP polity, some believed that the RGC system might be salvaged once again through constitutional renovation. In preparation for the election of the eighth RGC in fall 1974, a new series of constitutional amendments, designed to enhance both the responsibility and the responsiveness of the system, was presented to the population. This had resulted in more than a months's delay in holding these elections, while inmates in barely sufficient numbers were being induced to offer themselves as candidates. The ballot listings, in quantity and quality, were a rather sorry showing, not encouraging in the drive for renewed credibility.

A key figure in the prison administration, associate superintendent for treatment Robert Freeman, gave his evaluation of the governance experiment while the elections were in progress.

> I think it's fair to say that the general feeling is that RGC is not working as it should—that, if it is to work, there has to be some changes in the thing. You see, when they came in they had great expectations that all sorts of certain wonderful things were going to happen. They didn't come about. Some of them . . . felt that there were going to be keys to the wing doors and that they could go out on speaking trips any time they wanted to and, you know, a lot of goodies they thought were going to come about and they didn't. And, as a result, there was an initial feeling that RGC wasn't any good. [But], really, if you look back on it, RGC has been effective in a number of things. . . . I happen to feel it could be a very effective group if some way you could get away from the wheeling and dealing and I don't know how to do that.[63]

The most striking innovation in the amended constitution was the creation of a new body called the "house of representatives." The objective, sound in principle, was to bring the prison club system into closer coordination with the RGC. This HR, as defined in the document, was essentially a consultative organ, not a legislative body. Within a structure reminiscent of the United Nations Security Council, it was to consist of five permanent members—representing the three racial-ethnic organizations (blacks, Indians, Chicanos) and the two largest specialized groupings (Lifers and Bikers)—plus two nonpermanent members selected by the big five from among the numerous smaller clubs and associations.

The vice-president of the seventh RGC, who was running unopposed for reelection, referred to the HR as "a watchdog," that would "keep an eye on us," meaning the councilmen.[64] But as Freeman pointed out, "They [the members of the HR] don't have power that I can see."[65] Moreover, the major clubs had long since established their own lines into the prison administration. And by this time the RGC had slipped to such a degree, both absolutely and in relation to the clubs, that it had virtually lost its function as a principal inmate channel for communication with the administration.

A second major innovation involved the introduction of a two-stage election system, consisting of a primary followed by a general election. By the time of the March 1975 general election, only the presidency was a two-way contest, while every other candidate on the primary ballot was uncontested.[66] Freeman gave his opinion on the reason for the paucity of good candidates for RGC positions: "There are certain people [inmates] I've talked to, that I know I've felt would be good men, that aren't interested at all. They're not interested in putting themselves in the position of being hassled all the time. Or being put in the position of negotiator or mediator or whatever it is."[67]

The RGC's vice-president, a Biker who was about to win his second term unopposed, argued that a principal impediment to the success of self-government lay in the lack of preparation of the inmates for running it. He spoke candidly in informal discussions:

> What do I know about elections and things? I've been a thief for eleven years. I understand hard-headed rule, you know, just a form of outlaw rule, I can understand that. . . . We need classes—these guys are going to have to be taught.
>
> We are thieves, armed robbers, you know, whatever you want to call us, and all of a sudden they expect us to be legislators, or self-governing—if we couldn't govern ourselves out on the streets, the majority of us, and then they come in here, and gave us self-government, [and said] do what you want with it. It's like giving kids a candy store.[68]

In mid-December 1974, the council presented the administration with an elaborate reorganization agenda, which appears, in retrospect, to have been a final effort to revive the representative system. This document could be read as a semi-ultimatum, making January 1, 1975, the deadline for carrying out most of the key demands. The agenda began by insisting that "the Constitution for Self-Government be strictly adhered to" and that the administration "agree to provide a more accurate interpretation" of the constitution for the participants in the current political-awareness class.

The long list covered the gamut from issues of classification and segregation to visiting policies and the hospital. The inmates were pressing for the replacement of the unpopular associate superintendent of custody and the removal of two of the medical staff. The agenda hit especially hard at the controversial issue of involuntary transfers carried out by custody.[69]

This broad agenda, even given its tough terms, could have served as a basis for negotiation; but by this time the bargaining arena had been decidedly narrowed and the RGC retained little of its former clout. Well aware of this, Warden Rhay was not inclined to yield on key insistences. And he was all the more ready to believe the worst when the events of December 30 occurred during the meeting called to discuss this particular agenda. The very weakness of the eighth RGC's position, so the reasoning went, could induce the council, or some of its more hot-headed members, to utilize a violent incident as a way of forcing the issue. Whatever validity there was in such an analysis—and Rhay clearly gave it credence—these events showed that the inmate system had deteriorated badly. Much more than the constitutional superstructure stood in need of repair.

On the eve of the RGC's dissolution, Superintendent Rhay expressed the view that he did not think "there is much future in self-government" in light of the experiences over the last several months. He pointed to the apathy of the population (20 percent turnout in the latest primaries), criminal charges pending against some RGC officers, and, in the state capital, the swing toward the view that inmate self-government at Walla Walla had run its course.[70] The warden's power position had been enhanced both by the RGC's decline and by the clear signal Rhay evidently had received from his superiors in the state capital that the decision on the future of inmate participation was now his to make. At this crucial juncture, he expressed his attitude toward the RGC system in the following way:

> I agree that input from the prison population has to be there; but what form that takes should be left pretty much up to the administrator. I certainly don't think something of this magnitude should be imposed on any institution at any level except those who want it. In other words, the state capital should never do it. If we learned anything in the world we learned that—and I think probably I'm more capable of judging it than most people around. I'm senior warden of the U.S.[71]

The state of mind of the few remaining representatives of the inmates' parliamentary system can be discerned in discussions that took place at RGC headquarters about three weeks prior to dissolution. Political renewal was, in principle, about to be launched in the new elections for a ninth council. The president—alone in not standing for election since he was midway in a twelve-month term— remarked:

Being on the RGC is a very frustrating experience. . . . You get tired of banging your head against the wall after awhile. . . . We had hoped by allowing people to run for a year [term] and staggering it every six months that the administration would lose their ability to play past people, in other words, to make you start all over again [every six months] to build up your credibility, because there would be certain people on the Council that already had this credibility and knew what was happening within the institution.[72]

The rationale of a two-stage electoral system was given as follows:

The general idea of having a primary election was that, once you become a candidate for this general election, then you went to school on the constitution . . . Then, when you became elected, you had a working knowledge of what the government was and what your capacity would be as a Council member . . . so that a man could have a little schooling and wouldn't go on to the Council cold.[73]

The one distinctive power of the house of representatives was its role on recall moves:

The HR would advise the RGC as a whole, give the clubs a chance to voice their opinions since they did represent certain segments—or a large majority of the population—and also handle the recall procedures. In the event that a staff member or another RGC member or a member of the population felt that somebody wasn't doing his job, this person would be investigated and given a hearing by the House of Representatives, which in turn would either quash it or make a recommendation for recall to the Council.[74]

Warden B.J. Rhay, basically dissatisfied with the RGC system—and now deeply irritated by the HR's failure to oust those whose actions Rhay felt warranted it after the December 30 events—made the decision to abolish these four-year old inmate institutions and precipitate a political regrouping.

The Fourth Constitution: The RC

From an institutional point of view, the structure of the Resident Council, which replaced the RGC in mid-1975, was yet another variation of the constitution for self-government first adopted in 1971. As the original constitution had reemerged in a revised form in the spring of 1973 and again in the fall of 1974, so the post-RGC version can be perceived as once again carrying through an exercise in constitutional revisionism.

The symbolism of governance had undergone drastic alteration, signaling fundamental changes that the prison administration and Harold

Bradley, the state's head of corrections, had insisted upon. The new council and its competence was described in the "Guidelines for Conduct of Resident Council," outlining a framework several steps removed from quasi-constitutional government. The words *government* and *constitution* had been removed, and the opening section on concept, replacing the preamble, contains the following explicit disavowal: "The Council is not intended to usurp any authority of the Superintendent of the Penitentiary, or the Director of Adult Corrections in the exercise of their ultimate responsibility for the management of the penitentiary."

These guidelines provided again for the familiar elected eleven-member council. Five officers, constituting an executive council, were elected each in a separate race; and the six remaining members were individually chosen to chair six special committees, each elaborately described in the document. Annual elections (late in the spring) with annual terms for council members reflected the trend of the previous revision toward longer terms. There were also provisions to invalidate elections in which fewer than 60 percent of the population voted and to require attendance at training courses between the primary and general election, on "Political Awareness, Adult Corrections Procedures and W.A.C. [state administrative code] Rules." The most novel articles set up a joint staff-resident arbitration committee (primarily to monitor the RC system itself) and a staff liaison group to advise the council. The committee structure of the RC features some name changes: the former People's Action Committee, charged with dealing with the immediate needs of the population, became the Area Liaison Committee, while the Race Relations Committee was redesignated the Equal Interaction Committee.

Not long after the RC had set up shop, it issued a "Statement of Policy" to the inmate population, indicating the nature and limits of its mandate:

> . . . It is the responsibility of this Council to act as intermediaries between the administration and population for purposes of communications and grievance resolutions. As it was very clearly pointed out at the Council's first meeting with the Administrative Staff, the Resident Council is not intended to function as a governmental body, but rather as a negotiating team or body, to negotiate resolutions to grievances, and to present to the Administration resident-initiated proposals.[75]

During the course of the initial RC (1975–1976), its members constantly debated the nature of their body and its role as the successor organ to the RGC. One analysis came from a black inmate member of the RC who compared the RGC and RC in the following conceptual terms:

> I think the whole RGC was considered more or less a government body, that they made policy and different things for the rest of this population. . . . This is the concept, I think, that the whole RGC worked under. I don't

think Mr. Rhay was ever really in accord with that particular concept. He naturally always maintained that he was the Superintendent, that anything that happened within the institution, he had the last say-so over whether it would happen or not. And in some cases, his say-so wasn't accepted, I don't believe, under the old Government Council. What is being done now is that we are not a government body, we are negotiators. We mediate situations, we don't make policies, or anything of this nature. We suggest things, we make proposals and present them to the administration, and we hold conferences in regards to the things we're trying to get.[76]

Some of the inmate leaders and politicians professed to have found a rationale for their new council. This same RC member saw the change as possibly salutary:

[The RGC] brought a lot of freedom in, but then it waned to the point where it was not controlled; nobody could control that self-governing situation. So by maybe this Council [RC] starting a new era, on another plane, another attitude, it could have the impetus to create another whole system, following up the freedoms that we have already achieved.[77]

An older white inmate, however, described the change from RGC to RC:

The great change is that the power is not possessed by the residents that was possessed. The RGC, we had the total government . . . with the RC, I don't feel that they have the power. . . . [Their] hands have been tied, you know, and that's not good. . . . The administration just doesn't recognize the RC the way they did the RGC, for the simple reason they don't have the power. Its just more or less a liaison committee now and . . . functioning the way the administration wants them to function.[78]

In fundamental ways, an era of constitutionalism in inmate governance had reached its end with the demise of the RGC. It was an inglorious conclusion to an initially hopeful participatory experiment. There had been a special mystique in the use of the term *government,* quite apart from any reality that this term may have described. While the inmates doubtless invested too much in the term itself, the prison administration, for that very reason, bridled at the term and could scarcely wait to expunge it.

But terminology aside, despite the similarities in structure between the RGC and the RC, the latter marked a lowering of expectations and a narrowing of functions. The RC was not taken very seriously; it stood as a token of participation rather than participation itself. It came to be viewed by the inmates as a facade behind which the prison administration was moving to reestablish, as far as it dared, certain features of that custodial and autocratic rule that had characterized the pre-1970 regime. Superintendent Rhay himself noted the similarity between this advisory council and the one that had existed in the prereform era.

Balance of an Era

Clearly WSP is today living in the shadow of the past decade and must come to terms with the bruising experiences through which it has passed. Rigid polarization between inmates and staff, deep antagonism among inmates and their groupings, contradictory pulls between participatory and authoritarian patterns of governance: these are the legacy of the 1970s. Not just at Walla Walla but across the country, the collaborative regime—the model held out by the 1967 President's Crime Commission—has gone into eclipse.

But the need to find a way out of the cycle of destructive conflict within the prison polity remains undiminished. In the era of the interactive prison, interventions of the federal judiciary can be helpful but can do little more than construct a floor of basic decency under the prison regime. By themselves, such measures will not repair the organizational and group life of the prison polity. Moreover, if not an exercise in futility, it is exceedingly difficult at the least to achieve even a barely humane milieu in the kind of warehousing fortress exemplified by WSP. Amos Reed, secretary of Washington's new Department of Adult Corrections, expressed "a feeling of desperation" concerning overpopulated and obsolete institutions such as Walla Walla.[79]

There are many reasons for discouragement and the violence which marks the present political life within WSP is undoubtedly one of the most important. On the plane of superstructure—that is, the level on which the building and operating of constitutional systems takes place—WSP's inmate polity was notably unsuccessful. The various RGC constitutions had a short life span, marked by an ongoing revision process. The various replacement models were doubtful improvements over the earlier ones.[80] There was a progressive loss of confidence in the workability of a parliamentary system, a trend that brought the reform program as a whole into disrepute. Yet tattered as its banner became, the ethos of political *liberalization* was never wholly discredited. The most fruitful approach to the rehabilitation of inmate participation, within some sort of representative framework, is likely to lie in the gradual strengthening of lines of communication into the prison polity's policy-making arenas, coupled with the re-emergence of respected inmate leadership.

Organizational and group life blossomed for a time but in the longer run failed to live up to its promise. Its development was uneven, warped by serious flaws, never able to find a secure basis of common interest. The result was degeneration into an internecine "war of all against all," a shattered inmate polity, a polycentrism spun out of control. At an early stage of the reform era, observers had noted a sharp drop in inmate-on-inmate violence, compared to the prereform period.[81] But beginning at mid-decade, the volume of violence increased sharply.

In looking for the sources of the deterioration of the group life of

WSP's inmate polity, we find serious deficiencies in the politicization process. An effectively operating political pluralism assumes the functional equivalent of political parties, which then moves the class struggle into the political arena, making possible the reconciliation and compromise of conflicting interests. At WSP the inmate polity succeeded in doing this only for a year and a half to two years. After that it depended upon a precarious balance of power which was subject to frequent breakdowns. Nevertheless pluralization and *democratization* remains a fact of life at Walla Walla. Even with the progressive weakening of the club system, (for example, through deprivation of "turf"), the inmate organizations still function substantially above ground. The prison polity is not unresponsive, in some sense of the term, to these groups and their interests. What is lacking at this juncture is the capacity to integrate these multiple groupings into a responsible system of inmate governance.

On the broadest and most basic level of development of any polity—the structural level—*detotalization* goes forward. In retrospect, it seems clear that WSP's political culture was evolving in a more open direction, parallel to the trend in many other American prisons following World War II. In the 1960s as the pace quickened toward a more radical politicization of inmates, Walla Walla lagged behind California and other centers of unrest. Then at the beginning of the 1970s, WSP made its "great leap forward." Its leap was primarily a reformist one, and it was seen in a somewhat exaggerated light. Even so, the myths and artifacts of this reform era left a lasting imprint on Walla Walla's inmate political culture. The prison administration's later efforts at retrenchment could not succeed in fundamentally altering the political arena that had emerged from these earlier processes.

The attempt to reverse the cultural thaw brought on violence. Just prior to the four-month crisis of summer 1979, a news report was circulating that the authorities were seriously considering turning the clock back on hair and dress codes and in other liberalized areas.[82] This proposal was quickly buried in the ensuing furor. The administration might deprive the inmates of a governance council without much protest, but reinstituting the former cultural rigidities would bring on a bitter fight. For the inmates, changes in these areas were the symbols of a new order of prison life. Inmate councils could come and go, but these were truly "the freedoms that we have already achieved."[83]

Plainly the inmate polity has developed unevenly with respect to detotalization, democratization, and liberalization. This evolution, of course, took place neither wholly on its own nor in isolation. The larger context was the prison polity as a whole, which in turn functions within the overall political system. In earlier chapters, we have frequently pointed to considerations stemming from this total environment; and in this summation, one or two salient points bear repeating.

After Conte's departure in 1971 as head of the prison system, the reforms did not have consistent or strongly committed leadership to keep them going. Conte's reform-minded successors at the state level had grave doubts that the ground had been adequately prepared for liberalizing a traditional institution such as WSP. They had concluded that it was already too late (in 1974) to revive the experiment. Here the issue of what was *believed* about the pre-1970 preparations becomes all important. Conte had, in fact, worked since 1966 to bring reform into the institutions, yet administrators such as B.J. Rhay felt that the reform program had been thrust upon them—suddenly, in 1970—and officials who later came to Olympia generally accepted Rhay's interpretation. Their approach was to allow the great experiment in inmate participation to wither. Its direct repeal was far too risky.

From the beginning, the larger prison polity—inmates, guards, treatment staff, administration—had been fragmented. Incompatible subcultures fed into conflicting interests and seemingly irreconcilable goals. Here the search for some basis of common interest was hampered by the breaks in continuity at higher governmental levels and the weakness of commitment to the reform program at all levels.

Historically prison-reform experiments have been made through the leadership and nurturing of reform wardens, Osborne and Gill among them. When support at the system's center was withdrawn, their projects could not survive. It was, however, typically the warden who was central to the making of the experiment, not the state director. Thus the fact that WSP's long-term warden was ambivalent in his commitment to the reforms may well have been decisive.

In addition, the almost unremitting hostility of the custodial staff towards the reforms was also an important factor in their failure. The prisoners, as we have seen, made their own contribution to the result. But, given their backgrounds, their grim environment, and their lack of preparation for the radical change, what is perhaps most astonishing was that they were able to keep the Walla Walla experiment in self-government going for more than four years; that, almost overnight, some of the self-styled thieves and armed robbers indeed became legislators.

Notes

1. See John P. Conrad and Simon Dinitz, "Position Paper on the Isolated Prisoner" (Columbus, Ohio: Academy for Contemporary Problems, 1977).

2. Ibid., p. 33.

3. Ibid., pp. 7–9. See also James B. Jacobs, *Stateville* (Chicago: University of Chicago Press, 1977).

4. Personal communication.

5. The changing relationship between authority and force in the prison society is reflected in the treatment of the issue in the 1950s by Sykes, a leading sociologist, and views expressed in the 1970s by a younger political scientist, Berkman. (See Gresham M. Sykes, *The Society of Captives* (Princeton: Princeton University Press, 1958), pp. 46–48, and Ronald Berkman, *Opening the Gates* (Lexington, Mass.: Lexington Books, D.C. Heath and Company, 1979), pp. 11–12, 159–160. Taking as given that inmates did not regard the prison administration's authority as usurpation, Sykes observed that the prisoners' lack of "an inner moral compulsion to obey" requires that they be "forced, bribed, or cajoled into compliance." Berkman rejects the dissociation between inmates' behavior and their views about authority; he perceives recognition of the legitimacy of the regime as steadily decreasing; the prisoners' compliance, then, can be obtained only by force, requiring a much more coercive system, ironically, than Sykes contemplated. Moreover, according to Berkman, the prison administration has not only been delegitimized in the inmates' eyes, but it is now widely seen as a lawless agency, resisting the courts and covering up its illegal activities.

6. In addition to Berkman, *Opening the Gates,* see John Irwin, *Prisons in Turmoil* (Boston: Little, Brown, 1980); and John Pallas and Robert Barber, "From Riot to Revolution," in *The Politics of Punishment,* ed. Erik Olin Wright (New York: Harper & Row, 1973), pp. 237–261.

7. Irwin, *Prisons,* pp. 62–63, argues that an important factor in the delegitimization of correctional institutions lay in this disappointment with rehabilitation. The indeterminate sentence, in particular, became very unpopular. But this disaffection with the treatment model applies more to white prisoners than to minority inmates whose principal grievances lay elsewhere.

8. James B. Jacobs, *Stateville: The Penitentiary in Mass Society* (Chicago: University of Chicago Press, 1977), p. 59.

9. The importance of the Muslims' legal challenges, which initially stimulated the judiciary's abandonment of the hands-off doctrine, is emphasized by many analysts. See ibid., pp. 59–70, 255–256.

10. *The Autobiography of Malcolm X* (New York: Grove Press, 1964); Eldridge Cleaver, *Soul on Ice* (New York: McGraw-Hill, 1968); George Jackson, *Soledad Brother: The Prison Letters of George Jackson* (New York: Bantam Books, 1970) and *Blood in My Eye* (New York: Bantam Books, 1972). See also Etheridge Knight, *Black Voices from Prison* (New York: Pathfinder Press, 1970).

11. Discussion, August 1972.

12. On the political attitudes of the early 1970s, among selected Wash-

ington State prison inmates, see Erika S. Fairchild, "Politicization of the Criminal Offender: Prisoner Perceptions of Crime and Politics," *Criminology* 15 (November 1977):287–318. For more detail, see Fairchild, "Crime and Politics: A Study in Three Prisons" (Ph.D. diss., University of Washington, 1974).

13. Frank Browning, "Organzing behind Bars," *Ramparts* (February 1972):40–45.

14. "Walla Walla," KING (TV) Seattle 1971.

15. Ibid.

16. The administrative directive, applying to all adult correctional institutions, issued in November 1970 spoke only of making "available . . . *opportunities for participation* in democratic government" (Emphasis added). It is clearly stated that the competence of the Residents' Government was recommendatory and that "it is to be understood that the final responsibility and authority for the operation of an institution is vested, by law, in the superintendent." *Prison Law Reporter* 1 (January 1972):96.

17. Discussion, October 1975. Later in the discussion, this inmate formulated the "only difference" as being that in pre-RGC days, "the leaders of the joint got together and went . . . [to] Bob Rhay. Now you got an elected body that does exactly the same damn thing—it's just an arbitrating committee."

18. Discussion, March 1973.

19. Interview with Rhay, March 1973. "You can't imagine the void that was created by this." Rhay's concern appeared to be that his authority was undercut, particularly in the eyes of the guard staff.

20. For example, James Madison, in no. 10 of *Federalist* (1788), singled out "faction" as a prime threat to the budding United States constitutional system.

21. American political scientists have been debating over many years how realizeable this ideal can ever be. The dispute has been between those who argue the perfectibility of grassroots democracy within the given system in the United States (Dahl) and those whose perception of the status quo equates it with the pervasive rule of a "power elite" (Mills). See Robert Dahl, *Who Governs?* (New Haven: Yale University Press, 1961) and *Pluralist Democracy in the United States: Conflict and Consent* (Chicago: Rand McNally, 1967); C. Wright Mills, *The Power Elite* (New York: Oxford University Press, 1959).

22. Richard R. Korn and Lloyd W. McCorkle, *Criminology and Penology* (New York: Henry Holt, 1959), p. 525. See also Lloyd E. Ohlin, *Sociology and the Field of Corrections* (New York: Russell Sage Foundation, 1956), p. 14.

23. Irwin, *Prisons,* p. 35.

24. See Milton Burdman, "Ethnic Self-Help Groups in Prison and On

Parole" *Crime and Delinquency,* (April 1974):107–118, concerning the "potential value" of these kinds of groups in attaining the aims of corrections as against their "potential for violence."

25. An inmate (interviews, March 1975 and April 1978) stresses the interconnections between inside and outside: "The BLP is an organization that started outside of the pen primarily by the ex-convicts who have become members of the Black Panther Party [and] of a couple other liberation black movement parties outside . . . Underneath the BLP we were all Panthers. There was a branch formed inside but we could not just come out and say we're parts of the Panther Party. We stayed under the banner of the BLP . . . We were the first group inside the joint to hold closed meetings [no guards present] with people from the outside."

26. Interview, August 1972.

27. Ibid.

28. Interview, March 1975.

29. Interview, April 1978.

30. Ibid. The White Citizens Council was not recognized, but the Bikers became official (WSPMA).

31. Ibid.

32. Ibid.

33. Quoted in Barry Farrell, "A New Way to Run the Big House," *Life,* September 8, 1972, p. 41.

34. Interviews, March 1973, March 1975.

35. Discussion, August 1972. One inmate, interviewed in 1978, estimated a year and a half (1971–1972) as the period during which, despite administrative divide-and-rule tactics, inmate unity remained intact.

36. This was embarrassing to the guards and may have been premature for WSP. See "Inmates Back [Guards'] Strike," *Seattle Post Intelligencer,* February 19, 1975.

37. Discussion, April 1976.

38. For a recent empirical study, see James G. Fox, *The Organizational Context of the Prison: A Study of Five Maximum Security Prisons* (Sacramento, Calif.: American Justice Institute, 1980).

39. See Berkman, *Opening the Gates,* pp. 114–116, for an analysis of the restriction of inmate groups to the nonpolitical. For background, see R. Theodore Davidson, *Chicago Prisoners: The Key to San Quentin* (New York: Holt, Rinehart and Winston, 1974).

40. Interview, April 1978.

41. See Gabrielle Tyrnauer and Charles Stastny, "The Changing Political Culture of a Total Institution: The Case of Walla Walla," *Prison Journal* 57 (Autumn–Winter 1977):43–53.

42. Rhay's views were most explicitly stated in a March 1975 interview, conducted just before the RGC was abolished by him.

43. On the rise of "gangs" and "super-gangs" in maximum-security prisons, see Jabobs, *Stateville,* pp. 138–174.

44. *Unique People/VOP,* February 1977.

45. "B.J. Rhay on Tour," ibid., (March 1977).

46. According to Robert MacIver, a political theorist, the party system is "the democratic translation of the class struggle." R.M. MacIver, *The Web of Government* (New York: Macmillan, 1947), p. 217.

47. See Arnold S. Kaufman, "Human Nature and Participatory Democracy," in *The Bias of Pluralism,* ed. William E. Connolly (New York: Atherton Press, 1969), pp. 178–200. Kaufman argues that the participatory and representative systems serve distinct functions, making necessary a choice between the two. Here we make no such distinction but find both necessary for guided prison democracy.

48. See Peter Bachrach, Morton S. Baratz, and Margaret Levi, "The Political Significance of Citizen Participation," in *Power and Poverty: Theory and Practice,* eds. Peter Bachrach and Morton S. Baratz (New York: Oxford University Press, 1970), pp. 201–213.

49. Under the terms of the DSHS Memorandum on Residents' Government of November 6, 1970, the superintendent "will have veto powers. It is to be understood, further, that the exercise of that veto power will require great wisdom and will demand a clear supporting statement of why the veto has been found necessary." *Prison Law Reporter* 71 (January 1972):76.

50. RGC, "Self-Government Statement," mimeographed (1972). The following discussion is based largely on this document.

51. *Prisoners Coalition,* newsletter (March 1972). The newsletter also states: "Everyone in this institution is a political prisoner because each is a victim of the corrupt, exploitative society and culture of Amerika [sic]. Only a small percentage of the prisoners are currently aware of their political status, but the rate is increasing."

52. Jo Moreland, "Irresponsibility Pervades Prison, Report Charges," *Walla Walla Union-Bulletin,* September 15, 1972. The authors of the report included two correctional sergeants working in the minimum-security building; two former RGC presidents, both now residing in the Building; the president of the MSB-Lifers; and the Citizens' Advisory Council (CAC) chairman.

53. The revised constitution, prepared by the joint staff-inmate committee in the months prior to its ratification in March 1973, included a new preamble referring to a "common contract" and a "frame-work of understanding" embracing both residents and staff. As a statement of the principle of collaborative governance, this was a distinct advance over the original charter. A code of ethics for RGC members was also contained in the proposed draft. There was, however, no basic alteration in the fundamental structure of the governance machinery that would establish actual mechanisms for inmate-staff collaboration.

54. Discussion at RGC Headquarters, March 1973.

55. Ibid. That same month (March 1973), the inmates filed in court for a writ of mandamus to compel the penitentiary to provide them with drug treatment. See *Prison Law Reporter* 2 (March 1973):242–243.

56. Discussion, March 1973.

57. RGC, "Weekly Report," February 1972, esp. pp. 38–45. Informally, inmate leaders suggested on numerous occasions that the prison administration was attempting to scuttle the furlough program through its loose screening. A few days later, Governor Evans, responding to demands to curb the program and the threat of possible legislative action to terminate it, issued a directive restricting furlough to those classified for minimum security. RGC Public Relations reacted by thanking Evans for having "just saved the furlough program from being completely removed." The RGC press release stressed the need for selection by "collaborative decision" with residents: "Collaborative management . . . stressed as check-balances against escape prone or potentially dangerous offenders. . . . Residents strongly recommend citizens from community and members of law enforcement to be a part of selecting process."

58. Ibid., pp. 22, 42, 45.

59. Summary of WSP Superintendent's Meeting, March 16, 1973.

60. See *Voice of Prison*, January 11, 1973. The project involved filing in the courts for legal incorporation of Rhayville. Associate Superintendent Freeman evidently tried to quash the *VOP* article, but the authors of the scheme reportedly appealed to Warden Rhay's vanity, telling him that "in naming this place Rhayville we're talking about a tribute to you. So he says, 'OK, OK, go ahead.' " Rhayville seemed to many to be essentially a stunt and the proposal soon died. Still, the blueprint stands as the principal example of a utopian project constructed by WSP's inmates, near the high point of their hopes for prison democracy. The internal regime of Rhayville was to be concerned exclusively with treatment and education, except for a police department drawn from among the residents, which would "maintain law and order within the limits of the city." Other than that, custody would move to the perimeter. Rhayville, in short, gave scope to both custody and treatment, within a framework of legal order protecting normal patterns of social and economic activity.

61. Discussions in minimum-security building, March 1973. During this discussion one inmate alleged: "We asked Bob Rhay and the Captain if they were ready to go up on stage and say, 'Okay, kiddies, the game's over. You either function or you don't leave the penitentiary [on Council business]. You either elect the proper people on the Council or there is no Council' . . . Rhay says 'that's a fantastic idea; let me think about it.' . . . Two days later some people in the population said [to him], 'let us handle the situation.' So they're handling it and they've gone back to the same garbage." This view was expressed shortly before the election for the fifth

RGC. Rhay went at least part way in his speech at the subsequent installation dinner to make the kind of public exhortation urged by this MSB resident: "We have to produce or stop talking like we are going to produce," the warden said to the newly elected councilmen. "Resolve that you will not become any more bogged down in petty grievances or individual cases, that you will look at things that are good for the population as a whole, the institution as a whole, and the administration as a whole" (RGC Banquet, March 29, 1973).

62. For discussion of this referendum and the surrounding circumstances, see Tyrnauer and Stastny, "Changing Political Culture," p. 46. Another ballot question, which was supposed to be answered only by those who responded no on the query about their confidence in the RGC, concerned support for alternative representation. Some 40 percent indicated a preference for being represented by the heads of inmate clubs or by an outside neutral group. However, the question was posed in a confusing way; and the total figures indicate that about one-third of those who expressed confidence in the incumbent RGC cast a vote on this issue as well.

63. Interview, October 1974, (Robert Freeman).

64. Interview, October 1974, (vice-president of RGC).

65. Interview, October 1974, (Freeman).

66. The electoral system called for twelve nominees for councilman to emerge from the primary, of whom six would be chosen in the general election. The field, however, included only fifteen names, of whom one was currently on escape. The top three offices—president, vice-president, and secretary—were to be chosen separately. Of the three candidates for president, one would be dropped out by the primary; the vice-presidential candidate (a Biker) was unopposed; and the two candidates for secretary would both appear on the general election ballot. Thus the significance of this primary election was minimal.

The rationale presented by RGC officers just after the primaries of March 1975, for which there was a 20 percent turnout, consisted of the claim that between the primary and the general election, nominees "went to school on the Constitution . . . [so] when you became elected, you had a working knowledge of what the government was and what your capacity would be as a council member." Discussion with the eighth RGC, March 1975. This was apparently the implementation of the following clause: "Once elected, a candidate will be required to attend available classes in the fundamentals of administrative responsibilities, political awareness of the elected position and RGC Constitution," Art. 2, sec. 2(C). Somewhat similar reasons explain the adoption of a system of one-year staggered terms, certain offices in the eighth RGC having been designated for a six-month term and others (including the presidency) for a full year. The RGC president maintained that "self-government had deteriorated simply because every time you had an election . . . they had to start all over—they didn't have any rapport with the administration." But while his case rested on the concept of extended overlapping terms, it developed that the other council members with year-long terms were no longer serving and that he alone was to continue on into the ninth council. Discussion, March 1975. It seems evident that to make such an elaborate electoral system function meaningfully requires a competitive political arena and a degree of political sophistication that the inmates clearly lacked. Putting this two-stage vote into operation risked exposing the level of apathy.

67. Interview, October 1974. During the term of each of the RGCs, there had been a number of resignations followed by the co-opting of other inmates to fill the vacancies until the next election. This method was used to keep the balance among the inmate groups but obviously changed the results. A persistent pattern, it tended to intensify from council to council.

68. Interview, October 1974. In a statement for publication this vice-president described the RGC as being "as good as it will ever be"; but if it is to be "effective," it "must be willing to make a firm stand with the administration." *"It's Happening at WSP"/VOP,* October 1974.

69. WSP-RGC, "Re-Organization Agenda," December 19, 1974.

70. Interview, March 1975.

71. Ibid. In the context of this discussion, Rhay was careful to exclude the pluralistic club system from his strictures concerning "self-government" as it was embodied in the RGC: "Even if I were to abandon what is known as RGC, I would certainly not lose the communication device that is presented by the clubs. In reality, I think the clubs more accurately represent the population than any elected group could. The clubs represent anywhere from 75–80% of the population. The strength of the whole movement is that very thing—the ethnic and club movements are the strength of the institution."

72. Discussion with eighth RGC, March 1975.

73. Ibid. This rationale for a term of tutelage is in accord with what has been termed "co-optative participation."

74. Ibid.

75. Residents Council: "Statement of Policy" (August 28, 1975), printed in *Voice of Prison* (September 1975):5. Emphasis added.

76. Discussion with RC members, April 1976.

77. Ibid.

78. Discussion with RC members, October 1975. This inmate went further to claim that, when the change-over occurred, the RGC had deteriorated to such an extent that there was widespread disillusionment with self-government itself: "Most [of the population] were so disgusted that it took a lot of selling just to get the present RC ratified, you know, the guidelines, constitution. . . . They didn't want anything really, they had no faith in

anything. And to be quite frank, they have no faith in anything at the present time.''

79. In an interview with Tom Wicker, at the 1981 convention in Miami of the American Correctional Association: "How to 'Revulse' the Public," *New York Times,* August 21, 1981, p. 31.

80. Thomas Murton divides participatory-management models, broadly gradated by the inmates' increasing share in governance, into four types: token, quasi-governmental, governmental, and full participation. Measured by this typology, Murton rates the RGC system at Walla Walla as quasi-governmental. Murton, *Shared Decision-Making as a Treatment Technique in Prison Management* (St. Paul: Murton Foundation for Criminal Justice, 1975), pp. 13, 107–116.

81. See Shelby Scates, "Prison Reform," *Seattle Post Intelligencer,* June 4, 1972. The writer notes, among other things, "a remarkable lack of racial tension."

82. See Hilda Bryant, "Prison Inmates Riled at Talk of Tougher Rules," *Seattle Post Intelligencer,* June 14, 1979.

83. Discussion with a black inmate leader (and others), April 1976.

8   A Penitentiary and the Constitution

In the course of a few years, the prison community we have described lost whatever coherence it may have once had. The traditional order of overt custodial control and covert accommodation between rulers and ruled was shattered by the reforms and the social changes underlying them; the new collaborative regime proved ephemeral. The administration's drive to restore the old authoritarian order unloosed a torrent of violence, which was countered with violent repression. Even while the administration proclaimed its retaking of the penitentiary, a number of forces assured that its victory might be a pyrrhic one. The most dramatic of these was intervention of a federal court, which attempted to apply strict controls on this restoration process.

The Debate over Judicial Intervention

The actual impact of court decisions on American prisons over the past two decades has been highly controversial. Clearly, there is often a large gap between the rulings of the courts concerning prisoners' rights and their implementation.[1] In addition, after a period of massive judicial intervention there has now begun a retreat. The courts, in a time of increasingly conservative judicial appointments and in the wake of the conservative swing of public opinion, have found ways of reinstituting the "hands-off" policy in all but name.[2] Courts in any event have a limited capacity to monitor administrative decision-making and enforce standards within the prison. As a noteworthy exception, James Jacobs relates a case in which financial damages were assessed against prison officials, the "most effective remedy," for failure to attend to an inmate's medical needs.[3]

Nevertheless, as Jacobs shows, even where the courts' commands are applied, they are often blunted. Perhaps the best example of this has been in the area of internal punishment for infractions (typically consignment of inmates to isolation or disciplinary segregation) and the disciplinary processes leading to such punishments.[4] Jacobs and Gordon Hawkins have both drawn on the study made in the early 1970s by Harvard's Center for Criminal Justice of the implementation of Federal Judge Raymond J. Pettine's order establishing detailed procedures on disciplinary matters at Rhode Island's Adult Correctional Institution (ACI). One of the key findings of the Harvard study was that, while the court-prescribed "procedural due process model" aims to install a process of fair and honest fact-finding, the disciplinary procedures at the Rhode Island prison were "pervasively dispositional" in deciding who goes to the "hole" and for how long. It is not surprising, therefore, that this study concludes that the "disciplinary . . . procedures at the ACI, observed . . . after the imposition of the decree, did not meet the expectations of the court."[5] The way in which the due process model is undermined in actual practice provides a general lesson on the prospects for virtually any new prison project:

> The success or failure of any new correctional program depends upon the . . . attitudes of the custodial as well as the administrative staff toward the change. Where there is antagonism, no amount of care in drafting meticulous provisions and structuring intricate processes will achieve . . . a fair and impartially administered disciplinary system.[6]

Thus the effective carrying out of a court's mandate necessarily assumes a substantial amount of good faith on the part of the prison administration and staff; for, as Jacobs and others have argued, courts are in a poor position to control the myriad of administrative decisions that make up the daily life of the inmate.[7] Thus, juridical norms often will be attenuated and mangled as they enter the prison. Nevertheless, direct judicial intervention, such as Judge Pettine's imposition of due process requirements in disciplinary proceedings, does make a considerable impact on both inmates and prison administrators. The Harvard study reports a "positive inmate response" to the concern shown by the judiciary. It reflects a change in the status of prisoners, which cannot fail to be transmitted to the political sphere. This same study finds also "a growing recognition by administrative and custodial staff that inmates do have rights, rights that would be contested and enforced."[8] Consciousness of these changes acts as a restraining influence on the prison's authoritarianism.

The 1970 Rhode Island case applied narrowly to the reform of one particular area of prison practices, as governed by *due process* standards (the Fourteenth Amendment). Almost simultaneously, in a more encompassing example of judicial activism, a federal court was invoking the Eighth Amendment to order Arkansas "to make a prompt and reasonable start toward eliminating the conditions that have caused the Court to condemn the system [at the state penitentiary]."[9] This case marks the beginning of the *cruel and unusual punishment* rulings as applied to the entire range of conditions within American prisons. Over the succeeding decade, the Eighth Amendment motif appeared in cases involving half the states, including Rhode Island.[10] The effect of such broad judicial intrusion was to place the federal courts squarely into the prison political arena, and give judges a role that could not fail to raise controversy.

Yet even the most restrained assessments of the potentialities of judicial involvement, such as the 1972 Harvard study, had insisted that the "courts must continue to intervene . . . because no viable alternative exists."[11] Courts obviously have limits to their role, but they remain vital to the process. As Herman Schwartz has put it, "Change still seems very risky to many administrators, and few are willing to surrender any power to inmates. Since prisoners have almost no independent sources of power, change will have to be externally imposed, and only courts can—or are likely to—do this." Schwartz sees the courts' activism as helping to legitimize prisoners' grievances by putting "a moral imprimatur" on these complaints; it provides an "excuse" for reform-minded prison administrators, since "courts can relieve sympathetic but fearful administrators of the responsibility for making changes."[12] On the other side, critics of the "imperial judiciary," such as Nathan Glazer, are not only skeptical of the beneficence of judicial intervention in social policy but fearful of undermining the administrator's policy-making authority. Glazer singles out Federal Judge Frank M. Johnson, Jr., who among other things had ordered Alabama to install a classification system in the prisons. Glazer argues that, in view of the philosophical debate then going on over the efficacy of rehabilitation, this should be "a matter of prison policy . . . rather than a matter of right."[13] The charge that Judge Johnson was intruding improperly into administrative prerogatives came not only from academic sources. But despite sharp modification of this initial order by an appeals court, Johnson persisted. The stubborn resistance of Governor George Wallace, exacerbated by the long-standing political feud between Johnson and Wallace, further politicized the issue and stiffened legislative resistance to the costs of reforms.[14] Fully three years after Judge Johnson's original Eighth Amendment prison ruling, the issue of compliance took a unique turn. Wallace was out of office and Johnson had negotiated with Governor Forrest James to place the prison system into receivership, naming the governor as the court-appointed receiver, with full authority but responsible to the judge.[15]

The implementation of judicial orders has proved to be a problem not only in Alabama. In the shadow of this ongoing debate over the propriety of these judicial intrusions, the courts on the whole have been cautious. Much of the resulting deference to the states' authority derives from a frank appreciation of the practical difficulties in implementing judicial decrees in the prison setting. These limits of judicial action are seen by radical critics of the prison system as inherent in the nature of courts and law. To bring about "real reforms," asserts Brian Glick,

> Judges would have to transfer authority over prisons to prisoners themselves, or to black, brown, and poor white communities, since only people with the same cultural background and class interests as prisoners can be

counted on to respect prisoners' rights. Such a substantial change in power relationships is obviously beyond the legal or political capacity of a court. . . . The U.S. political and legal system gives [judges] neither the power nor the inclination to enforce basic changes in the internal power structure of prisons. As a result, court rulings can have little significant impact on prison life.[16]

Glick and Glazer represent two opposing critical positions. Glick would require much greater judicial activism in pursuit of certain ideal ends. Glazer would preserve the discretionary authority of the custodians and thus block the expansion of inmates' rights at the expense of administrators' power.[17] Yet the norm of a collaborative regime, while not contemplating the complete transfer of authority to prisoners, would surely require some redistribution of power. Inmates almost universally welcome the symbolic change in their status enunciated by judicial decisions, quite apart from the actual implementation of court decrees. They sense that the courts have shaken a hierarchical pattern of authority, nudging it in the direction of a somewhat more coordinate relationship.

The deep involvement the inmates have had in the legal culture before landing in prison has been essentially oppositional. Trial, sentence, release process—all reflect the outside society's hostility and rejection. Until recently this negative experience was compounded by the essential arbitrariness of the prison regime. The very idea that there can be regularized restraints—that is, constitutional checks—on prison officials alters the prison order in a more positive direction. Nor does the adversary framework of lawsuits in itself represent a revival of hostile confrontation; rather it marks the assimilation of culturally-sanctioned forms used for the resolution of disputes.

The litigious quality in American culture is notorious and, even in previous eras, inmate culture to an extent reflected it. The "jailhouse lawyer" was long a fixture of virtually every prison. Lawbreakers resisted finally severing their relationship to the law, however futile their efforts to utilize legal channels for their own benefit. Yet the pursuit of prison lawsuits had little point so long as the hands-off judicial doctrine prevailed. Today, whatever the deficiencies or excesses of judicial decision-making, prisoners throughout the country have become aware that they have been at least partially readmitted to the legal-political culture.

Walla Walla in the Legal Arena

Early Cases

As early as 1961 a prisoner at WSP had filed a suit against Superintendent B.J. Rhay, which hinged on a claim under the Thirteenth Amendment that prison rules requiring him to work, prior to the final disposition of his appeal in the state supreme court, amounted to "involuntary servitude."[18] The case, which went up to the Ninth Circuit Court of Appeals before being dismissed, reaffirmed that the Thirteenth Amendment provides little help to prisoners. Forced labor tied to "punishment for crime" is explicitly excluded from the amendment's coverage.[19]

Toward the end of the 1960s, an inmate sued Rhay for intercepting correspondence to the prisoner's attorney, the correspondence assertedly violating prison regulations that barred "complaints about institution personnel, inmates or policies." The district court judge dismissed the case, observing that the inmate's interdicted letter exhibited "a pathological fixation with the subject of sodomy."[20] Six months later, WSP's reform program would abolish all forms of censorship.

A year into the reform era, a group of inmates fought a civil rights action against Governor Dan Evans together with the entire correctional hierarchy. Three months after the filing of this omnibus complaint, the district judge peremptorily dismissed it as "frivolous" and as involving nothing more than "a rehash of the same prisoner gripes that have been presented to this Court [before]."[21] But the period of the reforms seemed congenial to the use of the legal arena and such setbacks failed to dampen the inmate's litigious spirit. Another complaint attacking prison conditions at WSP was pressed as far as the federal appeals court, which promptly sent the case back to the district court with the admonition that a prisoner was entitled to his day in court.[22]

Inside Walla Walla, inmate leaders, in an effort to clarify their new rights, began to question the formal legal status of the RGC constitution, together with the availability of remedies for its violation. During a special meeting in early 1974, assistant attorney general William Collins informed inmate leaders that the RGC constitution was not a binding legal contract. Rather it was "something the institution has promised to live up to."[23] But these inmates were less interested in promises than in enforceable legal commitments.

Encouraged by Conte's philosophy of corrections, Washington prisoners were also turning to the courts to assert a right to treatment, especially in the area of drug addiction. Litigation began in 1973 with a suit on behalf of the inmates of all of the state's adult penal institutions aimed at compelling treatment for drug addiction.[24] The initial suit was displaced by the *Bresolin* case, which led to a distinctly favorable state supreme court ruling in 1975.[25] The court seemed prepared to mandate an effective program at WSP. But *Bresolin* v. *Morris* was based on statute rather than constitutional grounds; so the state legislature responded by promptly modifying the law that had established such treatment in institutions. And when the *Bresolin* case again reached the state's highest tribunal in 1977, a divided court decided that the establishment of a drug treatment program was purely discretionary, not mandatory. The dissenting opinion argued strongly that "the power of the courts to intervene to protect inmates from conditions which threaten their health or safety" must apply to an addict held within "a closed setting," who has shown "a willingness and desire to cure his addiction." The majority opinion, however, pointed to the ongoing debate, with its burgeoning literature, that questioned "the entire concept of rehabilitation as a practical goal of confinement . . ." The state's highest court, adopting a posture of judicial restraint, then fell back on the observation that "courts are ill equipped" to administer prisons and therefore must give "deference to the appropriate prison authorities."[26]

Hoptowit

The opportunity to test the degree of deference that the courts would concede to the prison officials of Washington State was soon to come. Prisoners' rights issues, especially as they touched on the U.S. Constitution, were being extensively litigated in the lower federal courts, with an occasional intervention by the U.S. Supreme Court. Judges were cautious on the whole. The boldest ventures, into the Eighth Amendment area, were linked to the names of a small band of federal district judges, who had ordered sweeping prison reforms in such states as Arkansas, Alabama, and Rhode Island. Washington State became one of these as a result of the events surrounding the prolonged WSP lockdown of summer 1979.[27]

In October the case of *Hoptowit* v. *Ray* was launched in Federal District Court of Eastern Washington.[28] At the time, no judge was assigned to that district; as a consequence, the chief judge of the court of appeals (Ninth Circuit) designated the judge who would sit on this case. The jurist thus fortuitously chosen was Jack Tanner, who ordinarily presides in Tacoma, Washington, some three hundred miles from the Spokane courtroom where this drama was to be enacted. Judge Tanner's first act was to appoint the Department of Justice and the U.S. Attorney in Spokane, James J. Gillespie, as *amicus curiae* to "participate in the case with the full rights of parties."[29]

During the six-month period that Tanner allotted for the parties to submit documentation on their case, a large quantity of expert testimony was compiled, much of it solicited by the U.S. Attorney. Among the large number of professionals who toured WSP were psychologist Craig Haney, an associate of Stanford's Philip Zimbardo; criminologists Richard Korn and Paul Keve; and psychologist Peter Suedfeld (University of British Columbia). Judge Tanner, in the findings he first announced orally in May 1980, relied heavily on the reports of Haney and Korn. Haney had made two separate visits to WSP in February and March, totaling six days, and

Korn spent three days there in March.[30] Overcrowding, which played a major role in the *Hoptowit* case, was succinctly documented in Haney's report to show that more than four-fifths of WSP's living units violated minimum standards adopted by both the American Correctional Association and the American Public Health Association. According to Haney, "Overcrowding has been reliably shown to produce interpersonal violence, psychopathology, and breakdowns in normal patterns of social interaction and communication."[31]

But Judge Tanner rested his decision on many factors in addition to crowding. The high level of violence at WSP, particularly the links of the guard force to this violence, he judged of crucial importance in the Walla Walla environment. Tanner held that overcrowding, idleness, deteriorating physical plant, inadequate physical and mental health care all "caused pervasive psychological deterioration of prisoners," which led directly to violence. "This high level of violence," he wrote, "forces prisoners to live in an atmosphere of fear, anger, and frustration, which, in turn, leads to more violence."[32]

Concerning guard behavior, Tanner found a "pattern and practice" of misconduct "uncontrolled by the administration at WSP."[33] The court also relied for its findings of guard brutality on a report compiled by investigators from the state attorney general's office, following the "guard riots" of July 1979. The state's own probe of those events had found "an almost unbelievable lack of communication" between the guards and the administration.[34]

Among the strongest findings in Tanner's legal opinion were those relating to the inmates' lack of "effective and legitimate" grievance procedures, all of which contributed "to the general atmosphere of fear, anger, frustration, and powerlessness." The judge saw the greatly reduced role of inmate leaders as a negative factor because it closed off lines of communication to the administrators. He obviously disapproved of the current prison regime:

> Superintendent Spalding believes that a central purpose of the lockdown in mid-1979 was to gain administrative control over prisoners and to disband the various prisoner organizations. . . . He testified that . . . riot team guards [were] yelling: "We're running this Penitentiary now" and "This is a new Institution" while they were beating Seg Unit prisoners.[35]

In approaching his judgment as to the lawfulness of the regime at WSP, Tanner found "inadequate," "deficient," and "intolerable" conditions in several other important areas, among them a lack of programs, inadequate medical facilities, and intolerable conditions in segregation and protective custody.[36] Thus he concluded that, in spite of certain efforts of the Spalding administration to make improvements, *"the totality of conditions* at WSP still falls far below minimum constitutional standards.'' He then announced that he would appoint a ''special master'' to oversee the court-ordered changes.[37]

A picture emerged that placed Walla Walla in the not-so-elite company of Arkansas and Alabama. And with seeming inevitability, Washington would join the parade of states whose prison regimes had been branded as constituting cruel and unusual punishment.

With a broadly based array of factual findings relating to the ''totality of conditions,'' Judge Tanner built his legal opinion on the developing Eighth Amendment case law as it then stood. Noting that the prison problem is ''complex, intractable, and . . . not readily susceptible to resolution by decree,'' he conceded that courts are ''ill-equipped to deal with the increasingly urgent problems of prison administration.'' He observed that the requirements for committing resources, making comprehensive plans, and applying expertise to these matters places the prison problem ''peculiarly within the province of the legislative and executive branches of government.'' This admitted, Tanner asserted, in words borrowed from the U.S. Supreme Court, ''a policy of judicial restraint cannot encompass any failure to take cognizance of valid constitutional claims whether arising in a Federal or state constitution.''[38]

The Eighth Amendment applies, Tanner ruled, citing an appeals court opinion on overcrowding in Oklahoma prisons: ''The Eighth Amendment . . . [is] intended to protect and safeguard a prison inmate from an environment where degeneration is probable and self-improvement unlikely whether physical or mental.''[39]

Judge Tanner clearly had concluded that WSP's environment produced such degeneration. He cited the cases from Alabama and Rhode Island for the proposition that the ''Court's remedial power includes the power to order compliance with nationally accepted minimum correctional standards.'' Tanner then proceeded to find what features of prison life at WSP affronted the Eighth Amendment standard.[40]

Constitutional Standards in the Prison Milieu

The court's order in the *Hoptowit* case was stringent but not unreasonable in view of the seriousness of its findings.[41] Tanner adopted the general pattern of requiring the correctional authorities to propose plans for the remedying of unconstitutional situations. An overall comprehensive plan was to be submitted within sixty days. In a few areas where specific standards were imposed, these were not formulated by the court but were drawn from professional sources, such as the ACA wardens' team's recommendations on guard recruitment and training, ACA standards on segregation, and

AMA standards on prison health care. But the most interesting and novel feature of Tanner's approach was the requirement that state officials draw up these plans, which were then to be reviewed by the special master and finally presented to Judge Tanner with the special master's recommendation. This pattern would seem to be conducive to a pragmatic working out of the problems in each area, as distinct from the imposition of court decrees. Nevertheless, on one particular issue—on which the court flatly mandated that there was to be no harassment or retaliation against any inmate plaintiffs—a confrontation between the court master and the prison authorities soon developed.

Despite the promising features of Tanner's approach, the issue of compliance remains problematic. Inescapably the area that has received the most prominence is the overcrowding. Even with the pressure felt from the court's decision, Walla Walla's population at first actually increased and then was gradually reduced, but by the summer of 1981 the inside count was edging upward again and had passed the 1,000 mark in an antiquated institution with a rated capacity much below 1,000.[42] The political mood in the state supported the building of more prisons as the primary way to solve this problem; but issues of where to locate these new constructions and how to pay for them hindered that solution. The new secretary of adult corrections, Amos Reed, advocated more construction and was cool to the exploration of alternatives. Legislators, who were resistant to the high costs of implementing the court decision, called them "Tanner appropriations". In addition, the newly enacted statute instituting "presumptive sentencing", designed to lengthen sentences, would push the prison population upward. Inevitably, the state would be wrestling with its problem of crowded prisons for a very long time, quite aside from any interventions by a federal judge.

On the implementation of many of the other provisions of Tanner's order, the picture was mixed. Some observers felt mildly encouraged by the assignment of a new warden to WSP, one who was not tied to the earlier resistance to the court's intrusion and who appeared amenable to working gradually toward a less authoritarian prison regime. At the same time, the state-level officials were determined to fight the Tanner decision through the courts. The first secretary of adult corrections, Amos Reed, dislikes any kind of supervision, judicial or otherwise. He strongly opposed a bill proposed during the 1981 legislative session that would have created a statewide corrections advisory board. He firmly believes that optimum administration flows from an autonomous secretary and department. And he has made efforts to withdraw the state from the judicial consent decree covering the Monroe Reformatory (agreed to after the Spokane trial on Walla Walla).

In July 1981 argument on this appeal of *Hoptowit* v. *Ray* took place in Seattle before the Ninth Circuit Court of Appeals.[43] Between the original trial and this subsequent courtroom confrontation of the two sides, the U.S.

Supreme Court handed down its decision in the case of *Rhodes* v. *Chapman,* which pointed to a decidedly less inmate-oriented interpretation of the ban on cruel and unusual punishment. Five justices joined an opinion by Justice Powell that viewed the district court's findings of fact—supporting its holding that the Southern Ohio Correctional Facility (SOCF) was in violation of the Eighth Amendment—as tending rather to refute that conclusion. The Powell opinion drew a distinction between overcrowding and any particular celling arrangements. Then, pointing to the fact that the SOCF, Ohio's only maximum-security prison, had cells of the most modern design, the Court majority downgraded the "expert" opinion that double-celling in these conditions would lead to the evils predicted from overcrowded conditions generally.[44]

The Powell opinion further argued that the considerations that the district court had weighed to reach its result "properly are weighed by the legislature and prison administration rather than a court."[45] Three of the remaining justices joined in a concurring opinion, written by Justice Brennan, that insisted "that judicial intervention is *indispensable* if constitutional dictates—not to mention considerations of basic humanity—are to be observed in the prisons." The remaining justice, Thurgood Marshall, in dissenting, put in even stronger terms his belief that the Powell majority was taking "far too limited a view of the proper role of a federal court in an Eighth Amendment proceeding and . . . far too sanguine a view of the motivations of state legislators and prison officials."[46]

In analyzing the *Chapman* decision in relation to a case such as *Hoptowit,* the high court's insistence on the judiciary's deferring to administrators on such matters as celling arrangements to meet problems of overcrowding, together with the Supreme Court's minimization of the role of expert court testimony in such matters, suggest the kind of arguments that would work on Washington State's side on appeal. Still it seemed improbable that the main lines of Judge Tanner's decision could be reversed or substantially altered. The Appeals Court, however, in announcing its decision (mid-February 1982) harshly rejected Tanner's "totality of conditions" approach, terminated WSP's court-mastership, and returned the case to the district court for separate determination of each alleged constitutional violation.[47] Yet, whatever the result of the remaining battles in the courts, *Hoptowit* could still play a prominent role in this period after *Rhodes* v. *Chapman.* Now that the Supreme Court has pronounced on the prison issue in relation to the Eighth Amendment, the further spelling out of the meaning of "cruel and unusual punishment" reverts principally to the lower courts. *Hoptowit* will be one of the important cases to be resolved.

The importance of this case hangs on yet another consideration, a symbolic one. Let us remember it is Walla Walla that is the object of this protracted judicial battle over the meaning and substance of "cruel and unusual punishment" of prisoners. This is the same fortress penitentiary that a decade earlier was held up as marching in the forefront of progressive reform. These dramatic shifts in the conditions at Walla Walla marked the completion of yet another circle of reform and reaction in America's penal history. The intervening of the courts, on the other hand, appears to be an aspect of a more basic structural change in what had once been the most isolated of total institutions.

Notes

1. See, for example, Gordon Hawkins, *The Prison: Policy and Practice* (Chicago: University of Chicago Press, 1967), p. 144.

2. For example, in dealing with habeas corpus petitions, state courts have usually disposed of them either summarily or by simply accepting the statements of prison authorities. See the discussion in ibid., pp. 145–148. Hawkins cites examples principally from California.

3. See James B. Jacobs, *Stateville: The Penitentiary in Mass Society* (Chicago: University of Chicago Press, 1977), pp. 113–114, citing *Wright* v. *Toomey,* a case involving Stateville (Ill.) administrators (affirmed 7th Cir., 1974/74-1106). Legally, inmates can sue for personal damages under section 1983 of the Civil Rights Act; in 1981 an estimated 10–15,000 prisoners' suits were filed in federal courts under this section.

4. See ibid., pp. 114–116.

5. Harvard Center for Criminal Justice (CCJ), "Judicial Intervention in Prison Discipline," *Journal of Criminal Law, Criminology, and Police Science* 18 (1972):200–228. The case is *Morris* v. *Travisano,* 310 F. Supp. 857 (1970). See the discussion in Jacobs, *Stateville,* p. 260, and Hawkins, *Prison,* pp. 144–145.

6. Harvard CCJ, "Judicial Intervention," p. 227.

7. Jacobs, *Stateville,* p. 116; Harvard CCJ, "Judicial Intervention," p. 227. The Harvard study adds (p. 227) that, in the area of prison discipline, "most courts will lack the expertise necessary to understand [this] unique problem," and "any such decree requires a massive burden of supervision." Leonard Orland, *Prisons: Houses of Darkness* (New York: Free Press, 1975), p. 108, believes that many of the issues of daily life in prison cannot be adequately dealt with through existing constitutional doctrine but require action by state legislatures, which have largely shirked this responsibility.

8. Harvard CCJ, "Judicial Intervention," p. 222. See also Hawkins, *The Prison,* p. 149.

9. See *Holt* v. *Sarver,* 309 F. Supp. 362 (1970). For a brief discussion

of the context of this decision, see David Rudovsky et al., *The Rights of the Prisoner,* Rev. ed. (New York: Avon, 1977), pp. 27–29.

10. *Palmigiano* v. *Garrahy,* 443 F. Supp. 956 (1977). In connection with this decision, Judge Pettine appointed a court master to oversee implementation of his order.

11. Harvard CCJ, "Judicial Intervention," p. 228. The report also urges that "active intervention by concerned and knowledgeable correctional officials and legislators as well as courts is essential to effect long overdue institutional reforms."

12. Herman Schwartz, "Protection of Prisoners' Rights," *Christianity and Crisis,* February 17, 1975, pp. 29–30. Schwartz played a prominent role as an Attica observer in 1971 and also as legal counsel to inmates.

13. Nathan Glazer, "Should Judges Administer Social Services?" *Public Interest,* no. 50 (Winter 1978):64–80. See also Charles S. Prigmore and Richard T. Crow, "Is the Court Remaking the American Prison System?" *Federal Probation* 40 (June 1976):3–10. Judge Johnson had held in an earlier case that the Eighth Amendment ban applies to inmates deprived of adequate medical care. *Newman* v. *Alabama,* 349 F. Supp. 278 (1972).

14. See "Alabama Prisons," *CJ Bulletin* (March 1976).

15. Ray Jenkins, "Judge, at Governor's Request, Puts Alabama Prisons into Receivership," *New York Times,* February 4, 1979, p. 26. This innovative governmental arrangement bypassed the state board of corrections, a political body created by statute, as well as cutting across lines of separation of powers.

16. Brian Glick, "Change through the Courts," in Erik Olin Wright, *The Politics of Punishment* (New York: Harper & Row, 1973), pp. 306–307.

17. Glazer, "Should Judges Administer?" pp. 76–77. Glazer (p. 74) does concede that "many rights are demanded simply from the point of view of justice and human dignity," but he appraises judicial activism in many social service areas as having gone well beyond the "simple-justice basis."

18. *Draper* v. *Rhay,* 315 F.2d 193 (1963).

19. See Ronald Goldfarb and Linda Singer, *After Conviction* (New York: Simon & Schuster, 1973), p. 394.

20. *Rhinehart* v. *Rhay,* 314 F. Supp. 81 (1970) at 82. During the 1960s the most significant case in correctional law, formally tied to Walla Walla but not involving the prison regime directly, was *Mempa* v. *Rhay,* 359 U.S. 128 (1967). The U.S. Supreme Court ruled that legal counsel was constitutionally required in revocation-of-probation proceedings. See Goldfarb and Singer, *After Conviction,* pp. 241–242.

21. U.S. District Court for the Eastern District of Washington, No. 2806, mimeographed (April and July 1972). When this same judge had earlier dismissed without a hearing an individual prisoner's complaint that he was being denied treatment for a medical condition, the federal appeals

court reversed, saying the inmate was entitled to a hearing. *Riley* v. *Rhay* 407 F.2d 496 (1969).

22. This followed the precedent of *Riley* v. *Rhay*. The case was *Thomas* v. *Evans,* no. 72–1708 (9th Cir., June 8, 1973), 2 *Prison Law Reporter* 399.

23. *Voice of Prison* (January 1975):4. Questions discussed concerned not only the enforcement vis-à-vis the state of the RGC constitution but also how administrators could be held to the state law and administrative regulations that inmates felt were being violated. The inmates' own legal-services attorneys pointed out to them that they were the subjects of an evolving body of rights, but that broad authority for administrators derived from the claim of security needs, acting as a kind of elastic clause.

24. *Fetty* v. *Smith* (Wash. Sup. Ct., filed March 22, 1973 [2 *Prison Law Reporter* 242, March 1973]). It is an interesting commentary on this period that it was the inmates who were the least hesitant in proclaiming the rehabilitation motif.

25. *Bresolin* v. *Morris,* 543 P.2d 325 (1975).

26. *Bresolin* v. *Morris,* 558 P.2d 1350 (1977) at 1352–1354, 1356, 1358. The following year, the same court followed essentially the same reasoning in a case involving alcoholism rather than drug addiction. *Aripa* v. *DSHS,* 588 P.2d 185 (1978).

27. Supporters of prisoners' rights in the state, representing a variety of views, had long been searching for a strategic legal opening, especially at WSP. The deterioration of general living conditions at Walla Walla, plus the evidence of serious guard misconduct during the July 1979 events, appeared to make the time ripe for a legal test. The American Civil Liberties Union (ACLU) of Washington, which had been considering litigation and discussing legal strategy since 1972, now decided that it could no longer hold back. In mounting the challenge, the ACLU joined with legal-services attorneys (Evergreen Legal Services) who had wide experience in prison legal matters.

28. Frederick Hoptowit, an American Indian, and fourteen other WSP inmates filed a class-action complaint on October 12, 1979, which "attacked past and present conditions of confinement" and "sought damages for theft or destruction of personal property and for brutality" during the June-October 1979 prison lockdown. *Hoptowit* v. *Ray,* Memorandum Opinion, U.S. District Court, Eastern District of Washington, Docket No. 79–359, mimeographed (June 23, 1980). The list of defendants was headed by Governor Dixy Lee Ray and included the entire correctional hierarchy.

29. Judge Tanner at that same time issued, on motion of the inmates' attorneys, a temporary restraining order barring harassment or intimidation of inmates in the lawsuit.

30. Craig Haney, "A Report on Conditions of Confinement at Wash-

ington State Penitentiary," April 15, 1980, U.S. District Court, Eastern District of Washington; Richard R. Korn, "Report on Conditions at the Washington State Prison at Walla Walla," filed in the U.S. District Court, Eastern District of Washington, April 17, 1980.

31. Haney, "Report," pp. 17–18.

32. *Hoptowit,* 10. The Haney report (pp. 26–27): "A largely punitive, authoritarian attitude now dominates the correctional philosophy of WSP ... While conceding that violence actually increased at the outset of its own tenure, the [Spalding] administration chooses to interpret that fact in terms of inmate leaders or 'troublemakers' who resented their loss of power. . . . Yet the violence has not appreciably abated . . . Perhaps out of over-sensitivity to the reputation of this Penitentiary as one whose past administrations have been 'soft' on prisoners, this policy of toughness has been followed singlemindedly."

33. *Hoptowit,* 11.

34. Korn, "Report," p. 27. Korn relates that this passage—together with a further statement of the so-called Jackson/Russell Report that the custodial staff from top to botton clung to a "cover-up" mentality—were read by him to the associate superintendent for custody, eliciting a vehement denial of their accuracy. However, this report seems also to buttress the ACA Report of July, 1979. See also the Haney report, pp. 12–16, which asserts that "guards have tremendous autonomy" (p. 15).

35. *Hoptowit,* 21–22. See also Haney report, pp. 30–31. Haney argues that the lack of a legitimate grievance mechanism threatens gross disruption: "Under these circumstances inmates feel powerless and frustrated. . . . Some of the prisoners . . . give up in the face of powerlessness. . . . Others attempt last ditch actions designed to call attention to problems illegitimately." See also the Korn report, p. 30. The problems involved in poor screening of guard recruits and the growth of a "guard clique" are discussed in the Keve report (p. 2) and in *Hoptowit,* 16–17. Korn recounts several revealing episodes of guard behavior throughout his report.

36. *Hoptowit,* 22–47.

37. Ibid., 47, 48. Emphasis added. Subsequently Michael Lewis of the Center for Community Justice (Washington, D.C.) was appointed the special master.

38. Ibid., 5, 6. See *Procunier* v. *Martinez,* 416 U.S. 396 (1974).

39. *Battle* v. *Anderson,* 564 F.2d 388 (1977), quoted in ibid., p. 6.

40. *Hoptowit,* 49, 50–55. Judge Tanner also held that WSP's conditions and practices violated art. 1, sec. 14 of the Washington State Constitution, which prohibits cruel punishment.

41. Ibid., 56–60.

42. See the figures cited in ibid., 7–8. The state submitted to the court at the time of the trial a figure of 872 for its rated capacity. Judge Tanner

arrived at a figure of 492, "consistent with ACA minimum standards." In actual planning, the target figure was 850, to be lowered eventually to 750.

43. *Seattle Post Intelligencer,* July 7, 1981. Senior assistant attorney general William G. Collins argued in the appeals court that Tanner's order was "excessively intrusive" and the district court itself "excessively enmeshed in the minutiae of prison operation," resulting in dissension, lowered morale, and confusion. Counsel for the inmates made the point that Tanner had stepped in only because the state was operating "an unconstitutional prison" at WSP.

44. *Rhodes* v. *Chapman,* 29 *Crim. Law Reporter* 3061 (1981) at 3064. See especially the discussion in notes 13, 14, 15. "Generalized opinions of experts cannot weigh as heavily in determining contemporary standards of decency as 'the public attitude toward a given sanction.'"

45. Powell noted further: "Courts cannot assume that state legislatures and prison officials are insensitive to the requirements of the Constitution or to the perplexing sociological problems of how best to achieve the goals of the penal function in the criminal justice system." Ibid., 3065.

46. Ibid., 3065, 3069, 3071. The three concurring justices agreed with the result (but not the reasoning) on the basis that, in this particular instance, mandating minimum cell dimensions that would end double-celling would as a practical matter lead to transfer of many inmates to a worse prison.

47. Personal discussions with Michael Lewis (former court master) and others. Appeals court citation: *Hoptowit* v. *Ray,* 80–3366 (9th CA-1982- remanded to Dist. Ct.).

9 Conclusion: Who Will Rule the Joint?

We are firm in our resolve and we demand, as human beings, the dignity and justice that is due to us by right of our birth. We do not know how the present system of brutality and dehumanization and injustice has been allowed to be perpetrated in this day of enlightenment, but . . . we cannot allow it to continue. —Attica Liberation Faction, September 1971

Whoever's in power runs the joint. —WSP prisoner, October 1975

A decade and more has passed since the prisoners' demands rang through Attica's D Yard. It has been a decade of vast changes in American society, few of which, by the decade's end, had proved favorable to prisons and prisoners. When we began our research, the tremors of Attica were still reverberating throughout American society. As we conclude, the shadow of Santa Fe lengthens across all American prisons. The voices calling for a return to a more punitive system of incarceration have been growing louder and more insistent, supported by a conservative political tide.

The bold experiment with self-government that briefly transformed one American fortress prison in Washington state into the semblance of a democratic community is today only a memory in the minds of old cons and a scapegoat for politicians and administrators who have despaired of finding solutions for that state's continuing prison crisis.

The persistence of the penitentiary in America in the face of the many indications of its inefficacy in either reducing crime or rehabilitating those who pass through its gates is often cited as a puzzle. In the study of "primitive" societies, to which early researchers often compared the prison, it is an anthropological truism that institutions that do not serve some function—economic, political, or psychological—are unlikely to survive periods of rapid culture change. Prisons, when seen only in relation to their stated objectives, seem eminently dysfunctional. The penitentiary in particular, progeny of Enlightenment humanism and the Puritan ethic, seems an anachronism today. And yet it persists, its achitechture, its regulations, and its routines almost unchanged for a century and a half.

The United States has the highest incarceration rates and longest sentences in the Western world, as well as one of the highest crime rates. Some recent studies have shown that imprisonment rates in fact are more closely correlated with levels of unemployment than with any variation of the crime rate.[1] The present era of economic uncertainty and rising unemployment seems a timely one for the revival of ideas such as those of Georg Rusche in the 1930s. The concept of less eligibility, for instance, linked the institutions of incarceration with the labor market.[2] (The principle holds that the prison inmate's standard of living should be no higher than the lowest stratum of free labor.) In this perspective, prisons have a latent function as instruments of social and economic control, dumping grounds for surplus labor, their conditions adjusted to remain just below those of the lowest of the working class.

Whether one accepts the ideological premises of the work of the New Criminologists, who have been responsible for the revival of Rusche and other Marxist thinkers, one must welcome a methodology that examines the criminal justice system in relation to other institutions in American society. The very rarity of this kind of holistic approach to corrections leaves many important questions unaddressed and unresolved. It also lends credence to the accusation that much of criminological research, in ignoring interconnections, serves the status quo.[3]

In the era of the interactive prison a prime lesson to be drawn from the study of the penitentiary in mass society is that better methodological tools must be developed to comprehend the changing role of a detotalized institution in a rapidly changing society. Both the overt contradictions and covert functions of incarceration in that society must be grasped if change is to become controlled and goal-oriented or even if, at some distant future, prison abolition is adopted as a societal aim. We must also develop more understanding of the positive role of conflict—now seemingly coextensive with senseless and pervasive violence—in effecting structural changes in institutions.

Our principal focus in this study has been on power and its changing locus in the American maximum-security prison in general and in a particular historical case, WSP at Walla Walla. We conclude with some observation on these changes and the forces that are effecting them. The crisis of legitimacy, which overtook the prison as it did other American institutions, has been a catalyst in the transformation of social and political relations behind the walls. Prisoners' groups and organizations become politicized interest groups; and the conflict between these newly formed interest groups led to fundamental changes in the social structure.[4] Thus, even as the memory of the reforms at Walla Walla wanes, many of these changes in structure and consciousness persist.

Power and Legitimacy in the Penitentiary

The penitentiary was conceived as the ultimate symbol of a lawful and orderly society. Those who had violated the law were sent there to repent their breach of the social contract and, by healing it, to heal themselves. Since that society was "conceived in liberty and dedicated to the proposition that all men are created equal," there was no question but that its legitimacy should be recognized even by those who trespassed against it. The Principal Keeper, as deputy of that society, was supreme and unquestioned authority. Silent meditation and then silent labor were the instruments by which the sinner was to be restored to a state of civil grace.

As the silence of the penitentiary was ruptured, so also, it seemed, was the consensus. The relationship between rulers and ruled changed from that of more or less benevolent despotism to a polarization and suppressed warfare. It remained suppressed by covert collusion between the two hostile parties, neither of which could gain from open battle. The polarization was expressed by a well-developed counterculture complete with a language, a set of roles, myths, and a "charter," known as the convict code. While oppositional to the dominant caste, it did not question the larger society in which the system was embedded. Agencies of that society, having built and staffed the prison, preferred to forget it and entrust the details of its daily operation to the person who knew it best, the warden.

In the 1960s, a period of social ferment, the legitimacy of the penitentiary, as that of nearly every other social institution, was called into question. Imprisonment was seen by many as an instrument of social control, a method of eliminating political opposition. The result was polarization between keepers and kept, a feeling that each represented a life-threat to the existence of the other.[5]

This, in turn, led to a closer scrutiny of life in the penitentiary by other agencies of the society: the courts, the schools, voluntary citizens' groups, by state and Federal government. Religious groups, as well as radical political ones, questioned the legitimacy of the prison as an instrument of punishment. Ironically the founders of the penitentiary, the Quakers, became in the early 1970s, its severest critics. They joined the abolitionists, arguing that there can be no criminal justice without social justice and that social justice can never be achieved in an institution—and a society—based on racial and class bias.

The crisis of legitimacy that characterized the 1960s and early 1970s opened many doors in the fortress prisons of America. Despite the best attempts of politicians and administrators bent on recapturing the prison from the inmates, they have not been closed yet. What we can see through those doors, often with the eye of a television camera, is the brutality that reached its zenith at Santa Fe. And the penitentiary, which once stood as the symbol of a lawful society, has in many places now been declared unconstitutional by judges of the same criminal-justice system that created it and operates it.

The "lawlessness" of the contemporary prison has several facets. These include the physical and psychological conditions of confinement in a crowded, understaffed, and underfinanced institution. In addition, there are instances of illegal retaliatory actions by increasingly angry and militant guards, who perceive themselves as competing with the inmates for scarce resources. Also in the category of lawless are the violent prisoners who have filled the leadership vacuum left by the administrative removal of politically active prisoners. At Walla Walla these were represented by the Bikers, at other prisons by gangs. The administrations that favored these elements, either to counter the politicals or to pursue the time-honored precept of *divide et impera* contributed to the problem.[6]

Who then will rule "the joint?" Some argue it will ultimately be the courts, with their special masters to oversee judicial decrees. Others see the state legislature with their control of the purse strings as the decisive power.

In the post-reform period at Walla Walla, no one seemed sure who was in charge. During the course of the lawsuit, which declared WSP in violation of the Eighth Amendment, expert testimony stressed both this uncertainty as to who was in control and the lack of communication between different segments of the prison population.[7] This situation led to a chronic frustration and a sense of impotence, often expressed in a "my hands are tied" theme. Thus, for example, Amos Reed, the head of corrections in Washington State, who had taken over in early 1981 with the assurance from Governor John Spellman that he would have a free hand, complained to the local Council on Crime and Delinquency that "we have no real control over the intake or outgo" and warned that "we cannot absorb that kind of [budget] cutting and run institutions on a constitutional level."[8] Reed's words contained a veiled message for both the federal judge whose verdict he was appealing and the legislature with whom correctional officials were in perpetual battle over finances.

Superintendent Spalding, despite his "get-tough" demeanor vis-à-vis both prisoners and renegade guards, also emphasized his helplessness. Like many other administrators, he placed much of the blame on judicial interference, while simultaneously expressing the hope that the court orders would induce the legislature to allocate the funds for programs and purposes he deemed essential.

The inmates, particularly those who were veterans of the reform period, also expressed their sense of powerlessness. Their organizations dissolved, their incipient union movement destroyed, they felt victimized by both fellow inmates and angry guards. No longer could they freely hold

press conferences to air their grievances. The guards, in turn, felt a pervasive sense of physical danger in their work and often cited stress-related ill-
ness, in addition to violence, as occupational hazards. At the same time, the
officers' union was growing in power and militancy at the institution.

In its plunge from a beacon of reform and prison democracy to its present status as an "outlaw" prison, WSP exemplifies the cycle of reform and
reaction so familiar throughout penal history. We seem to be left, as has
been suggested, with a two-hundred-year history of reform without
change.[9] And yet on another level, we have seen the diffusion of power, the
experiment with participative democracy, the increasing contact with the
outside facilitated by communications technology—all have promoted
lasting structural transformations in the prison.

Reform and Rehabilitation

Where these more fundamental changes will eventually lead, and whether
they are indeed irreversible, will depend less on the correctional system than
on changes in American society beyond the walls.[10] The conservative tide
that is sweeping the United States is not favorable to prisoners' rights and
prison reform. Without a supportive external environment, reform programs, no matter how well designed, are doomed to failure.

The critics of the rehabilitative concept, many of them academic liberals, believe that by abandoning the indeterminate sentence, treatment programs, and parole, they are enhancing the autonomy and self-respect of the
prisoners and establishing justice within a failed institution. Few of them
have themselves done time.

By contrast, even the most radical prisoners have focused their demands on the immediate conditions of their existence. Prisoners call for
treatment programs long after they cease to be fashionable in penological
circles. While the patronizing attitudes of "rehabilitators" may be rejected,
the amelioration that they bring to bleak conditions of imprisonment is welcomed. As Schwendinger and Schwendinger have pointed out, it was the
rehabilitation concept that legitimized struggles against intolerable prison
conditions.[11] And even ex-felon academician John Irwin, an outspoken
opponent of the rehabilitation idea, acknowledges how it contributed to his
own intellectual development and transformation from a convict into a
sociologist.[12]

Similarly, Malcolm X, in his autobiography, records his indebtedness
to the prison library and to the "rehabilitators" who encouraged his
reading.[13] The split between prisoners and their professional supporters is
revealed at a conference in Norway:

The discussions . . . shifted as ex-prisoners sought to direct attention to specific events that distressed them and to specific staff members . . . The scholars, journalists, and lawyers present tried to direct their attention toward systemic problems. This conflict between the here-and-now concerns of the prisoners and longer-term changes in economic and political systems in which prison systems are embedded threatened to divide the reform groups.[14]

Another point conceded even by many critics of rehabilitation is that the philosophy has never been effectively implemented in maximum-security prisons. Even while it gained widespread acceptance, the institutions were never created, the resources never invested, to implement the treatment objectives of correctional institutions. The treatment staff itself, while enjoying theoretical leadership, was in fact relegated to an isolated and powerless position by the custodial staff.[15]

While critics have accused the treatment staff of being either useless or exponents of control more sinister than the custodians, our experience at WSP suggests that treatment was simply a philosophy of corrections that was never seriously tried. Significantly enough, one of the principal demands of black radicals during the turbulent reform period was for the treatment that was proclaimed as an institutional aim long before. This need was felt so strongly and the staff provisions were so inadequate that a number of inmate-initiated self-help programs were set up with outside grants in order to attempt to deal with the severe psychological problems stemming from ghetto poverty, drug addiction, and alcoholism. The treatment personnel were regarded by the most radical prisoners as their natural allies, particularly as the older paternalistic teachers, counselors, and chaplains were succeeded by a "new breed" of political activists, often veterans of the civil rights and peace movements.

It is interesting to note that commentators with widely divergent viewpoints, after ostensibly rejecting the rehabilitative model, then salvage the remedial idea in some form. Fogel takes what he terms Gill's joint-venture model as the first principle of his justice model. Irwin, citing the use of the term *help* by the team writing the AFSC-sponsored *Struggle for Justice*, accepts that term in place of *rehabilitate*. And Schwendinger and Schwendinger justify remedial programs as "elemental rights."[16]

Thus despite the vehemence with which many liberals and radicals reject the rehabilitative model, when it comes to specific reforms aimed at the amelioration of prison conditions, they often find themselves on the same side with treatment personnel—and with militant prisoners.

The Legacy of Prison Democracy

A lifer and officer of the first Resident Government Council at Walla Walla summed up the meaning of self-government for many of the prisoners with the story of the People's Park, a patch of grass inside the walls, which was, until the reforms, off-limits to the inmates.

> The grass over there was always tempting. Macklin [former associate superintendent for custody] said you have to stay off it. . . . Well, we always wanted to get on the grass. . . . If you could run across the grass and get away with it, you tried . . . a lot of guys went to the hole over it. So finally when this new concept of self-government came in we just said, "Well, we got to live here. The piece of grass is inside the penitentiary and we feel that we should have it." And so we went up and argued and got it.[17]

One of Superintendent Spalding's first acts in response to the disturbances of 1979 was to have this grass paved over, ostensibly for practical purposes of preventing further escape attempts. But to many of the prisoners, it bore heavy symbolic freight.

Superintendent Spalding, who had been a guard during the reform period, blamed many of his problems as superintendent on the liberal experiment. He regarded it as a "pandora's box," which continued to spill out its contents until the strongest measures had to be taken to put the lid back on. Spalding believed that it was his mission to take those measures. At the same time, he credited the reforms with having prevented an Attica at Walla Walla.[18]

Perhaps that is the most significant assessment that has been made of the reforms—and by a hostile insider. The promise of that dramatic moment in 1971 when inmate leaders leaped to the stage of the old auditorium and cooled the fires of frustration and racial hatreds—that immediate promise was kept. This cannot be said for many other promises in that grim setting.

The four-year experiment at Walla Walla changed the lives of a few and the perspectives of many more. It will be remembered by outsiders who came into contact with it as a moment of light and hope in the dark annals of penal history. And perhaps it will be resurrected when a prison reformer of a future generation is casting around for methods to make the lives of society's rejects more tolerable.

What concrete lessons can future reformers derive from this late twentieth century experiment in prison democracy? How does it relate to the experiments of the past and the events of the present? Can it give us any guidance in reshaping the prison? Can participatory democracy actually change the prisoner and the prison? Fragments of this history provide ideas: the simulation of community life, the process of civic education (Thomas Mott Osborne); shared governance (Howard B. Gill).

Why did prison democracy fail? Reformers like Gill believes that it has never been given a fair test. Many critics argue intrinsic causes of failure, such as the contradiction between custody and treatment. Others insist that no real change took place, that the co-optative effect of these attempts at democratic decision-making "within the existing social control system of the prison" simply legitimates the punitive status quo.[19]

The experiments of the past have generally been judged failures by administrators (except by those who initiated them). As we have seen, however, these historical reform experiments have as often succumbed to external assault as internal contradictions. We cannot say conclusively whether "democracy," any more than other forms of remediation, can be rehabilitative. We can only observe that, like "treatment" in general, it has yet to be fully tried.[20]

Outlook for the Future

The boldest experiment in inmate governance of its time faltered when faced with a deteriorating external environment compounded by its own internal mistakes and weaknesses. While the WSP polity was struggling to place its constitutional system on a solid footing in the context of an increasingly interactive prison, the world beyond the walls of Walla Walla was changing even more rapidly and not in directions favorable to the open prison. During a brief period in the early 1970s, the climate for inmate participation had become favorable. But then the vision dissipated, the few administrators supportive of the movement retreated, public interest waned, and the prisoners saw their goal recede. Prisoners, like others in American society, again became depoliticized and apathetic.

The ebbing revolutionary wave and the abolition of the reform program has not brought the interactive prison to an end, however. Quite the contrary. Its evolution continues, albeit along an uncertain course, characterized by a lull in political activity and an unstable balance among the prison subcultures.

It has become clear from the WSP reforms that any future experiments in self-government should include considerable participation on the part of the prisoners; the role of even a benevolent administrator during their initiation and development should be at a minimum. Its official authorization, of course, has to come from administrative or possibly legislative sources, even though the judiciary might also play a part.[21] Then there must be a motivation powerful enough to transcend the multiple ethnic and other divisions among the prisoner population. Equally important are supportive symbols, ideologies, and myths, together with some measure of consensus on the "rules of the game," which must not conflict with the norms acceptable to the larger society. In the meantime, the various components of the prison polity (prisoners, guards, administrators) must come to terms among themselves.

Thus the concept of a collaborative regime calls for an integrated system of cooperative relations between the prison administration and the inmates, between the inmates and the officers (particularly in an era of guard unionism), and between the prison polity itself and outside elements of government and public. This is a heavy agenda and could not possibly be attempted in a single leap. As for past trials and errors, they will not provide ready-made formulas but can point to pitfalls.

Who will take the lead in future ventures on this path? Experience suggests a negative observation: that when the warden fails to take the leadership role, any such undertaking will almost certainly prove abortive. As in the past, deep public skepticism will greet each new attempt. John Irwin, in observing the conservative swing of the last half of the 1970s, comments that "across the country the concept of prisoners' having the right to organize and participate in decision making now seems ludicrous to most prison administrators and the public." A law professor, focusing on David Fogel's "justice model,"[22] which includes inmate participation, expresses a familiar criticism: "On scant evidence Fogel believes that those who cannot act responsibly in free society will act responsibly in prison."[23]

Sixty years earlier, Thomas Mott Osborne expressed the contrary perspective, which has since been the philosophical cornerstone of democratic prison experiments:

> The sole aim of the Mutual Welfare League is to prepare men for real life in the free society of the world outside. . . . Over against the brutality of the old system . . . the moral, mental and physical pauperizing involved . . . [the MWL] throws each upon his own resources and upon his own responsibility and holds him strictly to it. . . . It does not wish to produce good prisoners, it aims to train good *citizens*.[24]

Clearly the prospects for any expansion of inmate power are at low ebb at the beginning of the 1980s. Lacking political support from the outside, inmates are, in desperation, turning to the courts to assert their basic rights and to preserve minimal standards for their environment. The courts, however, have given some signs that they may return more autonomy to prison administrations, retreating toward the old hands-off doctrine. The deep ideological and conceptual divisions among both correctional professionals and academics—over the purposes of imprisonment, over sentencing policies, over the reformability of the prisoner, and the prison—have compounded the general disarray. Governmental bodies, state legislatures in particular, have pushed toward increasingly regressive choices.

The 1980 elections placed in the White House a president determined to dismantle social programs reaching back to the New Deal. Speaking to the International Association of Chiefs of Police in September 1981, Ronald Reagan not only ignored the recommendation of the attorney general's task force to provide $2 billion in federal aid to states for building prisons to relieve overcrowding, but appeared to be resurrecting the concept of a "criminal class" that deserved nothing but warehousing. In his view, those who explained crime by pointing to social causes were "the same people who thought that massive government spending could wipe away our social ills."[25]

Although prisons have failed to make any significant impact on the crime problem, the use of incarceration is on the rise, to the exclusion of correctional alternatives. Further, while costs of imprisonment are becoming prohibitive, investment in anything other than cells and security has been mostly abandoned. And the discovery that virtually every one of America's fortress prisons is in violation of constitutionally accepted standards has not at all spurred policymakers to start breaking up these behemoths. Even so, the trend toward a less isolated prison milieu, toward the *detotalization* of the prison culture, which had its beginnings in a very different era, appears to be inching slowly forward. It is not irreversible. But with its advance it acts to create a context wihin which longer-range progress can be made. The first step in a constructive course of public policy will be to place much less reliance on imprisonment, except for the "dangerous." Next, the courts must stand firm in their insistence on constitutional standards. Finally, on the "inside," more open environments must be created, attuning the prison regime to democratic values. As the bankruptcy of present approaches to corrections becomes ever more obvious, there is a possibility that we will begin to learn the lessons of the past and pave the way for a more humane future.

Notes

1. Positive correlations have recently been established not only between incarceration and unemployment but with low income levels and high concentration of minority populations. See especially Ivan Jankovic, "Labor Market and Imprisonment," in Tony Platt and Paul Takagi, eds., *Punishment and Penal Discipline: Essays on the Prison and the Prisoners' Movement* (Berkeley, Calif.: Crime and Social Justice Associates, 1980), pp. 93–104. See also William Nagel, "On Behalf of a Moratorium on Prison Construction," *Crime and Delinquency* 23 (April 1977), and Harvey Brenner, *Estimating the Social Costs of National Economic Policy* (Washington, D.C.: U.S. Government Printing Office, 1976).

2. Georg Rusche and Otto Kirchheimer, *Punishment and Social Structure* (New York: Russell & Russell, 1968). For a Marxian interpretation of the significance of this work, see Dario Melossi, "Punishment and Social Structure, Platt and Takagi, "Punishment," pp. 17–27.

3. Melossi, for example, attributes the "surprising" neglect of

Rusche's work, in light of its quality and of the revival of other criminological classics, to the state of criminology as a "tool of power." Melossi, "Punishment and Social Structure," in Platt and Takagi, *Punishment,* p. 22.

4. See H.J. Krysmanski, *Soziologie des Konfliktes* (Hamburg: Rohwolt, 1971), p. 138 (Citing Rolf Duhrendorf).

5. The writings of the New York commissioner of corrections at the time of Attica, Russell Oswald, show clearly that he and other administrators considered the challenge presented by the new breed of prisoners not only a threat to their own authority but to the entire society. See *Attica: My Story* (Garden City, N.Y.: Doubleday, 1972).

6. The custodial administrations' suppression of radical political activity and their relatively tolerant attitude toward the gangs and violent cliques that took their place has been described for California by John Irwin, *Prisons in Turmoil* (Boston: Little, Brown, 1980); for Massachusetts by Herman and Julia Schwendinger, "The New Idealism and Penal Living Standards," in Platt and Takagi, *Punishment;* for Illinois by James Jacobs, *Stateville* (Chicago: University of Chicago Press, 1977); and for Washington by Tyrnauer and Stastny, "Special Report on Washington State to the Prisoner Organization Research Project" (Sacramento: American Justice Institute, 1980).

7. See Richard R. Korn, "Report on Conditions at the Washington State Prison at Walla Walla," filed in U.S. District Court, Eastern District of Washington, mimeographed (April 17, 1980) and Craig Haney, "Report on Conditions of Confinement at Washington State Penitentiary," U.S. District Court, Eastern District of Washington, mimeographed (April 15, 1980).

8. See *Seattle Post Intelligencer,* October 8, 1981.

9. See Alvin Bronstein, "Reform without Change: The Future of Prisoners' Rights," *Civil Liberties Review* 4 (September–October 1977): 27–45.

10. As precedent for reversibility: In Germany, for example, the pre-1933 penal system was regarded as one of the most enlightened in the world. "Increasing concern about prisoners' rights characterized the history of German corrections during the first half of this century," with the Hitler period as an aberration, according to Hans Joachim Schneider and Sebastian Scheerer, "Corrections in the Federal Republic of Germany" in Robert J. Wicks and H.H.A. Cooper, eds., *International Corrections* (Lexington, Mass.: Lexington Books, D.C. Heath and Co., 1979), p. 48.

11. See for example, Schwendinger and Schwendinger, "New Idealism," pp. 185–191. See also the discussion in Platt and Takagi, *Punishment,* p. 3.

12. See Irwin, *Prisons.*

13. Malcolm X, *Autobiography* (New York: Grove Press, 1964) pp. 172–173.

14. David A. Ward, "Sweden: The Middle Way to Prison Reform?" in Marvin E. Wolfgang, ed., *Prisons: Present and Possible* (Lexington, Mass.: Lexington Books, D.C. Heath and Co., 1979), p. 125.

15. Platt and Takagi, *Punishment,* p. 91.

16. David Fogel, "We Are the Living Proof," (Cincinnati: W.H. Anderson, 1975), p. 219; Irwin, *Prisons,* p. 237; Schwendinger and Schwendinger, "New Idealism," p. 188.

17. "Walla Walla," KING (Seattle) TV documentary (1971).

18. See Gabrielle Tyrnauer, "What Went Wrong at Walla Walla?," *Corrections Magazine* (June 1981):41.

19. On the contradiction between custody and treatment, see David J. Rothman, *Conscience and Convenience* (Boston: Little, Brown, 1980). On the co-optation theme, see R.G. Kasinsky, "A Critique on Sharing Power in the 'Total Institution,'" *Prison Journal* 57 (Autumn–Winter 1977):58.

20. Platt and Takagi, (*Punishment,* p. 2) observe, "For the post-1945 era, the prison literature suggests that convicts were involved in treatment/ rehabilitation programs. That assumption is simply not true. . . . Convict labor continues to remain the principal assignment." These authors view the treatment model, in practice if not in theory, as essentially a tool for "maintaining order within the prison" on behalf of the ruling class's hegemony. Ibid., p. 91.

21. A constitutional right of assembly (association) for prisoners have not been given recognition by the courts. One observer, in comparing the status of prisoner organization in Sweden as against the United States states that: "Movements toward these more advanced issues [of political action] require that American prisoners first win . . . the right to organize on behalf of their own interests." Ward, "Sweden," p. 126.

22. Irwin, *Prisons,* p. 246. Although Ward ("Sweden," pp. 116–127) believes the Swedish experiment in prison democracy has itself failed, he cites it as "an experiment [in inmate participation] that would not have been given serious consideration in any American prison system."

23. Herbert S. Miller, "Current Perspectives in Corrections: A Cacophony," *Law and Contemporary Problems* 41 (Winter 1977):162.

24. Thomas Mott Osborne, "Self Government by the Prisoner," in Julia S. Jaffrey, ed., *The Prison and the Prisoner: A Symposium* (Boston: Little, Brown, 1917):105–106.

25. See *New York Times,* September 29, 1981.

Bibliography

"Adult Corrections in Washington State." *American Journal of Corrections* (November–December 1962):5–7, 10, 17.

"Alabama Prisons." *C.J. Bulletin* (March 1976).

Alper, Benedict S. *Prisons Inside Out.* Cambridge, Mass.: Ballinger, 1974.

American Correctional Association. "A Report of Conditions at Washington State Penitentiary." College Park, Md.: ACA, July 1979.

American Friends Service Committee. *Struggle for Justice: A Report on Crime and Punishment in America.* New York: Hill and Wang, 1971.

Bachrach, Peter; Baratz, Morton S. and Levi, Margaret. "The Political Significance of Citizen Participation." In Peter Bachrach and Morton S. Baratz, *Power and Poverty: Theory and Practice,* pp. 201–213. New York: Oxford University Press, 1970.

Bachrach, Peter, and Baratz, Morton S. *Power and Poverty.* New York: Oxford University Press, 1970.

Bacon, Corinne, ed. *Prison Reform.* White Plains, N.Y.: H.W. Wilson Co., 1917.

Bagdikian, Ben H. *Caged: Eight Prisoners and Their Keepers.* New York: Harper and Row, 1976.

Baker, J.E. *The Right to Participate: Inmate Involvement in Prison Administration.* Metuchen, N.J.: Scarecrow Press, 1974.

———. "Inmate Self-Government." *Journal of Criminal Law, Criminology and Police Science* 55 (March 1964):39–47.

Barnes, Harry Elmer. *The Repression of Crime: Studies in Historical Penology.* New York: George H. Doran Co., 1926.

Barnes, Harry Elmer, and Teeters, Negley K. *New Horizons in Criminology.* 2d ed. Englewood Cliffs, N.J.: Prentice-Hall, 1951.

Barry, John Vincent. *Alexander Maconochie of Norfolk Island.* London: Oxford University Press, 1958.

Beaumont, Gustave de, and Tocqueville, Alexis de. *On the Penitentiary System in the United States and Its Application to France.* Translated by Francis Lieber. Philadelphia: Carey, Lea and Blanchard, 1833.

Becker, Carl. *The Heavenly City of the 18th Century Philosophers.* New Haven: Yale University Press, 1932.

Berk, B.B. "Organizational Goals and Inmate Organization." *American Journal of Sociology* 71 (March 1966):522–534.

Berk, Richard A., and Rossi, Peter H. *Prison Reform and State Elites.* Cambridge, Mass.: Ballinger, 1977.

Berkman, Alexander. *Prison Memoirs of an Anarchist.* New York: Schocken, 1970.

Berkman, Ronald. *Opening the Gates: The Rise of the Prisoners' Movement.* Lexington, Mass.: Lexington Books, D.C. Heath and Company, 1979.

Bowker, Lee H. *Prisoner Subcultures.* Lexington, Mass.: Lexington Books, D.C. Heath and Company, 1977.

Brenner, Harvey. *Estimating the Social Costs of National Economic Policy.* Washington, D.C.: U.S. Government Printing Office, 1976.

"Bridge, Inc." *Corrections Magazine* 1 (November–December 1974):257–259.

Brockway, Zebulon R. *Fifty Years of Prison Service: An Autobiography.* New York: Charities Publication Committee, 1912.

Bronstein, Alvin J. "Reform without Change: The Future of Prisoners' Rights." *Civil Liberties Review* 4 (September–October 1977):27–45.

Browning, Frank. "Organizing behind Bars." *Ramparts* (February 1972): 40–45.

Burdman, Milton. "Ethnic Self-Help Groups in Prison and on Parole." *Crime and Delinquency* 20 (April 1974):107–118.

Carleton, Mark T. *Politics and Punishment: The History of the Louisiana State Penal System.* Baton Rouge: Louisiana State University Press, 1971.

Carlson, Rick J. *The Dilemmas of Corrections.* Lexington, Mass.: Lexington Books, D.C. Heath and Company, 1976.

Carroll, Leo. *Hacks, Blacks and Cons.* Lexington, Mass.: Lexington Books, D.C. Heath and Company, 1974.

Chamberlain, Rudolph W. *There Is No Truce: A Life of Thomas Mott Osborne.* New York: Macmillan, 1935.

Chapman, John Jay. "Thomas Mott Osborne," and "Osborne's Place in Historic Criminology." *Harvard Graduate's Magazine.* (March–June 1927.

Christenson, Scott. "Prison Labor and Unionization." *Criminal Law Bulletin* 14 (May–June 1978):243–247.

Cleaver, Eldridge. *Soul on Ice.* New York: McGraw-Hill, 1968.

Clemmer, Donald. *The Prison Community.* New York: Rinehart and Co., 1958. (Reissue, first published 1940).

Cloward, Richard A. "Social Control in the Prison." In Richard A. Cloward et al, *Theoretical Studies in Social Organization of the Prison,* pp. 20–48. New York: Social Science Research Council.

Cohen, Albert K.; Cole, George F.; and Bailey, Robert G., eds. *Prison Violence.* Lexington, Mass.: Lexington Books, D.C. Heath and Company, 1976.

Commons, Walter H. "Official Manual of the State Prison Colony." In Carl E. Doering, ed. *A Report on the Development of Penological*

Treatment at Norfolk Prison Colony in Massachusetts, pp. 3–68. New York: Bureau of Social Hygiene, 1940.

Connolly, William E., ed. *The Bias of Pluralism.* New York: Atherton Press, 1969.

Conrad, John. "Milton Burdman, 1920–1980." *Crime and Delinquency* 2 (July 1980):434–436.

Conrad, John P. and Dinitz, Simon. "Position Paper on the Isolated Prisoner," Columbus, Ohio: Academy for Contemporary Problems, 1977.

Conte, William R. "Modern Day Reforms in Washington State Penal Programs." *American Journal of Corrections* (May–June 1971):27–30.

———. "Philosophy of Corrections." *Bulletin,* Washington State Department of Institutions, March 10, 1969, pp. 3–15.

———. "Reorganization for What?" Manuscript, n.d.

———. "Some Comments on the Administration of Healing Services in Governmental Operations." Manuscript, 1978.

———, ed. *Selected Writings of Garrett Heyns.* Olympia, Wash.: Sherwood Press, 1975.

Copeland, Vincent. *The Crime of Martin Sostre.* New York: McGraw-Hill, 1970.

Cormier, Bruno, M. *The Watcher and the Watched.* Montreal and Plattsburgh, N.Y.: Tundra Books, 1975.

Cressey, Donald R. "Adult Felons in Prison." In Lloyd E. Ohlin, ed., *Prisoners in America* (The American Assembly), pp. 117–150. Englewood Cliffs, N.J.: Prentice-Hall, 1973.

———. "Limitations of Organization of Treatment." In Richard A Cloward et al., *Theoretical Studies in Social Organization of the Prison,* pp. 78–110. New York: Social Science Research Council, 1960.

Dahl, Robert. *Pluralistic Democracy in the United States: Conflict and Consent.* Chicago: Rand McNally, 1967.

———. *Who Governs?* New Haven: Yale University Press, 1961.

Davidson, R. Theodore. *Chicano Prisoners: The Key to San Quentin:* Case Studies in Cultural Anthropology. New York: Holt, Rinehart and Winston, 1974.

Denenberg, R.V. "Profile: Washington." *Corrections Magazine* 1 (November–December 1974):31–44.

Dickens, Charles. *American Notes and Pictures from Italy.* London: Macmillan, 1903. (Originally published 1842.)

Doering, Carl R., ed. *A Report on the Development of Penological Treatment at Norfolk Prison Colony in Massachusetts.* New York: Bureau of Social Hygiene, 1940.

Duverger, Maurice. *The Study of Politics.* New York: Thomas Y. Crowell, 1972.

Elli, Frank. *The Riot.* New York: Coward-McCann, 1967.

Fairchild, Erika S. "Crime and Politics: A Study of Prisons." Ph.D. dissertation, University of Washington, 1974.

———. "Politicization of the Criminal Offender: Prisoner Perceptions of Crime and Politics." *Criminology* 15 (November 1977):287–318.

Faith, Karlene, ed. *Soledad Prison: University of the Poor.* Palo Alto: Science and Behavior Books, 1975.

Farrell, Barry. "A New Way to Run the Big House," *Life,* September 8, 1972), pp. 32–41.

Flynn, Edith E. "From Conflict Theory to Conflict Resolution: Controlling Collective Violence in Prisons." *American Behavioral Scientist* 23 (May–June 1980):745–776.

Fogel, David. *We Are the Living Proof.* Cincinnati: W.H. Anderson, 1975.

Foucault, Michel. *Discipline and Punish: The Birth of the Prison.* New York: Pantheon Books, 1977.

Fox, James G. *The Organizational Context of the Prison.* Sacramento: American Justice Institute, 1980.

Freeman, John C., ed. *Prisons Past and Future.* London: Heinemann, 1978.

Friedrich, Carl J.; Curtis, Michael; and Barber, Benjamin R. *Totalitarianism in Perspective: Three Views.* New York: Praeger, 1969.

Garson, G. David. "The Disruption of Prison Administration: An Investigation of Alternative Theories of the Relationship Among Administrators, Reformers and Involuntary Social Service Clients." *Law and Society Review* 6 (May 1972):531–561.

Gill, Howard B. "Correctional Philosophy and Architecture." In Robert M. Carter, Daniel Glaser, and Leslie T. Wilkins, eds., *Correctional Institutions,* pp. 110–127. Philadelphia: J.B. Lippincott, 1972.

———. "The Norfolk State Prison Colony at Massachusetts." *Journal of Criminal Law and Criminology* 22 (1931):107–112.

Gilman, David. "U.S. Supreme Court Ruling May Foreshadow Reduction of Judicial Involvement in Corrections." *Corrections Magazine* (December 1976):49–51.

Glazer, Nathan. "Should Judges Administer Social Services?" *Public Interest,* no. 50 (Winter 1978):64–80.

Glick, Brian. "Change Through the Courts," pp. 281–321. In Erik Olin Wright, *The Politics of Punishment,* New York: Harper & Row, 1973.

Goffman, Erving. *Asylums.* Garden City, N.Y.: Doubleday, Anchor Books, 1961.

———. "On the Characteristics of Total Institutions: The Inmate World" and "Staff Inmate Relations." In *The Prison,* edited by Donald R. Cressey, pp. 15–67; 68–106. New York: Holt, Rinehart, and Winston, 1961.

Goldfarb, Ronald L., and Singer, Linda R. *After Conviction.* New York: Simon and Schuster, 1973.

Gouldner, Alvin W. "Metaphysical Pathos and the Theory of Bureaucracy." *American Political Science Review* 49 (1955):496–507.

Greenberg, David R., and Humphries, Drew. "The Cooptation of Fixed Sentencing Reform." *Crime and Delinquency* 26 (April 1980):206–225.

Griswold, H. Jack; Misenheimer, Mike; Powers, Art; and Tromanhauser, Ed. *An Eye for an Eye.* New York: Pocket Books, 1971.

Grosser, George H. "External Setting and Internal Relations of the Prison." In Richard A. Cloward et al. *Theoretical Studies in Social Organization of the Prison,* pp. 130–145. New York: Social Science Research Council, 1960.

Haney, Craig. "Report on Conditions of Confinement at Washington State Penitentiary." U.S. District Court. Eastern District of Washington. Mimeographed. April 15, 1980.

Harvard Center for Criminal Justice. "Judicial Intervention in Prison Discipline." *Journal of Criminal Law, Criminology, and Police Science* 18 (1972):200–228.

Hawkins, Gordon. *The Prison: Policy and Practice.* Chicago: University of Chicago Press, 1976.

Hayner, Norman S. "The Prison as a Community." *American Sociological Review* 5 (August 1940):577–583.

Hayner, Norman S., and Ash, Ellis. "The Prisoner Community as a Social Group." *American Sociological Review* 4 (June 1939):362–369.

Haynes, Fred E. *The American Prison System.* New York: McGraw-Hill, 1939.

———. *Criminology.* 2d ed. New York: McGraw-Hill, 1935.

Helfman, Harold M. "Antecedents of Thomas Mott Osborne's Mutual Welfare League in Michigan." *Journal of Criminal Law, Criminology and Police Science* 40 (1950):597–600.

Heyns, Garrett, and Conte, William R. "A Philosophy of Administration." In William R. Conte, ed., *Selected Writings of Garrett Heyns,* pp. 75–80. Olympia, Wash.: Sherwood Press, 1975.

Hickey, Joseph, and Scharf, Peter. *Toward a Just Correctional System: Experiments in Implementing Democracy in Prisons.* San Francisco: Jossey-Bass, 1980.

Huff, C. Donald. "Prisoner Militancy and Politicization: The Ohio Prisoner's Union Movement." In David E. Greenberg, ed., *Corrections and Punishment,* pp. 247–264. Beverly Hills: Sage, 1977.

Hymes, Dell, ed. *Reinventing Anthropology.* New York: Vintage Books, 1974.

Ignatieff, Michael. *A Just Measure of Pain.* New York: Pantheon Books, 1978.

Irwin, John. "The Changing Social Structure of Men's Prison." In David Greenberg, *Corrections and Punishment,* pp. 21–40. Beverly Hills: Sage, 1977.

———. *The Felon.* Englewood Cliffs, N.J. Prentice-Hall, 1970.

———. *Prisons in Turmoil.* Boston: Little, Brown, 1980.

Irwin, John, and Cressey, Donald R. "Thieves, Convicts, and the Inmate Culture." In David O. Arnold, ed., *The Sociology of Subculture,* pp. 64–80. Berkeley: Glendessary Press, 1970. (The article first appeared in 1962.)

Jackson, George. *Blood in My Eye.* New York: Bantam Books, 1972.

———. *Soledad Brother.* New York: Bantam, 1970.

Jacobs, James B. *Stateville: The Penitentiary in Mass Society.* Chicago: University of Chicago Press, 1977.

Jacobs, James B., and Crotty, Norma M. *Guard Unions and the Future of the Prisons.* Ithaca, N.Y.: New York State School of Industrial & Labor Relations, 1978.

Jankovic, Ivan. "Labor Market and Imprisonment." In Tony Platt and Paul Takagi, eds., *Punishment and Penal Discipline,* pp. 93–104. Berkeley, Calif.: Crime and Social Justice Associates, 1980.

Kannar, George, "Thinking about Jail." Review of *Discipline and Punish* by Michel Foucault. *Harvard Civil Rights-Civil Liberties Law Review* 13 (1978):573–586.

Kasinsky, R.G. "A Critique on Sharing Power in the 'Total Institution.'" *Prison Journal* 57 (Autumn–Winter 1977):56–61.

Kaufman, Hilde. *Kriminologie.* Vol. 3. Stuttgart: Verlag W. Kohlhammer, 1977.

Kluckhohn, Clyde, "Covert Culture and Administrative Problems." *American Anthropologist* 45 (1945):213–227.

———. *Culture and Behavior.* New York: Free Press, 1962.

Knight, Etheridge. *Black Voices from Prison.* New York: Pathfinder Press, 1970.

Korn, Richard R. "Report on Conditions at the Washington State Prison at Walla Walla." Filed in U.S. District Court Eastern District of Washington. Mimeographed. April 17, 1980.

Korn, Richard R., and McKorkle, Lloyd W. *Criminology and Penology.* New York: Henry Holt, 1959.

Krantz, Sheldon. *The Law of Corrections and Prisoners Rights.* St. Paul, Minn.: West, 1973.

Kroeber, A.L., and Kluckhohn, Clyde. *Culture: A Critical Review of Concepts and Definitions.* New York: Vintage, 1952.

Kropotkin, Peter. *Revolutionary Pamphlets.* Edited by Roger N. Baldwin. 1927. New York: Dover, 1970.

Krysmanski, H.J. *Soziologie des Konfliktes.* Hamburg: Rohwolt, 1971.

Lawes, Lewis. *Twenty Thousand Years in Sing Sing.* New York: Ray Long and Richard R. Smith, 1932.

Lewis, O.F. *The Development of American Prisons and Prison Customs, 1776-1845.* New York: Prison Association of New York, 1922.

Lewis. W. David. *From Newgate to Dannemora.* Ithaca: Cornell University Press, 1965.

Lifton, R.J. *Thought Reform and the Psychology of Totalism.* New York: Norton, 1969.

Linton, Ralph. *The Study of Man.* New York: Appleton-Century-Crofts, 1936.

Liston, Robert A. *The Edge of Madness: Prisons and Prison Reform in America.* New York: Franklin Watts, 1972.

McCleery, Richard. "Communication Patterns as Bases of Systems of Authority and Power." In Richard A Cloward et al. *Theoretical Studies in Social Organization of the Prison,* pp. 49-77. New York: Social Science Research Council, 1960.

———. "Correctional Administration and Political Change." In L. Hazelrigg, ed., *Prison within Society,* pp. 113-149. Garden City, N.Y.: Doubleday, Anchor Books, 1969.

———. "The Governmental Process and Informal Social Control." In D.R. Cressey, ed., *The Prison,* pp. 149-188. New York: Holt, Rinehart & Winston, 1960.

McGee, Richard A. *Prisons and Politics.* Lexington, Mass.: Lexington Books, D.C. Heath and Company, 1981.

———. "Review of State of Washington Adult Corrections System." Report to William R. Conte, Director of Adult Corrections, 1971.

MacIver, R.M. *The Web of Government.* New York: Macmillan, 1947.

McKelvey, Blake. *American Prisons: A History of Good Intentions.* Montclair, N.J. Patterson Smith, 1977.

MacNamara, Donal E.J., and Sagarin, Edward, eds. *Perspectives on Corrections.* New York: Thomas Y. Crowell, 1971.

Malinowski, Bronislaw. "Man's Culture and Man's Behavior," *Sigma Xi Quarterly* 29 (Autumn 1941):182-197 and 30 (Winter 1942):70-78.

Mathiesen, Thomas. *The Politics of Abolition.* New York: John Wiley, 1974.

Malcolm X. *The Autobiography of Malcolm X.* New York: Grove Press, 1964.

Melossi, Dario. "Punishment and Social Structure." In *Punishment and Penal Discipline,* Calif.: Edited by Tony Platt and Paul Takagi, pp. 17-27. Berkeley, Calif.: Crime and Social Justice Associates, 1980.

Merton, Robert K. *On Theoretical Sociology.* New York: Free Press, 1967.

Michels, Roberto, *Political Parties.* New York: Hearst's International Library, 1915.

Miller, Herbert S. "Current Perspectives in Corrections: A Cacophony." *Law and Contemporary Problems* 41 (Winter 1977):132–163.

Miller, Walter. "Lower Class Culture as a Generating Milieu of Gang Delinquency." In David O. Arnold, ed., *The Sociology of Subculture,* pp. 54–63. Berkeley: Glendessary Press, 1970. (The article first appeared in 1958.)

Mills, C. Wright. *The Power Elite.* New York: Oxford University Press, 1959.

Mitford, Jessica. *The American Prison Business.* Harmondsworth, England: Penguin Books, 1977.

Morris, Albert. Review of Carl R. Doering, *Report on Norfolk. Federal Probation* (April–June 1942):51–52.

Morris, Norval. *The Future of Imprisonment.* Chicago: University of Chicago Press, 1974.

Murton, Tom, and Hyams, Joe. *Accomplices to the Crime: The Arkansas Prison Scandal.* New York: Grove Press, 1969.

Murton, Thomas O. *The Dilemma of Prison Reform.* New York: Holt Rinehart & Winston, 1976.

———. "Inmate Self-Government." *University of San Francisco Law Review* 6 (October 1971):87–102.

———. "Prison Management: The Past, the Present, and the Possible Future." In Marvin E. Wolfgang, ed., *Prisons: Present and Possible,* pp. 5–53. Lexington, Mass.: Lexington Books, D.C. Heath and Company, 1979.

———. *Shared Decision-Making as a Treatment Technique in Prison Management.* Minneapolis: Murton Foundation for Criminal Justice, 1975.

Nader, Laura. "Up the Anthropologist—Perspectives Gained from Studying Up." In Dell Hymes, *Reinventing Anthropology,* pp. 284–311. New York: Pantheon, 1972.

Nagel, William. "On Behalf of a Moratorium on Prison Construction." *Crime and Delinquency* 23 (April 1977).

National Advisory Commission on Criminal Justice Standards and Goals. *Task Force Report on Corrections.* Washington, D.C.: U.S. Government Printing Office, 1973.

New Mexico. *Report of the Attorney General on the February 2 and 3, 1980 Riot at the Penitentiary of New Mexico.* Parts I and II. Santa Fe, N.M.: Office of the Attorney General. 1980.

New York State Special Commission on Attica. *Attica.* New York: Bantam, 1972.

Norfolk Investigation. Hearing before the Massachusetts Commissioner of Corrections. Compiled by Sheldon Glueck, Harvard Law Library. Report of Francis X. Hurley. February 1934. Briefs of Howard Gill. March 1934.

Ohlin, Lloyd. "Conflicting Interest in Correctional Objectives." In Richard A. Cloward et al. *Theoretical Studies in Social Organization of the Prison,* pp. 111–129. New York: Social Science Research Council, 1960.

———. *Sociology and the Field of Corrections.* New York: Russell Sage Foundation, 1956.

Opler, Morris E., "Themes as Dynamic Forces in Culture," *American Journal of Sociology* 51 (1945):198–206.

Orland, Leonard. *Prisons: Houses of Darkness.* New York: Free Press, 1975.

Osborne, Thomas Mott. *Prisons and Common Sense.* Philadelphia: J.B. Lippincott, 1924.

———. "Self-Government by the Prisoner." In Julia S. Jaffrey, ed., *The Prison and the Prisoner: A Symposium,* pp. 99–114. Boston: Little, Brown, 1917.

———. *Society and Prisons: Some Suggestions for a New Penology.* New Haven: Yale University Press, 1916.

———. *Within Prison Walls.* New York: D. Appleton & Co., 1914.

Osborne Association. (Before 1932: National Society of Penal Information.) *Handbook of American Prisons.* 1926 (2d); 1929 (3d); 1933 (4th). New York: G.P. Putnam. 1942 (5th, vol. II). New York: Osborne Association. 1926 and 1929 *Handbooks,* edited by Paul W. Garrett and Austin H. MacCormick. 1942 *Handbook,* edited by Austin M. Mac-Cormick.

Oswald, Russell G. *Attica: My Story.* Garden City, N.Y.: Doubleday, 1972.

Pallas, John, and Barber, Robert. "From Riot to Revolution." In Erik Olin Wright, *The Politics of Punishment,* pp. 237–261. New York: Harper & Row, 1973.

Paterson, Alexander. *The Prison Problem of America.* Maidstone Prison, England, 1935.

Pierson, George Wilson. *Tocqueville and Beaumont in America.* New York: Oxford University Press, 1938.

Platt, Tony. Review of John Irwin's *Prisons in Turmoil, Crime and Social Justice,* no. 14 (Winter 1980):70–84.

Platt, Tony, and Takagi, Paul, eds. *Punishment and Penal Discipline: Essays on the Prison and the Prisoners' Movement.* Berkeley, Calif.: Crime and Social Justice Associates, 1980.

President's Commission on Law Enforcement and Administration of Justice. *The Challenge of Crime in a Free Society.* New York: E.P. Dutton, 1968.

———. *Task Force Report: Corrections.* Washington, D.C.: U.S. Government Printing Office, 1967.

Prigmore, Charles S., and Crow, Richard T. "Is the Court Remaking the American Prison System?" *Federal Probation* 40 (June 1976):3–10.

"Prisons of Tomorrow." *Annals* 157 (September 1931).

"Prisoners' First and Fourteenth Amendment Rights." *Journal of Criminal Law and Criminology* 68 (1977):593–597.

Radzinowicz, Leon, and Wolfgang, Marvin E., eds. *Crime and Justice.* Vol. 3: *Criminal under Restraint.* 2d ed. New York: Basic Books, 1977.

Ramsey, Bruce, and Gettinger, Stephen. "Washington State Seeks a Return to Normalcy." *Corrections Magazine* (June 1981):33–37.

Reagan, Michael V., and Stoughton, Donald M., eds. *A Descriptive Overview of Correctional Education in the American Prison System.* Metuchen, N.J.: Scarecrow, 1976.

Reid, Sue Titus. *Crime and Criminology.* Hinsdale, Ill. Dryden Press, 1976.

Reimer, Hans. "Socialization in the Prison Community." *Proceedings of the American Prison Association, 1937* (New York: APA, 1937), pp. 151–155.

Reiman, Jeffrey H., and Headlee, Sue. "Marxism and Criminal Justice Policy." *Crime and Delinquency* 27 (January 1981):24–47.

Resident Government Council. Washington State Penitentiary. Institute I. "A Search for the Prison of Tomorrow." January 1972.

Rhay, B.J. "Observations on European Correctional Systems." In "Planning Prospectus." Olympia: Washington State Department of Institutions, 1970.

Rossi, Peter H., and Berk, Richard A. "The Politics of State Corrections." In David F. Greenberg, ed., *Corrections and Punishment,* pp. 69–88. Beverly Hills: Sage, 1977.

Rothman, David J. *Conscience and Convenience: The Asylum and Its Alternatives in Progressive America.* Boston: Little, Brown, 1980.

———. *The Discovery of the Asylum.* Boston: Little, Brown, 1970.

Rudovsky, David; Bronstein, Alvin J.; and Koren, Edward I. *The Rights of Prisoners.* New York: Avon, 1977.

Rusche, Georg. "Labor Market and Penal Sanction." In Tony Platt and Paul Takagi, eds., *Punishment and Penal Discipline,* pp. 10–16. Berkeley, Calif.: Crime and Social Justice Associates, 1980. (Translation from the German, 1933 article.)

Scharf, Peter, and Hickey, Joseph. "Thomas Mott Osborne and the Limits of Democratic Prison Reform," *Prison Journal* (Autumn–Winter 1977):3–15.

Schneider, Hans Joachim, and Scheerer, Sebastian. "Corrections in the Federal Republic of Germany." In Robert J. Wicks and H.H.A. Cooper, *International Corrections.* Lexington, Mass.: Lexington Books, D.C. Heath and Company, 1979.

Schrag, Clarence. "Social Role Types in a Prison Community." Master's thesis, University of Washington, 1944.

Schwartz, Herman. "Protection of Prisoners' Rights." *Christianity and Crisis,* February 17, 1975, pp. 19–30.

Schwendinger, Herman, and Schwendinger, Julia. "The New Idealism and

Penal Living Standards." In *Punishment and Penal Discipline.* Edited by Tony Platt and Paul Takagi, pp. 185–191. Berkeley, Calif.: Crime and Social Justice Associates, 1980.

Scudder, Kenyon J. *Prisoners Are People.* Garden City, N.Y. Doubleday, 1952.

Selznick, Philip. Foreword to *C-Unit: Search for Community in Prison* by Elliot Studt et al. New York: Russell Sage Foundation, 1968.

Serrill, Michael S., and Katel, Peter. "Anatomy of a Riot: The Facts behind New Mexico's Bloody Ordeal." *Corrections Magazine* (April 1980): 7–16, 20–24.

Silberman, Charles. *Criminal Violence, Criminal Justice.* New York: Random House, 1978.

———. "Race, Crime and Corrections." *Proceedings of the American Correctional Association, 1979,* pp. 5–14. College Park, Md.: ACA, 1980.

"State Prison: A History of Adult Corrections in Washington." *Perspective* (Washington State Department of Institutions) 10 (Spring–Summer 1966):5–14.

Studt, Elliot; Messinger, Sheldon L.; and Wilson, Thomas P. *C-Unit: Search for Community in Prison.* New York: Russell Sage Foundation, 1968.

Suedfeld, Peter. "Report on Isolation/Segregation Unit and Protective Custody, Washington State Penitentiary." U.S. District Court, Eastern District of Washington. Mimeographed. April 1980.

Sutherland, Edwin H. "The Prison as a Criminological Laboratory." *Annals* 157 (September 1931):131–136.

Sykes, Gresham M. *The Society of Captives: A Study of a Maximum Security Prison.* Princeton: Princeton University Press, 1958.

Sykes, Gresham M., and Messinger, Sheldon L. "The Inmate Social System." In Richard A. Cloward et al. *Theoretical Studies in Social Organization of the Prison,* pp. 5–19. New York: Social Science Research Council, 1960.

Takagi, Paul. "The Walnut Street Jail: A Penal Reform to Centralize the Powers of the State." *Federal Probation* 39 (December 1975):18–26.

Tannenbaum, Frank. *Osborne of Sing Sing.* Chapel Hill: University of North Carolina Press, 1933.

———. "Prison Democracy." *Atlantic Monthly* (October 1920):433–445.

Tawney, R.H. *Equality.* London: Allen and Unwin, 1931.

Taylor, Ian; Walton, Paul; and Young, Jack. *The New Criminology: For a Social Theory of Deviance.* New York: Harper & Row, 1973.

Teeters, Negley K. *The Cradle of the Penitentiary: The Walnut Street Jail at Philadelphia, 1773–1835.* Philadelphia: Pennsylvania Prison Society, 1955.

Teeters, Negley K., and Shearer, John C. *The Prison at Philadelphia:*

Cherry Hill: The Separate System of Penal Discipline: 1829–1913.
New York: Columbia University Press, for Temple University Publications, 1957.

Thomas, C.W., and Petersen, David M. *Prison Organization and Inmate Subcultures.* Indianapolis: Bobbs-Merrill, 1977.

Thomas, J.E. "A 'Good Man for Gaoler'? Crisis, Discontent and the Prison Staff." In John C. Freeman, *Prisons Past and Future* pp. 53–64. London: Heinemann, 1978.

Thomas, Jim et al. (Prisoner collective.) "The Ideology of Prison Research: A Critical View of Stateville." *Crime and Justice,* no. 14 (Winter 1980): 45–50.

Toch, Hans. *Police, Prisons and the Problem of Violence.* Rockville, Md.: NIMH Center for Studies of Crime and Delinquency, 1977.

Tyrnauer, Gabrielle. "What Went Wrong at Walla Walla?" *Corrections Magazine* (June 1981):37–41.

Tyrnauer, Gabrielle, and Stastny, Charles. "The Changing Political Culture of a Total Institution: The Case of Walla Walla." *Prison Journal* 57 (Autumn–Winter 1977):43–53.

———. "Special Report on Washington State Penitentiary to the Prisoner Organization Research Project." Sacramento: American Justice Institute, 1980.

Van Schick, John, Jr. *The Community Within the Walls.* (Pamphlet). 1934.

Ward, David A. "Sweden: The Middle Way to Prison Reform?" In Marvin E. Wolfgang, ed., *Prisons: Present and Possible,* pp. 89–167. Lexington, Mass.: Lexington Books, D.C. Heath and Company, 1979.

Warren, Earl. *Memoirs of Earl Warren.* Garden City, N.Y.: Doubleday, 1977.

"Washington State Tightens Administration of Furlough Programs." *Prison Law Reporter* 1 (March 1972):203.

Weber, Marx. *The Methodology of the Social Sciences.* Glencoe, Ill.: Free Press, 1949.

———. *The Theory of Social and Economic Organization.* New York: Oxford University Press, 1947.

Weeks, Lloyd Allen. "The Background of Penal Democratization." In Resident Government Council (Washington State Penitentiary). Institute: "A Search for the Prison of Tomorrow." (January, 1972):vi–xviii.

Wicker, Tom. *A Time to Die.* New York: Ballantine, 1975.

Wieder, D.L. *Language and Social Reality: The Case of Telling the Convict Code.* The Hague: Mouton, 1974.

Williams, Vergil L., and Fish, Mary. *Convicts, Codes and Contraband: The Prison Life of Men and Women.* Cambridge, Mass.: Ballinger, 1974.

Wills, Garry. "The Human Sewer." *New York Review of Books,* (April 3, 1975, pp. 3–7).

Wilsnack, Richard W. "Explaining Collective Violence in Prison: Problems and Possibilities." In A.K. Cohen, George F. Cole, and Robert G. Bailey, eds. *Prison Violence,* pp. 61–78. Lexington, Mass.: Lexington Books, D.C. Heath and Company, 1976.

Wilson, Duff. "Can the State Corrections System Be Rehabilitated?" *Argus* (Seattle) 85 (April 14, 1978).

Wilson, James Q. *Thinking about Crime.* New York: Vintage, 1975.

Wines, E.C., and Dwight, Theodore W. *Report on the Prisons and Reformatories of the U.S. and Canada.* Albany: Van Benthuysen and Sons Steam Printing House, 1867.

Wines, Frederick H. *Punishment and Reformation.* New York: Thomas E. Crowell, 1923.

Wolfgang, Marvin E., ed. *Prisons: Present and Possible.* Lexington, Mass.: Lexington Books, D.C. Heath and Company, 1979.

Wright, Erik Olin. *The Politics of Punishment.* New York: Harper & Row, 1973.

Yahkub, Thomas. "A History of the State Prison Colony." In Carl R. Doering, ed., *A Report on the Development of Penological Treatment at Norfolk Prison Colony in Massachusetts,* pp. 71–206. New York: Bureau of Social Hygiene, 1940.

Yinger, J. Milton. "Contraculture and Subculture." In David O. Arnold, *The Sociology of Subculture,* pp. 121–134. Berkeley: Glendessary Press, 1970. (Article published 1960).

Court Cases

Aripa v. *Department of Social and Health Services.* 588 P.2d 185 (1978).

Battle v. *Anderson.* 564 F.2d 388 (1977).

Bresolin v. *Morris.* 543 P.2d 325 (1975).

Bresolin v. *Morris.* 558 P.2d 1350 (1977).

Chapman v. *Rhodes.* 434 F. Supp. 1007 (1977).

Cooper v. *Pate.* 378 U.S. 546 (1964).

Draper v. *Rhay.* 315 F.2d 193 (1963).

Evans v. *Moseley.* 455 F.2d 1084 (1972).

Fetty v. *Smith.* 2 Prison Law Rep. 242 (1973).

Holt v. *Sarver.* 309 F. Supp. 362 (1970).

Hoptowit v. *Ray.* 79-359 (ED Wash., 1980).

Hoptowit v. *Ray*. 80–3366 (9th CA-1982—remanding to Dist. Ct.).

Jones v. *North Carolina Prisoners' Labor Union*. 409 F. Supp. 937 (1977).

Meachum v. *Fano*. 427 U.S. 215 (1976).

Mempa v. *Rhay*. 359 U.S. 128 (1967).

Morales v. *Schmidt*. 340 F. Supp. 544 (WD Wis. 1972).

Morris v. *Travisano*. 310 F. Supp. 857 (1970).

National Prisoners Reform Association v. *Sharkey*. 347 F. Supp. 1234 (1972).

Newman v. *Alabama*. 349 F. Supp. 278 (1972).

Palmigiano v. *Garrahy*. 443 F. Supp. 956 (1977).

Procunier v. *Martinez*. 416 U.S. 396 (1974).

Pugh v. *Locke*. 406 F. Supp. 318 (1976).

Rhinehart v. *Rhay*. 314 F. Supp. 81 (1970).

Riley v. *Rhay*. 407 F.2d 496 (1969).

Rhodes v. *Chapman*. 29 Crim. Law Review 3061 (1981).

Sostre v. *McGinnis*. 334 F.2d 906 (1964).

Sostre v. *Rockefeller*. 312 F. Supp. 863 (1970).

Thomas v. *Evans*. 72–1708 (9th CA). 2 Prison Law Rep. 399 (1973).

Wolff v. *McDonnell*. 418 U.S. 539 (1974).

Wright v. *Toomey*. 74–1106 (7th CA-1974—affirming Dist. Ct.).

Index

Alper, Benedict S., 63
American Civil Liberties Union, 110
American Correctional Association (ACA),
3, 28, 109, 127, 196, 202; ACA wardens'
team report on WSP, 109, 111, 127
American Prison Association. *See* American
Correctional Association
Attica prison riot, 1–3, 205

Baker, J.E., 62–63
Bates, Sanford, 53
Berkman, Ronald, 181
Bikers (Washington State Penitentiary
Motorcycle Association), 100–103,
123–124, 125, 145, 158, 163, 173, 183
Black Liberation Party (BLP), 158–159, 183
Black Muslims, 37, 153
Black Panthers, 158, 183
Black Prisoners' Forum Unlimited (BPFU),
158, 159, 160, 161, 162; "Black
Manifesto," 94, 97, 121, 143–144, 153;
SAM, 97, 144
Bradley, Harold, 96, 99, 123, 106, 175–176
Bresolin v. *Morris,* 193–194
Bridge (self-help program), 97
Brockway, Zebulon, 28, 30, 61
Burdman, Milton, 96, 106, 120

Chadek, Steve, 105
Chicago School of Sociology, 131–132
Cleaver, Eldridge, 153
Clemmer, Donald, 25, 27, 132
Cloward, Richard, 28
Club system at WSP, 89, 92, 102; cross-
membership, 159–160; decline of,
110–111; Rhay on club system, 101;
types of, 158. *See also* Bikers; Black
Prisoners' Forum Unlimited; Ethnic
clubs at WSP; Lifers with Hope;
Organizations, prisoners'
Coblentz, Warden J.H., 79
Collins, William G., 112, 203
Community prison, 45, 46; medical model
and, 46
Confederated Indian Tribes (CIT), 158, 163
Conrad, John, 42, 151
Constitutionalism, 164–167; constitutional
revisions at WSP, 94–95, 172–175, 184;
constitutional standards, 4
Conte, Dr. William R., 61, 83–89, 152, 156,
179–180; "philosophy of corrections,"

118, 156; relationship with B.J. Rhay of
WSP staff, 83–87, 117–119
Contraculture, 133–134
Convict code, 70, 133–134, 141–142, 147
Cormier, Bruno, 70
Courts: hands-off doctrine, 37; intervention
of, 37–39, 101–102, 203; WSP and,
192–199. *See also Hoptowit* v. *Rhay*
Covert culture, 146, 148, 149
Cressey, Donald R., 41
Cross Revenge Squad, 109
Cruel and unusual punishment, 38–39;
court rulings on, 38–39, 190, 195–199;
WSP, 113
Culture concept, 131–132
Culture of prisons, 5, 36

Dahl, Robert, 182
Davidson, Theodore, 132
de Beaumont, Gustave, 15, 23, 45
Deccio, Alex, 106
Delmore, Larry, 81
de Tocqueville, Alexis, 15, 23, 45
Detotalization, 35–36, 152, 179;
distinguished from liberalization and
democratization, 178–179
Dickens, Charles, 40
Dinitz, Simon, 42, 151
Discipline, in prison, 11–15, 25–26, 59–61,
107–108; disciplinary procedures,
189–190
Doering, Carl, 57
Drugs in WSP, 102, 122, 160; treatment
program, 169

Education in prisons, 97, 122
Eighth Amendment. *See* Cruel and unusual
punishment
Enlightenment prison, 19–25; Beaumont
and Tocqueville's view of, 23; debate
over Pennsylvania and Auburn models,
23; decline of, 24; relation to
Enlightenment era, 11–12, 14–15
Ethnic clubs at WSP, 143–145, 158. *See
also* Black Prisoners' Forum Unlimited;
Confederated Indian Tribes; United
Chicanos; White Citizens' Council
Evans, Governor Daniel, 94, 97, 106, 126,
193

Fogel, David, 62, 210, 213

231

About the Authors

Charles Stastny received the Ph.D. in international relations and Eastern European studies from Harvard University. His current research interests center around prisoners' rights in the United States and various European countries. He has taught at universities in the northeastern and northwestern United States and lectured in India and Israel. He is currently a research associate at Harvard University's Center for European Studies and a visiting scholar at Nürnberg University.

Gabrielle Tyrnauer received the Ph.D. in anthropology and Asian studies from Cornell University. She specializes in international minority problems, particularly those of Gypsies in Europe and the United States. She is currently doing research on social and political change among the German Sinti Gypsies under a Deutsche Akademischer Austauschdienst fellowship and lecturing at Nürnberg University. In addition, she is doing freelance journalistic work. She is affiliated with Harvard University's Center for European Studies.